NOBLES STRONG

NOBLES STRONG
LESSONS IN DESTINY

JON NELSON

XULON PRESS

Xulon Press
2301 Lucien Way #415
Maitland, FL 32751
407.339.4217
www.xulonpress.com

Paperback ISBN-13: 978-1-6628-1123-4
Ebook ISBN-13: 978-1-6628-1124-1

For Patty
My love, heart, and soul...

And to Irwin County
May we all be Nobles Strong...

TABLE OF CONTENTS

ACKNOWLEDGEMENTS

There are a LOT of folks to thank for a project of this size...

You're talking to an entire community- that turns into more than one since you're looking at everyone who loves Irwin County football, loves the Nobles family, loves them in the town they live in ten miles away in Fitzgerald, and loves them from all their stops along the way in Florida and Georgia.

I can't thank all of you for being as open and honest as you have been in completing this version of what folks saw in being "Nobles Strong." To the coaches, administrators, family, friends, and loved ones this was a humbling assignment.

To all of you who have offered a phone number, a part of your afternoon (or evening), and gave me your perspective on one of the toughest years we have all seen, I am forever grateful.

There's an old saying: "Trust the local guides, for they know the terrain..."

David Pierce and Steve Carter are most certainly those- your help in getting local interviews and giving your perspectives were invaluable. And, for all the photographs outside of the ones the family provided for the book, Renee Owens Hartley gets all the credit with her amazing eyes for action.

More than anything, I can't thank the Nobles family enough for their hours and hours of talking to me through a time where they lost someone they love very much. The lessons we all can learn from being around a family like this are immeasurable.

FOREWARD

IMPACT!

It is such a football word. One of the definitions given for impact is, "to come into forcible contact with another object." This happens repeatedly during the course of a game under the stadium lights of a Friday night. We see it in the trenches at the snap of the ball as offensive line meets defensive line.

Impact occurs when opposing defense meets motivated ball carrier as they struggle for every inch of territory. It happens again as the ball carrier makes contact with the ground. Impacts on a field are seen by all, felt by some, and can often be heard up in the stands. Nothing brings fans to their feet and pumps up a sideline like a big hit, but this is only one definition of impact and not the particular definition that is the marrow of the message in this book. The better definition of impact is, "To have a strong effect on someone or something."

Every one of us could name people who had a tremendous impact on our lives; it may have been a parent, a family member, a friend, a teacher, or a coach. And every one of us have had moments that that have impacted us personally, perhaps a graduation, the birth of a child, passing the big test, a promotion, or a big win. In this book, you will get a glimpse into an unbelievably true story: a story about a man who had a tremendous impact on the lives of so many people. He impacted people as a football coach. Thousands of young men knew and loved this man. They did not love him just because he was a football coach; they loved him because they knew he loved them.

I love the quote from John Maxwell, "People don't care how much you know until they know how much you care." I heard this man tell his teams, "Coach loves you," on a weekly basis. This man impacted more than just his players. He impacted other coaches that he coached with and for. After almost every game, an opposing coach had something positive to say about him when the two teams met in the middle of the field. Parents of the players had the utmost respect for him. They saw first-hand that he was not only after helping their kids win high school football games. They knew that he wanted to empower them to be winners for life.

Other teachers admired the way he pushed his players to excel, both on and off of the field. He wanted them to be good students and great men. He cared not only how they performed in class, but he also cared about how they treated their teachers and each other. And he impacted every community he coached in. So much so that it was fairly common to see people from previous communities show up for games at his current school.

His name is Buddy Nobles, and from the day we met in 2001, he had an impact on my life. I served with him as team chaplain at Union County High in Lake Butler, FL, where he was the head coach. It was in this community that I also served as a student pastor and Buddy's Sunday school teacher at Sardis Baptist Church. In 2006, God moved me to another community in Florida and in 2007, God moved him to Fitzgerald, Georgia. In spite of the distance, we stayed close. Most Saturday mornings would include a phone call to Buddy to ask how Friday nights went for Fitzgerald, where he served as offensive coordinator. When my oldest son, Will, was in 4th grade, we began taking trips to Fitzgerald. Buddy and Kaleb, Buddy's middle child who was the quarterback at Fitzgerald High, would work my son on the mechanics of playing quarterback. Needless to say he made an impact on my son, too.

MOMENT OF IMPACT # 1:

Fast forward to 2014…

In the years leading up to 2014, Buddy and I had many conversations. We talked about everything from our families to our faith to our jobs. By 2014, Buddy and the bulk of the staff from Fitzgerald had moved to coach in Coffee County, GA. Buddy loved what he was doing, loved the kids on the team, and loved the coaches he coached with. But for years he had shared with me that he really desired to be a head coach again. He had applied for a couple of positions in years prior but always finished second in the running.

This time was different.

Irwin County High, one county over from Fitzgerald (and rival school), was in need of a head coach and Buddy was their choice. I will never forget the phone call when he called to tell me the good news. We prayed on the phone, thanking God for the opportunity He had provided.

MOMENT OF IMPACT # 2

Fast forward to March 2016…

Three months prior I met my father for the first time. Just take a guess where he lived… that's right——-Fitzgerald, GA. In March I had a conversation with Buddy informing him that I was about to be hired by a church in Fitzgerald. He thought I was kidding him. I remember him saying, "Are you kidding me?!" over and over again. After I ensured him that I was not kidding, he uttered a sentence that I remember with unbelievable clarity, "This community needs people like you and is going to be blessed by you being here."

That was typical Buddy.

He was such an amazing encourager. I asked if he could use a chaplain. He said yes, and our lives and ministries were reunited. I refer to his coaching as a ministry because to him it was. Not only was I getting the opportunity to be his chaplain, but my son that he invested in for years was getting the opportunity to play quarterback for him. We prayed together on the phone, thanking God again for the opportunity he had provided.

MOMENT OF IMPACT #3

It is the summer of 2019. Buddy has had an incredible run as the head coach at Irwin County. His teams have played for the state championship four times in his five years. There was no reason to think that 2019 would be any different. During a conversation in early July, Buddy asked me to pray for him because he was having some medical testing done. He didn't give a lot of detail, but I sensed that he was worried. On the day of the first game of the regular season, I was in my typical game day routine. On the day of a game I would usually arrive at the school at 3:30 PM for pregame preparations. Early that afternoon I received a phone call from Buddy, and he asked me if I could be in his office by 3:15 PM. I told him I would be there, but by the tone in his voice, I felt something was wrong and the 3:15 meeting was going to be a difficult one. I arrived that afternoon and he asked me to come into his office and close the door. I sat down on the couch in his office, and he delivered the news that rendered me speechless. He told me that he had been diagnosed with stomach cancer, and there was no cure. We cried, and then we prayed. After what seemed to be an eternity of silence, in typical Buddy Nobles fashion, he got the team on the bus, and we went and kicked off a football season that would be unlike any other. A season like no other team, perhaps in the history of football, has ever experienced. In the pages of this book, you will journey through this unbelievable season. You will get to look behind the locker room door at the TEAM OF DESTINY and an incredible man they called Coach Nobles. I have no doubt that you will be impacted by what you read.

MOMENT OF IMPACT #4

Billy Stephens

Chapter 1

BUILDING A FAMILY

Kevin Erwin is like, pretty much, every other Southern, younger brother you know. He's protective of his older sister, Tammy. He wanted to make sure that anyone that crossed his sister's path was worth it. Kevin wanted to make sure that anyone that wanted to spend time with Tammy passed his muster and that muster was a pretty deep list of specifications and character assessments.

But this guy named Buddy wanted to spend some time with Tammy- and had to go through Kevin's path of approval to do it. But there was something about this guy that told him he might be okay.

"He came and picked me up one day at school," Kevin said. "And the next day, he was talking to me about her and kind of just left it at that. I'm, kind of, from a rough family. We're pretty protective and I guess he went about it the correct way- thanking me for the information I gave him, We went for a couple days and he asked me again and I introduced them and they started dating.

"Even back then, he was a different guy. I could just tell he was different. It wasn't your normal, typical high school guy. I had no inhibitions at all about it. Actually, I'd had quite a few of my teammates asked me about going out with Tammy. And never... not a single time... did I say 'Yes.' Buddy was the only one and it turned out really good."

Sports, the Erwins, and the Nobles were a big deal growing up. For Buddy to gravitate from being an athlete to a coach, Kevin thinks he couldn't have found a better partner than his sister.

"Buddy always wanted to coach," Kevin continued. "He worked with my father who owned a construction business. He worked a lot of summers to put himself through to be able to get to where he wanted. Every step he took, Tammy was right beside him. If it was his dream- and that was what it was- it couldn't evolve any better than it did."

Buddy got better as a coach every season. His teams would get better, too. He was always a student of the game- reading books constantly, attending clinics, not afraid to call up another coach or strike up a conversation. If it was baseball, the sport he played in college, he would remember how he might have been bested the day before and spend hours after the next practice fixing what he thought the problem was. He could tell you the pitch that was coming on the diamond and he could equally tell you the play call coming from the other sideline. The ability to see a game in three-dimensions is a rare trait, but Buddy had it.

"He and I went to school together," Kevin continued. "He left there and went to University Christian- which is where I graduated from. I was not going to miss a game. Then, he's at Lake Butler and they're having the run they had down there. And, I mean, every Friday night I was in Lake Butler sitting with Tammy or was standing on the sidelines. That was what probably brought all of us closer together. Because you could tell everything he did... everything he said... was from the heart. There was no guessing.

"If anything went wrong for a kid, it affected Buddy. You can tell that it was not just a game and it made everybody else around him as deep into the situation as he was. There was no way you couldn't be friends with him and you just knew how important was."

It would even include families as they grew. When Kevin's daughter was born, she would be brought to football games as soon as she could. The family on the whole could be seen at football games and baseball games in the area- even if it was inside the state prison at Lake Butler.

"He's just magnetic. He makes you understand the situation with these little sayings and how you can watch something. Later, you think about how important it was. He had a gift of making you realize how important a situation was while you were in it and I don't know if that can ever be done by anybody else to me."

Kevin also had one other thought that was prevalent in his mind...

"He was probably the first guy other than my family that I ever told 'I love you' to. There are times where you'll still have guys sit there and not say that. Why can't you say it? It's not a big deal if it's how you feel. In my family, it wasn't really prominent. They say 'I love you,' but he made it a daily thing. Even towards the end, he would be at the house when I drive in on Friday night. I go to the house and sit with him.

"And the second I walk up, he would say 'I love you.' It makes you realize the whole 'man' thing. Yes, you're a man. But you've gotta be able to tell somebody how you feel. All of his kids felt it. All the players felt it. They knew that they could count on him inside-out. I knew I could count on him for any-thing. He would never judge me for anything. My family life was a little rough growing up. And he was showing me how to be a man, treating my daughter as his own. He was showing me how to be a man and still be a dad. He was showing love and showing me emotion.

"You could still be rough and tough and do whatever, but this is how it's got to be. I am a much better parent because of the lessons Buddy taught me over the years. I would truly hate to think of where I would be without Buddy. He was that strong to me."

Kevin also got to see Tammy working late nights and being what he called a "perfect mom." The kids never went without anything. They had to earn it, don't misunderstand, but anyone around here could count on Tammy and all the kids in her circle were treated the same- blood or not. She was always going to be there for anyone who needed it- no matter what your last name was.

"She is, probably, one of the best moms I've ever been around in my life," he admits. "My kid knows she can call 'Aunt Tammy' at 2 in the morning if something comes up. She can call her and talk to her and she's there most of the time. I don't know that she ever has ever missed a single one of her kids games or events in all this time, too. You can bet your behind she was going to be at a game and everyone got to see her sitting in a chair."

Mike Posey would go from being a friend of Buddy's from the age of 13 or so to being the best man at his wedding with Tammy. And he knew it going back to their high school days, frankly...

"That's what he had his sights on then," Mike says. "I don't know if Tammy had her sights on Buddy at the time. But Buddy knew just what he wanted when he met Tammy. Those two right there were clicking from day one. So, if two people were meant for each other, it was those two."

Andrew Zow came to know Buddy as a 15-year-old who had a lot of talent and was getting playing time as a Freshman at Union County High School. He learned a lot in a very short period of time. It has stayed with him ever since... even now as a high school football coach on his own at Sylacauga High in Alabama on his way to Clemson.

"I was a fifteen-year-old kid coming out of middle school and go in with the varsity at Union County under Coach Robby Pruitt and Coach Nobles," he remembers. "Coach Nobles always said he loves you. So, that was sort of different. I was just a hard country boy growing up. This guy comes in and he's just different."

If there was some work that had to be made up at Union County, you were part of the "Dawn Patrol." At 5:30 in the morning, you were running.

In the dark...

Buddy would yell at those students that were with him before the sun came up on those back roads. He was trying to remind you to keep going... at the top of his lungs... but it wasn't meant in the way you think. It was as a reminder to never give up on a task.

"Coach Nobles is always constantly pushing us to the edge so you could get better. And when he would always remind us to do the right thing, it is his fatherly way of trying to continue to make me a better Christian, a better man, a better husband, and a better father."

When Andrew graduated from college, Buddy hired him as a quarterback coach and they got to see a roster with Buddy's son, Kasey, CJ Spiller, and Kevin Alexander making early impacts. Andrew would eventually end up in Birmingham with his business interests before getting back into coaching. He would never be too far from staying in touch throughout the years.

"He was very impactful in so many ways," he continued. "We would always call, always text, or be in a group text. We would just chat as he was always working on that championship ring. But there was no doubt we always stayed in touch. I'll always love him."

Matt Thomas was another player for Buddy that would go into coaching after his schooling was done... and he's now head coach at his alma mater...

"Coach Nobles used to come pick me up and take me home," he admits. "We lived on the west side and I couldn't get school at University Christian on the south side of town all the time. He would come get me, looking fabulous, in this little, tiny Camaro that we barely fit in. But he was driven to get us to go to school there- pardon the pun.

"I think the first thing that you realize about Coach Nobles is that he's real. He wasn't political or blowing smoke. He was as real a person I have ever had in my life. He could tell you stories about his life. He could be a mentor. He could cry with you and he could tell you something as important as to live your life for Jesus Christ in about an hour. That takes people years and years, but it was all just natural to him."

Matt knew, probably, in his senior year of high school that he wanted to be a coach as well. He would go on and emulate those things he learned from being around Buddy and has applied them ever since. Kids have come back, as they have in Buddy's time as a coach, and told them what kind of an impact they have had as mentors. Everything is coming full circle for guys like Matt- and he's not the only one.

"He helped you all along to formulate who you were as a young man," Matt says. "Then, what he did was as someone when you were growing into an adult."

Life being the circle it is gives Matt that chance to give back at his alma mater. There are times at the school that he feels Buddy's presence inside the walls and in the hallways. It might be something that Matt does on the practice field. It might be something in a game situation. And he's walking those same steps all over again.

"I find myself saying, 'He said that to me as a player.' I'm very honored to be here in two halves of my life and I get to honor Buddy by doing a lot of the things that he taught me.

He, obviously, has a special place in my heart and my life and always will.

"He taught me not to look at the color of the skin and to look at every person's heart. We coach in a diverse sport and brotherhood. As a coach, we're leaders. Buddy taught me how to mentor kids outside of the football field and not just the X's and O's. You invest in their lives. I've had phone calls from players- past and present- that have nothing to do with football. When they talk to you, it could be anything from money for food, they need homework help, or you're having issues with girlfriends. Teenagers think about everything.

"I've always been open here at school and Buddy never told anybody 'I don't have time for you.' I see a little bit of him in me."

Matt also recalls going to the Nobles home growing up and the idea that Buddy and Tammy opened their house for everyone who wanted to come by and visit. Tammy was always loving to anyone and cared about everyone. What sticks with Matt is the loyalty they showed to each other. They love and treat each other as folks who love each other should. They were definitely pieces that made up a football family.

Top to bottom...

Rowland Cummings has been a part of the Nobles circle since their Florida days as well. He's gone from a football coaching career in high schools to, now, being an administrator one county over from Irwin. He's the principal at Coffee High in Douglas- where Robby Pruitt is head coach.

He was linebacker coach at Union County High teaching social studies and adding basketball duties at the time. The young puppy, Buddy Nobles, and Rowland would game plan the opposition every week when they were on the same staff.

"They were the quintessential American family," Dr. Cummings recalls. "Buddy, Tammy, and their children are a great family of great character. There's a lot of talk about 'How big is a football coach?' But, with Buddy, he knows who he is as a man, as a husband, and as a Christian. He's as great a person that I've ever met in my life. He, truly, loves kids, loves coaching, and loved his family. You just love this guy."

As for family itself, Kaleb is super-thankful for everyone around him every day. Playing for his dad, and with his dad in Fitzgerald, he admits to knowing he had more responsibility than other kids. But he was also in a position to ask his dad a lot of questions from close range.

"Dad had done a lot of the same things I've done," he admits. "There were good parts and bad. There was somebody there who was harder on me than other people. But, if there was a bad practice, it wasn't taken off the field. He wanted me to be a kid first and, then, a football player. There was pressure on me playing quarterback, but there was never pressure from him. The fun part was Dad being my Offensive Coordinator in high school.

"He taught me a lot growing up. There were plenty of times where we go into the spring and summer and it would just be me and him on the field for an hour and a half. So, everything that I really learned as a quarterback was with him on my own. I didn't go to all these big quarterback camps all these kids go to, so there was a lot of one-on-one time on the field by ourselves just working drills. Those are the moments you cherish more than anything because I loved to do it with the person I love the most."

Those father and son conversations you have yourself…? Kaleb got to have them on the football field- practice or otherwise. Those conversations about life…? They were there, too.

With a twist...

If there was a passing drill and Kaleb overthrew his dad, he would have to go retrieve the ball himself. It wasn't a game of "chase," remember... it was a game of "catch." And those lessons carry with him in his current job at the University of West Florida on his way to Clemson as well.

"Now, in my everyday walk being a college coach, obviously his schedule was different than mine and all that, but I didn't see Dad as a coach. That's a special relationship to have..."

Kaleb does hear both his dad and Robby Pruitt in his coaching voice in his head. But he understands what that voice is telling him at the same time. "They both can get on your pretty good, but they were not going to rip you in front of the other kids. If they needed to get after your butt, they're going to get it done. My dad was the best at doing that, but it was about making sure that you understand their point. It's about making sure that the lesson that you're trying to get across is something that they'll remember and take with them. It'll make them better because of it."

Kaleb can feel his dad talking to him when it comes to handling certain events he comes across with students and players. His dad made those tough decisions and he now has to as well. The phrases may not be the same coming out of Kaleb's mouth, but the messaging is the same.

That's how he walks every day...

Kasey remembers the importance of church and school growing up, but also recognizes how tough it is being a coach's son who played for him.

"We would get into it," Kasey recalls. "If I get in trouble at practice, it would carry over to home. I would get it twice and nobody else. At the same time, though, you see a lot of the kids that are on a team that don't even have dads that come to games. Having a dad that was so involved was really special. I definitely enjoyed it."

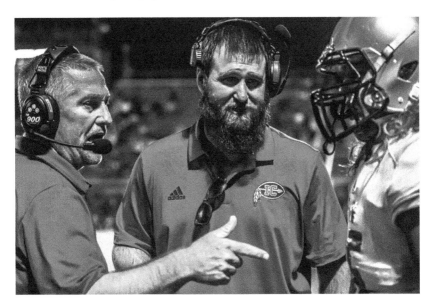

It evolved from coaching on Fridays to, with Kaleb to follow Kasey, doing all of those overnight drives to catch games on college football Saturdays. If you ask Kasey, one of his favorite photos, is a family photo with him in his Clemson uniform. You could tell the family was fully invested in seeing their children succeed- even if it meant a drive to a game involving his first stop at Rice before he transferred later in his career. That's anywhere from a six to a 13-hour trek that is an immediate turnaround the next day to get back to teaching and coaching back home.

Kasey, when he looks back at his parents growing up, knew his family was in a very fortunate space. You knew of friends and others that were children of broken homes and children of divorce. But his parents showed a love for one another consistently. They may fight about a particular topic, but at the end of the day they were still together as a team. They were a good example on how to raise a family and be a family unit that showed love in every direction.

"Everybody comes from different circumstances and you try not to judge," Kasey says. "You try to reach as many people as you can growing up. That's one thing I saw from my dad constantly."

He has loved every minute of coming home to be a coach on the staff his dad assembled. Although, it's even tougher at times to be a coach at Irwin as a player who learned from him growing up.

"There was a Friday night my first year where he, kind of, put me on restriction," he says. "I had to sit out a whole quarter without being on the headset because he said I wouldn't shut my mouth. I was very much like him and I am very opinionated. So we would disagree sometimes and I really enjoyed coaching with him. I'm glad I got two years of being able to do it."

Kasey has always struggled with his headset- by even his own admission. There's a certain point you can lift your microphone and the headset will shut off the mic automatically. Kasey has had problems almost weekly lifting the mic to that shut off position.

Buddy hears everything... regardless of location...

Dabo Swinney first got to see the Nobles family and philosophy back in 1996 during the Union County years. By 2003, he was recruiting in the Jacksonville area and they reconnected.

"That's when I heard about this young guy and all the success they were having at the school," he recalls. "We really started recruiting CJ Spiller at Clemson, so I got by there every chance the rules would allow me. I was bothering Buddy and we just hit it off. What you would get is so honest and he had a great love for CJ. What started the recruiting process was Kevin Alexander- who was a great player for us here as well.

"Kevin had committed early and CJ was the last minute for us. But Buddy was just awesome. He did things the right way and always told you that you can just love players and love them like they were his own kids.

"I just got to spend a lot of time with him and always thought he was one of the best people in the business."

Tucker Pruitt is currently the head coach at Fitzgerald High in Ben Hill County in Georgia. It's the county just north of Irwin County by geography- forever attached by rivalry. He played and learned under his dad, Robby, and Buddy with the Purple Hurricane. He went on to be a quarterback in college and has weaved his way in the coaching ranks back to one of the places where he grew up. His lessons have stayed with him as well...

"I remember back whenever my dad was coaching at University Christian where I was born," Tucker says. "I only lived there until about age 6 or 7, but I remember Coach Nobles and his son, Kasey, who is two years younger than me. We grew up together through Union County and here at Fitzgerald." So, it was like having an extended family all those years. There would be the trips to the Gator Bowl in Jacksonville- watching whoever was practicing or playing that year. There was Bobby Bowden's last practice for Florida State before he retired. There would be the Jacksonville Jaguars games or, just sitting around the house watching football.

"As kids, we're all wrestling and breaking things," Tucker remembers. "And they're telling us to go outside! They had a great family and it just kind of all linked up with Kasey being about my age and Kaleb being right around that same age. Obviously, everybody was great friends. Miss Tammy and my mom grew to be good friends as well, so they're just a great family and I'm glad to have gotten to be raised alongside them. I got to see Coach Nobles with the soft spot in his heart for all these football players he coached. Kasey, CJ, and I ended up being really good friends. Just like anybody else, we got adopted into the coach's family and they have people who share a bunch of love that are kind and gracious."

Tucker's dad, Robby Pruitt, now coaches at Coffee High in Douglas, Georgia- about 35 miles east as the crow flies from Ocilla. He's assembled a hall of fame career in two states with all the wins in Florida before his time in Georgia. Robby has been a mentor, a friend, and so much more with the Nobles family- as you just saw Tucker relay from his point-of-view.

Robby was head coach at University Christian for four state titles in six years from 1987-1992. He would leave there and take over the Union County program- winning three straight state titles from 1994-1996 and winning a state record 52 games in a row. The youngest coach to get to 100 wins in Florida high school history was inducted into the Florida High School Athletic Hall of Fame twenty years ago... and he saw something in Buddy.

Buddy was working in construction in the late 1980's trying to finish his education so he could teach and coach.

"He did that for several years because, if you didn't have a degree, you couldn't coach," Robby says. "He had a youth pastor job in addition to going to school full time. He was so hungry to coach and he became my rock. He ended up being my offensive line coach in 1990 and, when we moved to Union County, he worked there as my defensive coordinator."

There would be those times where Buddy would try to pursue head coaching jobs along the way. He would get frustrated about being passed over, but Robby was always there as his sounding board and trusted friend.

"Buddy would get really discouraged, but I would tell him that God has got a better place for you. Just keep your head down and keep praying to God. The Irwin job came along and I thought it was perfect for him. He was doing a great job there. Those people care for him a great deal."

Robby also got to see the Nobles family open their arms to anyone and everyone. The Pruitts and Nobles were, pretty much, inseparable through the years.

"I have two families that are extremely close," he adds. "And Buddy is like a brother." They got to see Robby's sons and Buddy's family merge- Tyler, Kenley, Trenton, Kaleb, Tucker, and Kasey- all moving as close friends and an extended family. They would play together- organized or in a yard. They would school together. They would grow together.

Robby also got to see Buddy go head-first into the rivalry involving a school they both coached at and the new job Buddy would take at Irwin. Robby had first-hand experience in rivalries outside of Ben Hill County and Irwin County and offered a parallel.

"I coached in the Warner Robins-Northside rivalry," Robby says. "So, I got a picture of it from that game. When Warner Robins hired me, that's the only thing they said: the one thing you've got to do is beat Northside. When Fitzgerald played Irwin, it's what I heard over and over. We played them, like, the second game of the year down in Ocilla and it was unbelievable. The old stadium was packed and people just kept coming in after the fire marshal headed them off. It was completely tight on the sidelines and there was not a spare place on my sideline.

"We beat them the whole time I was there, I think. We never lost but we had close games. Until two years ago, I think it was 18 wins in the last 20 years in the series. You knew every move the person on the other team was going to make and, when the game was over with Fitzgerald and Ocilla, you got a lot of hugs. There's no fear, no love lost... They're pretty good and the game was always pretty heated."

Robby got to see Buddy grow into being a head coach on his own and there would be seasons where they would both be runners-up. Robby is 7-3 in title games in Florida and Georgia and, if you ask him, he'll let you know any football coach would love to have that as a part of their resumes... even if the last thing you do, and maybe the last thing you remember, is going up first onto the platform to get the runner-up trophy.

But he would also see him chase after a title that a lot of folks thought Irwin County would be playing for in mid-December.

CJ Spiller has been a part of the Nobles family since his early years. There was the time in the Nobles family bunk beds, all the travel, shared meals, and getting coached starting in middle school. He spent his 2020 season as an unpaid grad assistant for Dabo Swinney's staff at Clemson. This follows a career in the NFL as CJ wants to pursue a Masters in Athletic Leadership.

"So, my 8th grade season, he got hired as a high school coach," CJ recalls. "Ever since I was little league age, I know my mom and Miss Tammy will be in the stands. When you hear parents yelling and screaming, you know you can hear Coach Nobles on the sidelines yelling and screaming. He was just a parent- watching and observing us- and then once I got to high school, we were so excited about him being announced as the new head football coach of Union County.

"We knew we were going to get ready for a great man and a great coach.

"I remember we started the JV season and you really didn't want freshmen to go straight up to the varsity. I also remember he had Kasey and Kevin Alexander play one game of JV as well with me. But I tell people I don't even know what it feels like to play a junior varsity game because Coach Nobles said that he can use us all at certain positions and he did.

CJ's junior season would be his most important as a high school running back that a LOT of schools wanted for their college backfields. The Union County team had lost in the state title game and they wanted to go back. Training started at 7AM and if you got there at 7:15 or 7:30, you may as well have not even tried to show up at practice in the first place. He would be late for a workout and Buddy would give no favor.

CJ would have to go through the same punishments as everyone else on the roster without a second thought. No one man was above the rest of the team at any time. It didn't matter if you had every Division I school in the country chasing after you or not, you are a part of a team and you will have the same repercussions.

When it came to where he wanted to go for college, that was the other lane of traffic that everyone had to handle as the team chased a trophy.

"I look back and I wish I, probably, should have had him more involved in recruiting- sitting in on those meetings with head coaches. Here I am a small-town guy, the first one of my family to even go off to college, and all this is foreign language to me. I guess you can say if I could change one thing it would be to have Coach Nobles and Miss Tammy in it with me and my mom when those coaches came in for those home visits to ask some of the questions.

"The day that he found out that I was coming to Clemson, I didn't tell him beforehand because he wanted to find out like everybody else. He said he didn't want me to think that he would try to influence me to go to a different school. He said he was proud of me because it was a hard decision and he knew how much pressure was put on me.

"He said, 'I'm proud of you, son. I'm glad you made the decision for yourself and that you weren't influenced by anybody else. Let's get this national letter-of-intent faxed off.' Everyone was blowing up my phone to check up on me that day."

Those conversations will be ones that CJ will always remember...

Gerard Warren was another key cog in those Union County teams to make sure the offenses that faced the kids from Lake Butler wouldn't get anywhere. And he was really good at it... He was ranked one of the top ten defensive linemen in the country by the time his days were done on the state title teams in the mid-1990's. He was recognized as one of the Top 100 players of the first 100 years of Florida high school football and would have a successful career in the pros in Cleveland, Denver, Oakland, and New England.

"What kind of a coach was he with Robby?" He thought for a minute...

"Oh, man," Warren exhales, "the closest one I can probably say would be a Jordan-Pippen or maybe a Bill Belichick and Bill Parcells relationship. I learned a lot more about life than I did about football. You learn about attention to detail, work ethic, integrity and taking pride in your work. Coach exemplified going above and beyond when it came to being a big brother, an uncle, a father figure, and Head Coach all balled into one."

Gerard also thinks Miss Tammy is the best right hand you could have. She was the backbone in a life that had sacrifices. She was always there and he thinks the Nobles family was different than, say, 90% of the high school coaches he's seen in his life. The lessons he learned then still help him out to this day.

"When I find myself at a crossroads in a situation," Warren says, "instead of overreacting, I'll say 'I don't know what to do.' And I don't want to do anything I'll regret. I'll go back to my room and think about Lake Butler and the lessons that I had learned. When I became a husband and a father, I now see that joy and elation on the faces of kids like Buddy. Now, being able to tell someone 'This is the reason why I work hard. This is the reason why I set a good example- not just for y'all, but for my children, too.' Trying to instill his work ethic is not about me. It's about what he passed on to me and carrying on with what they established, it's amazing."

Casey Soliday joined the Irwin County staff after being with his brother, Erik, up the road at Perry High as an assistant after the 2014 season. His first conversations were at a Chick-Fil-A in Cordele with Buddy and Thad Clayton.

"I thought they were well-organized and knowledgeable," Coach Soliday says. "Obviously, being in south Georgia, everybody knows about Irwin County and the successes. Irwin County is a program that was a really big step from where I was when it came to the fans, the parents, and the supporters. When I first got there, the knock was that Buddy hadn't won a state championship. I'm sitting here looking at the next couple of years saying, 'Man, I understand not getting the state championship.' But I'm sitting back looking at the success that he did have and I thought he was actually under-appreciated a little bit.

"I've talked to other folks and the comparison that we kind of came up with was like Marv Levy with the Buffalo Bills-where you get to the last game of the year and you don't win the last game of the year. But, with the Bills, they got to the Super Bowl four years in a row and that should never take away from what Marv Levy did as a coach and getting to all of those championship games."

Irwin County Assistant Drew Tankersley knew he was going to have more than just a football coach when he joined Buddy in Ocilla...

"We got a new head football coach, new head basketball coach, and new head baseball coach all at the same time," he admits. "I came in the spring of 2014, so we were kind of learning together as head coaches. I drove down from Perry one day and I was eating with my dad in Fitzgerald. I got a call from a strange Florida number on my phone. That was Coach Nobles who still wanted me to come to an interview there. Then, you know him. The rest is history.

"I interviewed with him and his wife," he continues, "and he told me when I got hired that when I left the room, he said 'I knew I had my guy right there.' He said we had two or three other guys interview and that meant a lot to me. I had inter-viewed with Irwin County before and, long story short, they hired another guy to be the head baseball coach. I really wanted the job and the job opened back up a year later. With Buddy now the head coach, hiring me, and telling me that...? That always meant a lot to me and I told his family that. I told his son, Kasey, that...

"That's pretty special for me that he would tell me something like that and I thought a lot of him."

Drew's wife always likes sitting in the stands with Tammy. Coach's wives stick together on Football Fridays. They always hear conversations and the slings and arrows that come with being on a staff, but they hear them together. Tammy always went out of her way to talk to Drew's son, make his wife feel special, and it didn't matter what sporting event we're talking about with Irwin County. He also got to see how tight the Nobles family is...

"When I first got there, when Kasey I think was coaching in Florida, and Kaleb... I want to say... was still playing at VSU," Drew says, "Kaleb would come up and you can tell they were a football family, too. He would follow his dad up and down the sideline. We would even have to push him out of the huddle sometimes. He'd be in there trying to hear what's going on and I thought it was cool to see them all work together.

"That's pretty special when you get to work with your dad coaching like Kasey does. You could tell that football is a big part of their life. They like to talk about sports, but every one of them has played a part. Kenley helped us as a Director of Football Operations, ran water to the players, and helped set up drills. It really is a special bond."

As Drew looked at the run of success Irwin had leading into the 2019 season, the appearances in the state finals went from the idea of "happy to be there" to "we need to go back next year." Clinch County would always be in the way in one aspect or the other- a regular season win or a championship would always be in the way. It would be a kick in the gut to being heartbreaking and frustrating all the same. The naysayers would be there after every loss telling anyone listening that Irwin couldn't win the "big one." The same thing happened in baseball on campus as well.

"I never lost hope," he admits. "There was one year they were trying to run him out of town. But, as the Bible says, you turn the other cheek. We didn't respond to any of them. We just had this feeling that, one day, it was going to happen."

Troy Fletcher has known the Pruitts and Nobles families through a lot of football seasons. Robby hired Troy and Buddy came in to coach and teach at the middle school for starters.

"They mean the world to each other," he says about Tammy and Buddy. "They're a really, really close loving family." His time working hand-in-hand with Buddy would be stretched to its emotional limits going into this season, but Troy would be there to show his love for a family that means a lot to him- on the field and off.

Irwin County High Principal Scott Haskins met Buddy first as a potential hire before his eventual job change.

"He always was just as pleasant as nice as he can be," Haskins says. "He always had great things to say about Irwin County schools and the kids that were there. He bragged on you constantly- even as he didn't know us and I didn't know him at all that point in the beginning. He didn't have to do that, but he bragged on our kids and wished me good luck."

After Buddy was hired at Irwin, the relationship between the two men would grow as well.

Rev. Dr. Lloyd Stembridge is the pastor at Arbor Baptist Church in Fitzgerald. His spiritual relationship with Buddy was only a small part of his love for the Nobles family. The fact that they were neighbors in Ben Hill County was a part as was Buddy's time on the staff in Fitzgerald. When Buddy got the head coaching job at Irwin, there would be no discussion of moving ten miles to the south and crossing a county line. Lloyd got to see this front and center.

"When he came to Fitzgerald, my first experience with him was meeting him on the field," he says. "He's very person-able and that's the start of our family's friendship." There would be the occasional trip to college football games in Tallahassee when schedules would permit and, in Tammy, he could always see a light that shone all the time and a love that was there within an entire family just the same. Lloyd would be there to help the family in their times of need going forward without a second thought.

And that's just a small part of a starting line-up that was there to walk with an entire family for the toughest season of their collective lives.

Chapter 2

A LONG SUMMER

In May, the Nobles family and some close friends go on a cruise to let their hair down for a little while before the next season's grind kicks in all over again. Kaleb wasn't able to go this time because of his own recruiting season for UWF, but everything seemed fine.

"We don't do traditional spring practice because we have the two scrimmage games in August," Kasey says. "But we did our workouts and our drills and stuff- putting the offense in and doing the yearly install early in the summer. They got some tests done and Dad had been wanting to go on a cruise since he had never been on one. He was sick for, I think, a couple days out of the cruise. He just wasn't feeling good and stayed in his room. So, that's when I started to think something was up.

"I knew he had been losing weight but I also know he had been trying to lose some weight. But I wasn't sure whether it was just that he was being really successful with his weight. But once we got back from the cruise I started noticing he'd have to take breaks at the summer practices. He would just be completely drained at the end of the work out and we'd only be out there for maybe an hour or two outside. On the return, for the next week-and-a-half or so, Dad didn't have much of an appetite or the energy that he's usually associated with as a coach.

He would become more fatigued as the day would go... and he was still losing weight."

These summer practices were in the mornings and the weather wasn't all that hot for the early mornings in south Georgia. It wasn't like everyone was drained, Kasey admits, but Buddy just wasn't keeping up with everyone else. There was a test taken in the late summer that showed some low hemoglobin levels. As a result, most of July turned into a test-taking month trying to get to the bottom of the problem.

"There was a point where you could tell he wasn't 100-percent," Principal Scott Haskins adds. "I guess we can go back to July 4th or somewhere in there. When I saw him, I knew that something wasn't just right. He had lost a lot of weight and just didn't look quite like himself. I guess that was the first real indication to me that he said he was not himself."

"Buddy, 100%, vomited a few times at practice and he said he was feeling weak," Drew Tankersley admitted. "He told the kids at practice he was proud of them pushing through. It was hot for him, but he wasn't one to put any problems out there. He didn't mention anything about any problems that you would have any discussions over. He would always say, 'Yeah, yeah, I'm okay. I'm good. I think I just got hot.' That's what the plan was and he would say he would take it easy. Then, there would be some rumblings and, yeah, it did start to progress the way it did."

"I also have a son who was a freshman this past year," Irwin assistant Pete Snyder said. "I would transition up to the high school after my practices with the middle school team. There would be some days where he was just kind of taking a knee out on the field and you could tell he did not feel well. He is super-duper tough and he will not tell you anything. He was not going to let on that he was not well, but you could certainly tell if he was not well.

"Then, I remember Tammy would do a lot of the lunch preparations for the team. They would do little sack lunches after practice in the summer. But she and some of the other parents would do special lunches. One of her big things was chicken and rice and it's really good. You could just come in and get a big plate of chicken and rice, sit down, and eat it. Buddy always talked about it and that he loves it. too. One day, they had fixed that and you can tell Buddy doesn't feel well because he's sick. He was trying to eat it and he just couldn't."

"We were doing simple things back in the spring- agility drills and stuff like that. In that 10 days, he was telling me then he just didn't feel well," Irwin coach Troy Fletcher said."He just didn't have the energy and he could tell something was not right. His stomach bothered him and he was losing some weight. His energy just was not there in that he just didn't feel something was right.

"I think that was, probably, before he really told anybody. I think he was starting to notice that something was changing. We went on the cruise and he likes to read books from other coaches. He brought the ones from Lou Holtz and Urban Meyer with him this time. There were about thirteen of us there on the cruise and he was just kind of relaxed and kept to himself. But, he had a doctor's appointment after we all came back and they thought he had an infection or something like that in the stomach."

"He had come back from the cruise and we talked," Robby Pruitt said. "I asked 'How you doin'...?' And he said, 'Man, not real good. My white blood counts are low.' He had to go and I told him that I would be thinking of him. And he asked to pray for him. He went and got tested and he was a little bit worried. The test came back and he called me and said he thought it might be a stomach infection in the lining of the stomach."

"We finally went and my wife got me an appointment for an upper GI and so we did all that," Buddy said during football season. "I'm sitting there, I guess, in the recovery room. My daughter's in the waiting room. My wife goes in to meet with a doctor. They asked her to come in and they told her the news. And I knew when they walked out of the doctor's office I knew something wasn't good. They came in and told me I had a tumor on my stomach. He did a biopsy on it right then sent it off and then two days later we found out that it was cancer."

"We just thought it was because of the change in medicine that was changing his appetite and changing his energy," Kaleb said. "So it didn't become a major-major worry until later. There weren't really any major red flags until he was diagnosed."

Kaleb was in the office staff room. They were watching game film, but he knew there was a doctor's appointment where everyone needed to know what was going on with his father. He would talk to his Mom or Dad every single day. If he's busy, he'll call back and they'll play phone tag- especially during this time of year. This time, Tammy would call rapid fire.

"That's when I stepped out of the Offensive Staff Room and walked to my office to talk," Kaleb continued. "She did not immediately tell me because she wanted to get me, Kenley, and Kasey on the phone and let us know at the same time. I knew that whenever she wanted to talk to us all three at the same time, you could just tell in her voice that something was not right."

When the words came out of Tammy's mouth- "cancer"- Kaleb went numb.

"You don't know what to say. I didn't even have words. I don't know if I said anything on the phone. I kind of just froze and you don't realize what it does to you until it's somebody in your family. Mom was talking about the appointment and the news and Dad comes on the phone. He's like 'We're going to be okay. We're going to fight this. God has a plan and God is putting his hand over me and he's going to take care of it. So we got a plan. We're going to fight this and we're going to keep doing as if nothing's happened.'

"So, in the midst of all that... in the midst of all of us are upset... I'm wanting to come home that day... I'm wanting to be there with Kasey and Kenley at the house... the calmest person and the one that is not worried as much is the one that has cancer, my Dad. You can say you're ready for it and you can say that you know you would be able to handle it but, in the moment when it actually happens, there's no words for it.

"There's no feelings, no emotions, no situations you can replicate... I've seen other people go through it and I've had friends that have gone through it. You always wonder 'What if it happened to so-and-so? Or what if it happened to my parents? How would I handle it...?' You think you're ready, but you're never prepared for that moment when it actually happens. I think that was why I went numb. Reality hits that this is really happening to the man you love more than anything in the world.

"I don't know what to do. I want to help, but there's nothing to do to help."

Robby and Buddy would talk about it daily as Buddy was going to the doctor quite often. On this longest day in this stretch of long days, Robby answered the phone...

"Buddy said, 'Hey, are you by yourself?'

Robby put him on speakerphone in his truck and got the news before anyone else.

"I didn't know what to say."

And he was, definitely, in the majority. But for Robby and the Pruitts, who have walked stride by stride with the Nobles family for a long time, it was some of the toughest news he had ever received. A dear friend and someone he loves was in the fight for his life.

Buddy also had to tell another circle of people- his coaches, staff, and administrators who had become a part of a very thick extended family. How do you tell those closest to you that are with you every single day that you've been given one of the toughest diagnoses you could ever be given...?

"He lost a lot of weight and lost it quickly," Luke Roberts remembered. "He didn't look bad. He just looked like he was trying to lose weight. But when he tells you he has Stage 4, inoperable cancer it was a rough day. Coach Fletcher had to, kind of, gather himself and walked out of the coach's office."

"It was one of those feelings that you got that you knew something was wrong," Irwin assistant Jared Luke adds. "Because you felt like it wasn't one of those things where you would have gotten a text that said everything came back great.

"Buddy is standing close to the office where he usually stood. He told us that he had stage 4, inoperable cancer. Terminal cancer. He said he had to go back to the doctor and see what the options were. The options were to try to cure this thing or find out what the best route to take is. It's a sobering moment when you sit there and you look at the guy that has been like a father to you to tell you that."

Buddy's talk would continue to focus on the unfinished business at hand on the field...

"It's just unbelievable to me," Luke says, "to watch him give that kind of talk in the coaches offices of, 'Look, I'm dying. But we're going to proceed forward with what we started.' He said he's going to be at everything he could be at and he didn't skip a beat. It was unbelievable to watch what unfolded the next few months day after day after that day in the office."

"We could tell something wasn't good," Irwin assistant Chip Rankin said. "He told us the diagnosis he had been given and it was very somber and still. Not a lot was said. After that, he went and told the players and this is leading right up to the Brooks County scrimmage. It was a pretty difficult few days there. But, at the same time, he maintained that this was not going to be a pity party. As far as he was concerned, he was going to be business as usual. We were going to do what we always do and it was not going to be about him."

"I knew something was up," Irwin assistant Dwayne Vickers adds. "I didn't know exactly what it was but he said he wants to talk. With everyone standing there, there was quiet and a lot of hurt feelings. But going through what he was going through, he was still showing a lot of courage and that we were all going to keep going forward. One other thing during this whole time was he would always mention Jesus Christ and how important he was in this fight."

"One thing about it," Irwin assistant Tim Talton says, "was he always kept Christ in his life. He said, 'I'm going to be okay. I will be okay.' That's what he told me. It was the same with the kids when he would talk to them, too, and me and it was pretty much all business all year."

"We never... I never... expected for those words to be said 'terminal cancer,'" Irwin Assistant Clayton Sirmans said. "When he explained it to us, that was very, very shocking. It was very emotional for everybody. I'm probably never going to forget that day because I know that everybody in the room got real emotional. It was, very much, a lot of grown men crying and being upset."

"The first night (after the diagnosis) was a Wednesday night," Buddy said. "My older son, Kasey, coaches with us and he stays downstairs. We, basically, have an apartment where he stays downstairs. He was upstairs and you could tell he was upset. My son Kaleb- he's on the phone with us. My daughter Kenley, she's right there, and my wife's upset. Everybody's kind of solemn- boo-hooing and everything- and, finally, I had enough of it. I said, 'You know what?' I said 'We ain't gonna be this woe is me.' I said we can't have it. I told them flat-out that I'm a winner.

"They were all looking at me just kind of dumbfounded. I said 'The only games I've ever lost are the games with a roof over my head. I said 'We ain't gonna lose this!' I said we're gonna fight it and we're going to get through it. I know we've got some great doctors. We talked about football and baseball, hitting the ball, running the ball, shooting the ball...

"There's a lot of people that don't count their talent. Doctors, nurses, people who change the oil in your car... They got a lot of talent. There's gonna be a lot of people taking care of Buddy Nobles. And there's been a lot of thoughts and prayers starting right off with my family and my wife. But it was kind of boo-hoo at the house. But we're getting through it now."

The doctors said that the tumor was in the stomach. But it wasn't something that happened quickly. It had formed over time. The doctors didn't know how long before it had reached the size it had. It couldn't be detected on any scans until it has fully engulfed the organ that is attached to- in this case, the stomach. It then appears in PET scans and, by then, there's nothing you can do. The cancer itself is very rare. Options were presented to the Nobles family- Mayo Clinic in Jacksonville, Emory in Atlanta, and Houston's MD Anderson. The family chose trips to Atlanta. The physicians want to make sure a family knows what the options are and what the choices can be at any stage of the fight.

"When he shared the results, he was very positive," Principal Haskins said. "He was going to try and do all that he could, but he also said he wasn't going to lie. He was very honest and open about how he was feeling and what exactly the doctor said. It was not a pleasant meeting, but nonetheless he held it in and did a good job with it the same time."

"The thing we want to see is the game plan with our doctors and everything- see what the game plan is so it's part of life now," Buddy said at the time. "I have to realize of this game plan I'm not in charge. That's the thing that's the hardest."

The plan of action was a combination of chemotherapy and radiation treatments.

"He told me what was happening and he was talking through it all," Superintendent Thad Clayton said. "He wants to be able to take care of his boys and let them know 'Hey, you know, no matter what comes, we're going to have a special year.' It was both an honor and a privilege to figure out how I can do whatever I can to support him and how he wants to take care of the staff. He would go and tell the team and let us take care of them on an emotional day. He took his coaches and told them and there were a lot of tears and a lot of hugs.

"There was a lot of 'I love you' and 'We'll do whatever we've got to do.'"

And, part of that... maybe the hardest part... was understanding that your life while it's yours, isn't yours anymore if that makes any sense... All the day-to-day work you have on your schedule now gets bumped by a higher priority...

"I told my wife, 'Well, we have an open date after Fitzgerald. Then we have an open date after I think it's Charlton," Buddy said. "And Tammy said, 'Well, just remember you're not in charge of this and we've got to get this handled.' She's the one in charge knowing where I'm supposed to be. She tells me she'll come by here and say we got to go. And that's what we've already figured out. So it's one of those things that's the hardest thing that I've had to realize I'm not putting this game plan together.

"But, you know what, I know God's in charge and he's gonna take care of me. He's given me some great doctors already and we're gonna see what happens. You know what...? I tell people I'm scared. But I'm not scared of my eternity. I know my security in Jesus Christ but what scares me is here on earth. I don't know what I'm gonna do.

"I have people calling me and texting me all the time now. Somebody called me the other night and we must have talked for 30 minutes and he said he'd gone through cancer and he said the chemo and radiation is, to use a phrase that we've all used around us because we don't cuss, is a h-e-double-l. It's really rough on your body."

Buddy would be 100-percent correct...

"Tammy reached out to my mom," Matt Thomas says. "So, pretty early on, my brother and Buddy got cancer at the same time. Obviously, one of the things- when I caught up with Buddy in early August after the cruise and he came back and they were getting ready for their first scrimmage game- he said to me that it wasn't going to be a pity party. I mean there he was like me and that's just who he was.

"My brother, Jeremy, has it actually the same way. My mom wasn't about pointing the finger and Jeremy was going to use the platform to share the gospel."

Matt and Buddy, since they were both coaching, would text on Sundays- since they both had Friday night games. Matt would want to know how Irwin County did in a back-and-forth with the Nobles family. It also served as a way to check in on how things were going off the field. Buddy had always been a great friend and resource when it came to coaching, recruiting season, interacting with other coaches or just in the day-to-day. Matt got a sounding board in an entirely different way now- and got to act the same.

Andrew Zow texted back and forth as well- trying to see if there was a point in the calendar where they could get together. He would get his early intelligence from the Pruitts and everyone else in his phone that was close.

Gerard Warren also called to check in once he heard...

"He told me he was in good spirits."

"You know what? We're going to fight! We were born fighters," Buddy told him.

"He told me that we had a 'little situation,' " Warren continued. "We got the fears out the way so let's get down to the battle. It's time to fight!"

A conversation with Gerard has all the fury of a football game attached. There's a quick pace. There's equal moments of introspection. There are tears. There's shouting. There's love and understanding. Especially when Miss Tammy talks about a triple overtime game their team went through in Buddy's Florida coaching tenure...

"I guess I was trying to be a role reversal with Coach Nobles," he admits. "I was trying to motivate him and let him know the road that we had traveled together in high school gives you a map for the future. Never give up! No matter the circumstances, no matter where you're at, if you have God in sight and you're willing to work at it, anything is possible."

After that triple overtime game in high school, that Lake Butler team never looked back. They won a state-record at the time 39 games in a row. The guys could have shut down after a demoralizing loss. But they didn't and they were able to have an incredible amount of success. It set everything in motion in front of them.

"I told Coach 'We're going to fight.' You have a choice in a time like this. Are you going to fight? That's what I want to hear." He and Buddy would catch up once or twice a month and wouldn't miss a game when he could see Irwin play on television.

"His body change because of the evil cancer really broke my heart," longtime friend Steve Hoard said. "I had a hard time with it. I was there for all the games that I could, but it was just so hard for me seeing his family suffer. What they were going through- his mom, his wife, his kids- but it wasn't about him. It's always about the kids, families, and coaches."

"Tammy had called me a couple times worried about it," her brother, Kevin Erwin, admits. "She wanted him to be eating better, but the stress about the football and wanting to win the state championship was there, too. They had gone to the doctor and that was the first real time I had seen him since the dramatic weight loss. I asked him how he was doing and he said he was doing well. I asked what he was doing and he said, 'I can't keep any weight on.'

"I think they went to one of the doctors up here and got some tests done. I don't think they got anything back from that and, then, maybe a week or two later Tammy called me at work to tell me about all the results and everything. That was a rough day. They found a tumor and they were going to test it, and then get two biopsies on them. They found out the results, but it didn't look good."

"The doctor said it was cancerous, but not to give up hope. The second biopsy came in maybe three days after that. Tammy called me at work and let me know that it was cancerous."

Kevin remembers the day when Buddy was cut open and doctors found what was wrong. There is a common area at Emory-St. Joseph's Hospital where everyone waits for answers-good and bad. He didn't have to know the family and the procession going in to know what they would be facing as they entered and, eventually, left Room D. You would be sitting there in the lobby all day with all the emotions and options running through your head at the same time. Is it? Is it not? What do we do now? All those questions in a room of emotions, folks lost in thought, and families facing futures of light and dark.

"They just come out bawling, crying, and hysterical. And at some point, it's your turn to go in."

Kevin went in with Buddy and Tammy in the room to get their answer...

The doctors thought Buddy had five to six months to live...

"Somebody said something the other day," Buddy said after the diagnosis. "A couple of people were talking to me and said, 'Man it couldn't happen at a worse time.' And, then, the other person goes, 'No it's good, because his mind's on football.' And that's true. My mind is on football, but I do map it out a little bit different now.

He would focus his conversation then on one person who was keeping him on the task at hand- his Director of Cancer Operations, Tammy...

"She's unbelievable. We've been married 34 years this year and she's always told me 'wherever you go, I'll go.' I told her one time, if she ever left me I wasn't staying with the kids! I was going with her! But, just to have her by my side, driving me to those places, taking notes, she's looking up stuff on the internet already. She's a full-blown math teacher- she's a real teacher. She's not like a weightlifting coach or a football coach. She still takes care of her classes. It's unbelievable to have her by my side. But you know what...? God put us together a long time ago and I thank her for that."

It's been a learning experience for everyone in the Nobles orbit by this time of the diagnosis. It's about what you can learn, where you can learn it from, and find as many people and places to learn as much as possible about the road you're about to travel on. No resource is turned away and all the information goes into some kind of mental database for use when you find that moment to ask a question.

It was a learning experience for Buddy, too...

"I've kind of Googled some things. I'm not very good at the internet and stuff like that. But I've kind of Googled some things- like learning about the PET scan. My wife told me some things that were going to happen, what they were going to do, and how they were going to inject the dyes into me. We've started looking at different places and getting informed, but I think my wife knows the most. I think also what this does is it reinforces that it's okay for guys and coaches and all of that macho stuff to just be put to the side. Now, it's okay if this is another example of 'Hey, it's okay for your friends to kind of speak up and sit there and tell you that they love you.'"

"I was on my way to Tennessee for a Fastpitch girls softball tournament bracket," his close friend Mike Posey recalls. "He was just calling to let me know about their spring and summer practices. It had to be right at the beginning of football season because my cousin, who lives up near Atlanta, called me and said, 'You may want to call Tammy. I don't think something's right with Buddy.'

"I didn't call Tammy at the time because, obviously, but I had talked to Buddy a little bit after the suggestion. He was having tests done, but never really went into it and kept it to himself. Once I found out about it, it floored me."

What Mike would do, when he would call down the line, is talk about other things- football, daily life, or anything else to treat the talk as normal as it could. Everyone else has the same thoughts in mind at the time. You want to talk and ask how someone is doing, but at the same time, you don't want to intrude considering the emotions of the moment.

"I guess he didn't want me or anyone else to really know the pain or suffering that he was in at the time. At the same time, Buddy wanted to keep everybody's spirits up. Buddy was not a down person as one of the hardest-working players and coaches I ever knew."

"It was just human emotions at that point," Irwin assistant Luke Roberts said. "They cried. I cried. There were hugs and a lot of loving one another in that moment. The next thought was on all the kids. They had to just get right down and focus on what was there in front of them. They did a great job, because Buddy doesn't want it to be a pity party. Buddy was just as concerned about the kids and still wanted to win that state championship. Honestly, I think that's what kept him going."

"It sends shivers down your spine," longtime friend and coach Rowland Cummings said. And he wasn't alone in that feeling. "I heard, subsequently, after that it was stomach cancer. My mother passed away of stomach cancer in 1971, so I kind of had a little bit of a background with that. I knew that he was going to literally- obviously- be in for the fight of his life. We all had the strength- and he would at the time- to get back with me always. Mainly, though, his message with you was 'always tell them how much I love you.' And I almost always told him how much I think of him as a person, a husband, a father and as a Christian."

Along those lines, Buddy would talk publicly about what weighed on him...

"The one thing that's affected me the most is my team, because I don't want my seniors to have their senior year messed up." He actually apologized to the players as the players first got the news. Their response was understandable in the emotion of the moment- putting their heads down and living in disbelief of what was in front of them with someone they all loved. But Buddy wouldn't let the emotion stay...

"I said we ain't playing this season for Buddy Nobles. We're not doing any of that. We're gonna play for each other. We're gonna play for the seniors. We're gonna play for Irwin County high school and we're gonna play for Ocilla."

Buddy also was never going to be one that was afraid of telling someone he loved them. He also wasn't afraid of letting his coaches coach as the season and the support he got from coaches, whether they were on his staff or not, was another humbling aspect of this fight.

"People are calling me and every place I've gone leading up to coming here... every coach I've run into... has said, 'Tell Buddy that we're thinking about him. Tell him that we love him. Tell him that whatever he needs just have him reach out and let us know.' I mean the coaching fraternity is that and this is one of those things, sadly, that reinforces it too much. What we have got to realize is that we are a coaching fraternity.

"I mean, I like getting after people on a Friday night. But when it's over, I want to be friends. I want to make sure that we get along and everything. Probably the one thing I'd like to do is make the final game and let somebody let me win... not really...

"But, you know, we are a fraternity. I think people don't realize that because when I got with a guy like Robby Pruitt, I mean, who would have known the friendship and the brotherhood that we've had for 30 plus years now. It's unbelievable. You've got guys like Mike West- who called me the other day. Randy Garrett, Mike Booth, Robby Pruitt... I got guys from Florida calling me and texting me. It's just so unbelievable.

"Chad Campbell called me today and just told me, 'Hey, I'm just thinking about you' and that's the tough thing because right there now... if you're gonna play for Chad you're gonna be hardcore. But for him to call me and say 'Hey, I just want you to know I'm thinking about you' that means a lot. I'm getting a lot of texts and a lot of emails. But we are a fraternity and it means a lot for people to care for each other. I know I want to get after people on Friday night out on our field or somebody else's field, but to know that they care that much about me means a lot."

And those relationships would only amplify and reinforce over the football season...

An entire community- on the field and off- would embrace another community altogether.

"Keep the faith!"

As in hold your chin up, don't quit, was just one of many messages from coach Buddy Nobles to a downhearted Indian nation following a loss to Clinch County in the 2015 state single-A title game. It was the second defeat in the championship game in as many years for the boys from Irwin County High.

The Indians had not won the prestigious state football title in 40 years. Nobles felt the frustration of the players and fans in this old community where football is a big part of the culture and winning still matters.

"We're going to beat that door down some day," the coach says in David Pierce's book, Our Boys, a team, a town, a history, a way of life."

And the Lord let Nobles live long enough to see it get done.

It didn't happen in 2016. That year, the Indians were knocked out in the quarter final by the fine team from Emanuel County.

But all hope was not lost. Nobles inherited a pipeline loaded with young talent when he took over the up-and-coming program in 2014 as kids from across the county were inspired to take up the sport that helped to put Ocilla on the map.

In 2017 and in 2018, bolstered by a massive line and a stable of fine backs, the Big Red rolled, including satisfying victories over border rival Fitzgerald, as the boys fought their way back to state both years but there again they were bitten by old nemesis Clinch when all the marbles were on the line. The 2017 game was supposed to be played at the Mercedes Benz stadium but was cancelled there due to snow and ice in Atlanta and the Indian buses, which had left for the game, were forced to return to Ocilla. Drawing home-field advantage due to their superior record, the No. 1-ranked tribe fought their guts out before the Panthers prevailed, 21-12.

The battle for state in 2018 went to Clinch 27-20 at the Benz.

Then came the 2019 season, which will be remembered as much for tragedy as for triumph.

David Pierce

Sometimes, teams in high school football will line up a scrimmage or two to see where you are heading into any season...

Irwin County paired up with a perennial power in the Double-A classification, Brooks County, for their scrimmage date in Ocilla. Maurice Freeman went to school there at Brooks and has come back to take the team to region championships as head coach in 26 seasons in his home town in Quitman. The Trojans finished 9-3 in 2018 with a run that ended in the second round of the playoffs. Traditionally, Coach Freeman will play anyone, any place, any time, and anywhere.

So, hosting a team from Ocilla was nothing out of the ordinary for a school looking for an early challenge.

"This was not your typical scrimmage," coach Freeman admitted. "I told my guys that Irwin could flat-out play. Their big, ol' fullback (DJ Lundy) wasn't going to play since he was injured for a while. The rest of those guys can flat-out do it, too, so we had to game plan normally. We don't gameplan for a jamboree where we would continue to work on ourselves. But we said we would game plan for them because those guys were the real deal.

"We could watch a little film on them and figure when you are supposed to clean something up. When we got there, Coach Nobles came over and talked to me and told me that he loved me. I've always enjoyed our times together in the past and he would tell me he had cancer. He said to me, 'I don't know how long I have, but I'm going to give it all I got.' I told him if I could do anything for him, just let me know. I told him, 'I'm in your corner, But you fight as hard as you can fight!' We got into the game and it was a hard-nosed game. Those guys were fast and strong and they looked great.

"After the game was over, you go your way, and you're playing your season."

"I'm thankful this went down in the fall," Kaleb admits. "I think Dad wasn't one to talk about it whenever this whole thing went down. It was tough to focus sometimes on what's going on in my life with football with everything going on with Dad. Where I had a little bit of dead time, I have more time to think about this and realize this is really happening.

"You hear this a lot from people, but I kept on just hoping I would wake up one morning and it would all be a bad dream. But every morning I would wake up and realize that this is really happening.

"When my Dad would come to Pensacola for games or practices, he would naturally strike up conversations with our coaches. We have had coaches from our staff sleep at our house in Fitzgerald. So everyone on our staff knew my Dad. It took me about a week to tell our staff at UWF about my Dad's diagnosis. Really, that was the first group or person I was having to tell and putting those words together were not easy.

"Obviously, with the season approaching I have to do my job, but I want to be home. I want to see Dad and come help as much as I can. I want to go to the doctor with him as much as I can. Growing up, whenever I would leave for Valdosta or Pensacola, Dad would tell me 'Hey, make sure you get your job done. Put your head down at work and do your job.' So even after his diagnosis, you still act like that even when this whole process was going on. It was tough."

Kaleb admitted practice time turned into a good time to get away as did something as basic as watching film. He waited for a week to tell the Argos staff about what was going on with his family and the entire staff understood and would give him the space he would need to do his job and be with his Dad, Mom, brother, and sister. The staff at UWF wanted to know what was going on and when he had to come home earlier in the month was one thing. But when you find out just what the prognosis is, it's another matter entirely. Kaleb had enough trust from his fellow coaches that he would game plan and get his job done to prepare the Argos- no matter his location.

"I knew he had a doctor's appointment that afternoon, so I made sure I had my phone close during our offensive staff meeting. When Mom called, I went to my office expecting to talk immediately. When she told me to hold on so she could get Kasey and Kenley on a conference call, I knew something was off and we were about to get some bad news. You just go numb when you get news like that. After the phone call, I just sat in my office in silence for about 5 minutes before I went back to our meeting."

Kasey would remember Wednesday, August 7th, too...

"I was at practice whenever my mom called and usually she doesn't call at practice," he says. "But I knew they had an appointment. We still weren't sure what was going on so I knew it was needed. When I answered, she told me to get somewhere away from the players.

"I know it's about to be pretty serious.

"She told me that they found a tumor in Dad's stomach that was really big. So that was rough being at practice finding that out. He didn't want the kids to know yet. He wanted to be able to tell them, but that was rough being at practice. I remember walking off and he told me not to tell any of the coaches. But, obviously, you can see it in my face. Coach Luke got it out of me and I told him what was wrong at the end of that day."

Buddy would make it back from the doctor's office in time for the end of practice. He would break the news to all of the coaches. All of the staff would break down and Troy Fletcher would have to excuse himself and leave the room. From there, it was telling the players.

Two days before the Brooks scrimmage... and it would get worse...

Friday morning, the team was preparing to go out of town when Kasey got his confirmation the tumor was cancerous. He would be at school and the conference calls were next with Kenley and Kaleb.

"You don't you don't see a lot of teenage boys crying, and especially considering they're trying to portray that tough macho football player look in the meeting room," Kasey continues. "That day, there were some of the toughest kids on the team that just had their head buried. You could see a majority of the team just crying, but Dad was about the strongest one in the room during that. He made sure that everybody knew that things were going to be as normal as possible."

"Buddy's desire was not to have any of this be about him," Thad Clayton says. "I remember that conversation and he wanted to find out how he could help make the team better men in addition to being a good football team. it's consistent with the man. It is consistent with his message- especially in post-game meetings- where I can read his heart. He wanted to pour energy into those kids and the kids that we played against and help them to be better people."

"Thinking about it," Irwin assistant Casey Soliday admits, "something just wasn't right. He wasn't feeling well in July and things didn't improve. Then, the week of the Brooks scrimmage was when he let everybody know, I had a feeling about it. When we were going to have this meeting, we didn't know exactly what we're dealing with. Cancer never crossed my mind and that night was unreal.

"Buddy couldn't do much because he was just so tired," Irwin assistant Pete Snyder says. "So he was just sitting and drinking Powerade trying to chill out a little bit, but you can tell he was not his normal self at all."

"We knew he was going back for another checkup at the end of the week before the scrimmage and that's when he found out," Irwin assistant Troy Fletcher follows. "We were having a meeting earlier in the day and, then, I found out we're having a big meeting. It was not just going to be just the football staff. I was worried and, I guess, expecting the worst.

"I'll be honest. I broke down and I left. I didn't stay in there and I was crying like a baby."

Coach Fletcher didn't go into the meeting with Buddy and the players but he noticed a still really strong Buddy at the time and Fletcher knew Buddy was not going to let this news and the situation overshadow the kids in the program.

"Other than him losing some weight, he did not let it affect the situation. He wasn't going to moan, 'Oh, woe is me. We won't fight this thing.' But, at the same time, there were still so many questions out there of how they were going to attack it and what they were going to do. And, then, the way you're trying to defeat this terrible thing and a football game at the same time.

"I'm not sure that they understood the severity of everything, but he coached that game just as hard as he coached any game and he kept his focus on the team."

"That meeting where he told the staff was a little emotional as anybody would be," Irwin Principal Scott Haskins said. "He's family and a friend. But, at the same time, everybody understood he was going to try to do his part and do everything that he could do in detail. He didn't want your pity. He wanted your prayers and your thoughts."

One of the things Haskins would be impressed with in this journey would be the outpouring of support from all the surrounding communities and it wasn't just the teams Irwin would play in 2019. It would be the Region 2-A schools. It would be ANY neighboring school doing whatever they could- thinking about the family and praying for them at every turn.

"It was just a beautiful thing to see."

"Kids are kids. They are pretty resilient," Irwin assistant Clayton Sirmans said. "They took it very seriously at the time. I don't think they understood the seriousness or gravity of this tough battle that the family was going through. But, Buddy? He would always explain everything in a positive way. And he knew he wasn't going to give in and give up at all."

"I got wind that he wasn't feeling too good and I sent him a text," Bill Barrs says. "He was really good about responding to my texts within just a few minutes if not immediately. This time, I didn't get a response. A few days later, I sent him another one and I didn't get an immediate response or a timely response. I went by the field house and he was sitting down there. About the time I walked in the door, his response comes through and I can tell just talking to Buddy that something wasn't right.

"After finding out later on, I was pretty much speechless beyond that."

"He called me and he was excited because he, initially, got a bad prognosis," Jeremey Andrews recalls. "Then, he saw a doctor and he got a little glimmer of hope. It's like the movie 'Dumb and Dumber' when they said 'So, you're telling me there's a chance?'

"I'm sure somebody else has brought up that story... I bet...

"He called me to let me know, to ask for prayers, and just wanted to make sure that we knew. He said he was going to fight it, and at the same time though, he said that it wasn't going to be any kind of a pity party. Not at all."

Buddy would exchange texts with Jeremey and other coaches that he impacted all season long with this as a beginning. They ask how he and the Nobles family were doing and he would go in kind. There would be football talk in the texts, but the talk about his health would always be a part of the discussion and the love that would follow.

It would be that way all season long- in multiple states across the country.

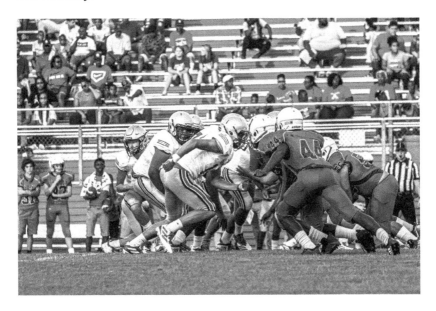

For a Georgia high school coach like Maurice Freeman, who was also chasing a title, he grew to know Buddy from speaking engagements where their athletes would cross paths. But, a few years ago, he had to be there as a rock for an entire community- football and otherwise. In July of 2013, three of his football players died in a single-car crash after morning workouts. A puddle of water caused a Ford Explorer to hydroplane and lives are changed forever. He has had to be that multi-leveled role in the summer of 2020 as one of his student-athletes was shot and killed through the outside wall of his family apartment.

"We all have big hearts as men. When it comes to Coach Nobles," he continues, "he called me in my time of need when I lost my three boys. He said 'Any time, you need me, you call me.' So, I did the same thing. This dude needs me and I have to call him to let him know I'm in his corner. If he needed anything, he just needed to let me know. And I'll be there.

"Everyone wanted him to pull through this. He was going to fight the whole time and it was incredible to see him still make it to practice and to games. He could have easily said, 'Look, man, I gotta get out of the way.' He didn't.

"The lesson for me in this as I look at it...? The world may rock you down onto your knees. You get on your hands and knees and crawl, but don't you quit."

Buddy Nobles certainly would not do that...

Chapter 3

AUGUST 23- AT BERRIEN/NASHVILLE, IRWIN 42-7

I t's a fairly straightforward drive from Ocilla to Berrien High in Nashville- about 30 minutes or so along US-129.

It was a fairly straightforward approach for the Nobles family after Buddy's diagnosis, too. Tammy, now adding what Buddy would call his "DCO- Director of Cancer Operations" to all the other titles she held over their time together, would make sure he would keep all of his appointments and do what he had to do health-wise to stay as close to 100-percent as he could.

Appointments were non-negotiable. Diet was the same way. And he had to be honest about how he felt physically- as much as he wanted to devote his full time to the team, town, and sport he loved- Buddy had to tell everyone around him what was going on and not hold anything back.

There are little moments you come across along the way that don't seem all that big to most folks. But, when you add that one moment into the framework of an entire season- those moments resonate and remind you just how much love can carry you through in a tough time.

One of those first moments came in the form of transportation. When you could see that Buddy was laboring, a lot of those close to him were trying to figure out how to have him focus on his job and not be spent physically...

Marty Roberts, the Irwin community, and the Booster Club helped out and didn't think twice...

"At the booster club meeting, they gave him a golf cart," Kasey recalls. "It made his preparation at practice a little easier. He was able to ride around and do his coaching like normal without wasting a bunch of energy. So that was a positive for that week. But it was definitely tough getting ready to start a regular season knowing your dad's sitting there fighting cancer and knowing football is not as important as what he's got going on.

"You also understand the fact that he's saying he doesn't want anybody to worry about it. He wants things to be normal. It was hard to balance that and that, to me, is this whole season in general. He doesn't want it to be a focus, but you can't ignore it. You know the team is going to be good and chasing after a State title, but at the same time, football isn't as important because of what's going on."

You're balancing a head coach who is suffering from stomach cancer with still trying to do game day preparation. There are meetings with the other assistant coaches to get all the game week elements done. It starts adding up, week after week, and then it keeps adding up that much more. Kasey, like the rest of the family, wasn't sleeping much.

"I was pretty upset about it for a while honestly," he continued. "I still am, but I've learned to deal with it. At the same time, I enjoyed being out at practice. I enjoyed coaching in the games. I knew that was a good release for me to be able to get out there and try to get my mind off of things. There's that two hour period every week where you want the kids to be focused and not stressed at practice, but then it starts happening to you. You start realizing this is real life. I really need this time at practice and need this time just to be able to get my mind off of things otherwise it's 24 hours a day I'm constantly thinking about it."

"I remember probably late July-early August, maybe after practice one day, that basically they found a mass," Irwin Assistant Drew Tankersley admits. "They didn't know exactly what the mass was or how bad it was. I can remember one day after practice, the coaching staff all got together behind the goal post right there on the practice field. It started becoming real before the Berrien game. He wanted to meet with all the coaches in the coaches office and he basically said he went to the doctor and they told him 'Stage 4 stomach cancer.'

"They said, worst case, 6 months best case- a year."

Drew looked around and saw several people crying. Others, like Assistant Troy Fletcher, had to leave the room entirely. The team finds out this news on Wednesday and they play their season opener two days later.

With the diagnosis now known to his Irwin County family, there was still a job to do and the first stop was Berrien. Tim Alligood, the head coach of the Rebels, had ties to Buddy through his ties to Robby Pruitt at Coffee, where he was an assistant, before moving one county over. The home team was coming off a 5-5 2018 season in a tough region- 1-AA.

"I didn't know a hundred percent of everything that was going on with Buddy," Tim said. "I had heard stories from other coaches, but I don't think at that time I realized it could be very serious. There was still hope that he would still get a decent chance to defeat it. I can remember going and talking to him. When I saw Buddy, I saw he had started losing a little weight. I will say this... every time you got around him, he was one of those guys who was a really optimistic guy. I told him: 'I know you are going through some things and we were all thinking of you.' He just looked at me and said: 'I appreciate it.' At the same time, we all knew there was a game to play and we talked about the game in front of us."

Coach Alligood knew they had their hands full with the visitors and thought they had to play a perfect football game against Irwin to have a chance to win at the end- even as he knew Buddy had a lot on his mind.

Kaleb wasn't going to hold anything back, either. He and Katy made an impromptu trip to South Georgia for the weekend to see everyone.

"We had already gotten the tumor and the cancer diagnosis about two weeks before, but we had not known the severity of the cancer. We had a scrimmage the night before at UWF and then had the morning to watch film as Offensive and Defensive staffs together. Again, I had to leave the staff room to take the call from Mom to be delivered the severity of the Cancer being Stage 4, terminal and non-operable.

"I wanted to walk out of the office and head to Fitzgerald right then. But, of course Dad was telling me to stay in Pensacola to keep working. I went back to keep watching our scrimmage film with the Offensive Staff, but obviously my mind was elsewhere. We had a staff meeting at 1:30 and our meetings are always ended with a prayer by Coach Shinnick. Right before the prayer, I told our staff about the newest news and it was very tough to actually put those words together. We had more film to watch after the meeting, but I eventually made the decision to go home for the weekend to see Dad and the rest of the family. It didn't feel right to be where I was and not be with my Dad at that time."

"It was the first time that I had seen him in person since he had been diagnosed," he adds. "We pulled in and got to the game I mean, literally, it was about five minutes before kick-off. I walked in right as Dad was ending his pregame speech in the locker room. We make eye contact- and I'll never forget this- because it's the first time seeing him since the craziness in mid-July. We had been on Facetime a lot the past few weeks, but seeing him was different because of how much weight he had lost. He paused his speech when I walked in and made eye contact. Once he finished his speech to the team, we had a very long hug and embrace and a few tears. But, of course, he had to get to the game quickly. There were a lot of emotions in that brief hug."

Kaleb is fairly certain that night in Nashville was only the second time he sat in the stands as a fan with his Mom, Kenley and Katy. As a coach, he feels out of place if he's not either in a booth or on the field in some capacity.

That lasted until a few minutes into the game...

"I was able to go on the field and stayed with Dad on the side-lines," he says. "I struggle sitting in the stands at his games because I don't like hearing complaints about play calling. That night was a little different in that I couldn't stay in the stands long because you could hear people talking about his diag-nosis and people were literally finding out the severity of it during the game. So I headed down to the sideline and stood beside him for a lot of the game."

"I have stood by him on a lot of sidelines for a lot of games but honestly, that was the most memorable game that I'll ever have stood with him on the sidelines. He was still calling plays but, while we were on defense, he and I stood together and talked. We were talking about the game going on in front of us but we talked about the diagnosis and everything going on as well. That's definitely the first time I have had tears in my eyes during the process of a game. I think we both kind of realized this is very serious. Obviously, this game is important but the time that we have together is even more important. I could put my arm around him during the game and be there with him on the sideline."

There was always the notion that he could be on the road and have to hop on a plane or be at West Florida and hop in the car to come home quickly. A night in Nashville, Georgia in late August was a welcome, albeit temporary family moment.

For Kasey, it was a reminder of taking care of business right in front of you when it's time to do so... the reminder of the lack of a "pity party" kept everyone focused on what Buddy thought Irwin County was capable of in 2019.

"We knew we were pretty talented," he admits. "We knew we had a chance to make another run for a ring, but I think Dad being selfless like that and him talking about not having any 'pity party' brought the team together more. We were already good, but I think that kind of gave a chance for the team to say,

'Alright, we're not going to get down over this. We're going to have the season we were planning on having where this is going to be special.'"

The night against Berrien was, whether the team knew it or not, a precursor for the season to come. Irwin held the Rebels to 54 total yards of offense, 2 of those were passing yards, and grabbed five turnovers on the night. Those early mistakes, Alligood says, cost Berrien and gave them a large hole to climb out of that night that they could never really recover. Irwin QB Zach Smith only needed to throw 10 passes- 8 were completed. Gabriel Benyard had three scores on the night combined and it was a 42-7 win for the 2nd-ranked team in Single-A Public.

There was one of "those moments" that you only have in high school football...

This time it happened in Nashville...

"It was halftime and Buddy tried to go into the locker room and the door to it was locked," Irwin Assistant Pete Snyder remembers. "It was really hot that game- like most Fridays in late summer. We had a small locker room, so he stayed outside on the side of this, kind of, corner of the end zone and right across from where that locker room door was. He had the offensive line out there and he was coaching out there. He had just been given a cancer diagnosis and he said it didn't matter. He's coaching his butt off with a 30-point lead."

There would be more scenes like that all season long...

After the events of the last week or two, Kasey had to do his own bit of research. A doctor can tell you one thing, but sometimes you have to do your own investigating to see what the future may hold yourself. It's part vigilance and it's part being a good advocate. There is, normally, a time where you have to stick up for that one you love and be as informed as possible when you're faced with tough decisions. On the one hand, you hope you never have to make those decisions you dread. But, at the same time, you have to be ready if those days come at you quicker than you would like under any circumstance.

"I had to look up 'stomach cancer' on Google," he said. "I had seen how dire the situation was and I knew the percentages. We knew it was going to be an uphill battle. But there's still a little bit of hope because we weren't sure yet whether he would be able to have surgery with the treatment options we were being given. There was still some hope, although it was tough."

"We were really encouraging, because we didn't know at that point what that sort of thing was." They had won big in Game 1 and, by some accounts, Buddy fell asleep on the drive back. The assistants were watching and noticing as far back as halftime and they could tell Buddy was really tired. From then, it was a real feeling and situation in front of them going forward.

"The meeting that week was an emotional one," Snyder said. "Buddy was trying to fight back tears and he was staring up at the ceiling a little bit. After he told us, he went and told the players. He told them the same thing he told us and he always said that he wanted to be as honest and open with them about what was going on as possible. He always was and he always told us he would let us know if he had any news- that was good or bad. He was always about those kids and would take care of their emotions- as well as everyone else's."

Berrien would win their next two non-region games against Atkinson and Bacon County, but the rest of the season was a long slog for Alligood and the Rebels. They wouldn't win another non-region game heading into their region schedule. And it didn't get any better for them as they lost all four games to Fitzgerald, Thomasville, Early County, and Brooks County to finish 2-8.

Coach Alligood would watch the title game in person at Georgia State. When Buddy would give his speech to those who came to see the Single-A final, it was a moment that hit Tim deeply.

"It was one of those moments that brings you to tears," he said. "With the emotion that he said what he said...? For him to be able to do that...? For him to muster the energy to get up there on the platform...? He probably knew that this is the last time I'm ever going to be able to do something like this again. He was trying to look out there at his community and his football players and let them know how much he loved them.

"I'm sure they looked up and thought the same thing. You can say what a blessing it was that he got a chance to finish the drill."

Irwin County 42

Indians

Berrien 7

Rebels

1	2	3	4	F
28	0	14	0	**42**
0	0	0	7	7

Chapter 4

AUGUST 30- FITZGERALD, 35-8

Every school has a rival... think about your own school- high school or college- and you know, instantly, who it is and what it means. And in the case of Irwin County and Ocilla, it's the team, county, and town ten minutes to their collective north.

It's Ben Hill County and Fitzgerald...

As Becky Taylor wrote in the Tifton Gazette as a preview:

"The rivalry between the counties dates back to before football existed in either. They first met on the gridiron in 1922 when Ocilla had its own city school system. Ocilla dropped football a decade later and games between Fitzgerald and newly-consolidated Irwin County resumed in 1954. Their series is one of the oldest continuous ones in the state. According to Georgia High School Football Daily, only three current series have been played for more consecutive years: Trion-Gordon Lee (which dates to 1946), Valdosta-Colquitt County and Ringgold versus Lakeview-Ft. Oglethorpe. Bowdon and Bremen have also played every year since 1954."

Fifty-one weeks out of the year, folks will live in one town (like the Nobles do), and work, shop, or socialize in the other. You could ask Marty Roberts about it as someone who lives in Irwin County and travels the ten minutes to work.

"51 weeks out of the year, we get along wonderfully," he says. "We eat together. We travel together... commune together. But that one week of the year, we absolutely despise them. If Buddy came directly from Fitzgerald to Ocilla, it might have been a little different. But, remember, he actually left here and coached at Coffee. He still lived here and attended church for a long time. When he got the head coaching job at Irwin, you know, you're an Indian.

"He was so close to the Pruitt family that it took a little bit of steam out of it, to be honest. When he thought about getting a job at Cook and one of the reasons he didn't want to do that was because they were playing the history of Fitzgerald every year. You had so much respect for him that made it a little tougher."

Buddy would drive to Marty's office at Fitzgerald Ford-Lincoln often and they would just sit and talk. Didn't matter about what... they would just sit and talk. This summer's "sit and talk" would be markedly different. The spring golf tournament for the football team came and went. The two of them would needle each other about their weight since they held it about the same. Initially, in the late spring they would laugh off Buddy's weight loss, but Marty knew something was eventually wrong.

He called Tammy.

"I said 'Is there something going on?' and she told me a little bit about what she thought it might be." He would learn more in short order...

"I was sitting at my desk one day and I knew he had been to the doctor. I saw his truck outside the office. I asked what's going on. Traditionally, Buddy would come by and we would leave the door open and talk. This particular day he walked in and asked if I had a second. But he wanted the door closed. I just felt something was wrong. He said he just found out he had cancer. So, from there, what's your game plan going to be for this? What are we going to do?

"He said we're not going to have a pity party for Buddy Nobles. He said we're going to move on and I'm going to get my treatment and we're just going to move right along."

Marty had visited Buddy one day at the fieldhouse on campus before the diagnosis. Coach knew something was wrong- just not to its eventual depth. He told Marty that he had never asked anyone for anything in his time in Ocilla. But he was going to ask for something personal- a golf cart to move around. It would be the best way for him to get around every day on campus.

Marty knew how much money the booster club had in the bank... it wasn't much...

"I needed $4,500 and, in a week's time, I had the money raised and got his golf cart ordered- tires, wheels and all that stuff. The next week, he wanted to give me a check himself. I told him that we're going to discuss it with the booster club."

What Marty didn't tell Buddy was that he had pulled the golf cart around where Buddy couldn't see. He walked around to the back door, apologized for being late, and wanted Coach to step outside.

"I had called Tammy and told her about it. She was outside and, when he came outside, tears started pouring down Buddy's face. That red golf cart was sitting there for him and it was one of the best things that I've ever been able to accomplish in my life." Money would come from as far as Atlanta would give a family something that would mean more than just four wheels and an "IC" logo. By the time the rivalry game with Fitzgerald came around, Marty would admit that having 4,000 people wearing white took his breath away. If you normally have an event like this one, maybe half of the folks on hand would participate.

Not this time... but it wasn't the only moment folks would carry with them...

Marty is a big Florida State football guy. There's always a moment in those home games at Doak Campbell Stadium where Chief Osceola and his Appaloosa, Renegade, will ceremonially ride with a flaming spear to the logo at midfield. Osceola will buck his horse and jam the spear into the ground to fire up the home crowd. There are rare instances where an important person for the program will accept the spear and drive that moment home. They do the same thing in Ocilla- just without the horse. And, for this game, Buddy would plant the spear himself.

But it would take some convincing...

"I made that spear at my house," Marty said, "and we use it before every home game. I'm in charge of that and pick out who plants it. We try to get everybody involved in it. It has been a star student or an alumnus. I will come up with a list of ideas at the beginning of the year. It just hit me just sometime during the first of the week to talk to him. By Thursday we had talked him into doing it. We told him that would be a perfect time to do it so the community could show its love to the family and for them to do the same.

"It was just unbelievable to be able to do it that way. It was great that both communities got together like that. I use the term 'one week out of the year, we don't like each other,' but what both Irwin and Fitzgerald did that night was amazing."

"It is flat-out warfare," long-time Irwin supporter Eddie Giddens admits. "We don't like you that week. But this year and this past season was different. Oh Lord, I was impressed. I have lifelong friends from Fitzgerald from even back to my high school days. It's kind of like we were united in every word. We will tell anybody that night that we're on your side."

Eddie has a picture saved on his cell phone, and it's easy to say he's not the only one, of Buddy planting the spear into the ground. There's not a week that goes by that he doesn't think about something Buddy said, something that happened from that 2019 season, or that big smile of his.

Safe to say he's not alone in that, either...

"It's fun for me," Irwin County assistant Clayton Sirmans says. "It's a rivalry that I've lived in Ocilla, graduating from here. We have friends from Fitzgerald and it's not a hatred from my time here, so to speak, but it's a rivalry in and out. I think it makes it even more of one when you have families that are connected and you're less than 10 miles away from each other. It's just a great rivalry because we know each other so well. I think that's a big part of it. A lot of people that were there this year loved Buddy and respected him. But seeing what happened before the game? Both sides got emotional. You know the feeling you get when you see that many people come together? It was just a pretty awesome moment- yet another moment that I will never forget."

You could ask Tucker Pruitt about it and what it means to live in it, play in it, and now coach in it...

"We live with each other pretty much the whole year," he admits, "and so bragging rights in that game is really big for the people around here. It gives you a little opportunity to brag against the other folks. Obviously, we're not in the same region anymore so it's not maybe what it used to be. But I think we're at a good spot in the rivalry, and it's still a big-time game for these people around here. I think Coach Nobles being from Fitzgerald and, then, going to Irwin County obviously bridges that gap, too. Everybody wants to win that game and after that we kind of put it behind us. And you wish the other side the best and try to go on to make the best of the rest of your year."

Tucker remembers his stomach dropping when he heard the news about Buddy and cancer. Bad stuff like that and getting news of that nature shouldn't happen to folks like that. When such a good guy who means so much to so many people is presented with a situation that you feel can't be true, it's a painful time.

"I know they were getting bombarded by everybody- all the people that care about him- in the church family, in the Fitzgerald Family, in the Irwin County family. So, most of the extent of my communication with them was a quick call here, a quick text message there, just to tell him that I'm thinking about him and praying for him."

There were also visits to the hospital and to the house to see the family when he could. But it was a difficult balance that was experienced and observed by most. He went over to the house a few times, hugged him and told him he was thinking about him and praying about him. But since they're getting communication from every possible angle and corner, Tucker wanted to make sure there was a sufficient amount of privacy as well. He would keep his distance throughout the football season, but the Pruitt family would always reach out to see if the Nobles family needed anything.

Tucker even thought the planting of the Irwin spear was awesome and something he would never forget after everything that had happened to the Nobles family.

And you could, definitely, ask the Nobles family about it. It goes from living, playing, and coaching in Fitzgerald to eventually coaching to the south- with a home built in that same town. A change in job didn't mean a change in address...

This week, while it was THAT week of the 52 where it's "purple" school and "red" school... while it was THAT week where conversations might be shorter than usual and bragging rights in that part of the state are on the line... It was also a week where a region showed a game week unity that would make everyone that didn't know what was happening off the field turn their head and pay attention from that moment going forward.

"We had gotten word early in the week that there was going to be a white out and didn't realize that Fitzgerald was going to do it, too," Kasey said. "So, stepping out of there and seeing pretty much both sides of the stadium home and away having a complete white-out was pretty special. Seeing all the shirts that said 'Nobles Strong,' that was a really, really special night for us- as a family and for the team."

Eventually, all of South Georgia would see what was witnessed in Ocilla in late August. Folks would wear the t-shirts, put signs up in front yards saying "We Got Your Back, Bud." You could go in most counties in that part of the state and you would know how the collective support was being spent. The Fitzgerald game was where it went to another level entirely.

"Dad had turned down throwing the spear at first," Kasey adds. "He said, 'There's no way. This isn't about me.' I told him it was about the kids, but he was still very adamant about not doing anything for him and focusing on the season. But my mom convinced him. She said 'These people are wanting to do this for you. People are here for you and this is something you need to do.' So he agreed to throw the spear down and you could just feel the energy in the air when he was out there in the middle of the field.

"He turned and raised the spear towards the Fitzgerald side to a standing ovation. You have got to understand. There's respect between Fitzgerald and Irwin. On that night, the Fitzgerald crowd gave him a standing ovation. They're going crazy for the head coach of their biggest rival. That was pretty special. Then, when he turns to the Irwin crowd, that's when you really think in that moment when he threw the spear down it solidified how special our year was going to be.

"That was crazy when he started crying when he threw the spear," Kevin Erwin remembers. "He felt everything that was given to him from everybody else in that stadium that night."

The vibe had changed...

This was a talented team in Ocilla. That was not in dispute. But, with all the doom and gloom that was hovering over a diagnosis there was an excitement with a group of men- young and old- that had a different mission. A mission for their coach, the family- blood and extended, and for everyone who was in touch with the program had been joined by faith in each other for the remainder of this journey.

No idea how long the journey would be, but everyone was walking as one...

"The 'white out' game was awesome," Andy Paulk admitted as he got to call it from the booth for radio. That thought was seconded by his broadcast partner, Kelly Wynn. "It was really an awesome night as both communities came together to support Buddy. We knew it was a special team from the very beginning before Buddy let everyone know he was sick. Coming off last year, we were going to be really, really good. But you could see this was a heck of a team right here."

"To see an event like last year- where the greater fraternity was the football fraternity- was a chance to see people wanting to love on their own," Irwin Superintendent Dr. Thad Clayton admits. "But it helps you to get back to what's good about high school athletics and what's good about high school football. It's much larger than just that Indian logo on our helmets or the Purple Hurricane logo. it's about people. It's about 'This is something good,' and when the chips are down and somebody needs love these combined communities will wrap their arms around you and love the people who had that need. It's greater than just what color you wear to go to work."

Dr. Clayton knows the image of all the white shirts in the stands will be hard to get out of his head- understandably so. The unified front you normally see 51 weeks out of the year carried over to a football game. It goes from "feuding and disputing," as Clayton says, and from fighting cousins to putting everything aside. The bragging rights over a year's time went away and there was an entire stadium rooting for Buddy Nobles. It didn't matter what magnet, license plate, car flag, or color you repped on a normal day. The message that night was one of unity, but there were other character traits that were on display: how to be a good man, how to represent your family name, how to be a good father, how to be a good husband, how to be a good employee, and tell everyone that you loved them.

"I may never experience another Irwin-Fitzgerald game that has that singular, combined purpose," Clayton admits. "And I may never see another game like that period. So, to be a part of that and to be just to be present was special."

Kenley noticed that the attitude rubbed off on everyone in that area and, eventually, anyone tied to the story- high school football fan or not. There was the white out. There were the signs. There were the t-shirts. The message and all of its love went from a town to two, from a school to two, and it would multiply as love often does when it's expressed and repaid in kind. If you walked into the local Wal-Mart in Fitzgerald, a Nobles would be befriended automatically- and be friends automatically. Buddy and the family connected everyone before a diagnosis and it was amplified with one.

People across an entire region would see him in an entirely different light.

"It's one of those things where I thought the rivalry kind of got away from us a little bit," Irwin assistant Jared Luke says. "Fitzgerald had beaten us 18 years in a row and it's like big brother up the road has your number. Tucker (Pruitt) is a great guy. He, his staff, and their school, Tucker's dad, Robby, and Buddy have been together forever. Tucker has a great relationship with Buddy as well and they decided they'd support him that night, too."

Coach Luke would tell anyone willing to listen that Buddy would let you know he loved you. He wouldn't ever be afraid to say it, either. And for this week out of the year on the football calendar, he would come at the rivalry from a different angle. He loved his church which was in Fitzgerald. He truly loved everyone in the town he coached in two stops before Ocilla. In one of Buddy's first couple of seasons at Irwin County, Coach Luke remembered talking badly about Fitzgerald in that week of the lead-up to the game. But Jared came to understand his head coach's perspective. He "got it," but he got it differently. It was through a different prism, but he got it.

"When Buddy holds the spear and he taps his chest," he continued, "he's letting everyone know 'I love you and I appreciate your support.' He does that for a minute or so to the Fitzgerald side. They're all standing up hollering and it is a great moment. All of a sudden, he turns around to the Irwin side and, I'm telling you, I still get chill bumps. It was indescribable. Our fans went crazy and everybody hollers as he plants the spear.

"BOOM!

"I was like, 'Dude, we're fixing to have a blowout. Absolutely! No doubt about it. The people that came out for that to support him were incredible. I couldn't thank our fans and Ben Hill County enough for what they did for him and his family supporting them in times of need."

"Tammy was sitting normally where she sits, about six or eight rows down from the Press Box," Irwin coach Chip Rankin recalls. "Buddy came off the field and he was not going to start coaching until he found Tammy and saw her. It was just one of the sweetest things I've ever seen. And the fact that you had folks from Ben Hill County wearing white and you had folks from Irwin County wearing white? That speaks a lot to how tight-knit that area really is. Everybody, I think, just wanted to show their support for Buddy. Everybody wanted him to get better and everybody was behind him and support him and that was a cool thing to see."

And when Irwin got to coaching, it was as Coach Luke had it thought out in his head after Buddy planted the spear...

For another game, Irwin County really didn't need to pass the ball. They ran up 400 yards on the ground and Jamorri Colson, Kam Ward, and the Benyards each ran for a score. Nathan Roberts caught one of Zach's three completions for a 28-yard touchdown in a 35-8 game that took Irwin to 2-0 and put another win with meaning in the books for Irwin County.

For Bill Barrs, it was another chance to see Irwin County up close and put another piece of a rivalry in his memory.

His oldest daughter, Abby, played recreational softball and met Buddy over a decade ago at those games. He would keep working at the police department in Fitzgerald, but call Irwin games on the radio with Andy and Kelly. Much like the Nobles family, he gets to see the game through that different prism.

"I got to know him through those times," he says. "It's rare to have a coach who's involved in both sides of a rivalry that is as close as this one is- considering it's pretty much the Twin Cities of Fitzgerald and Ocilla. It's a lot of 'getting along.' Both communities off the football field, off the basketball court, and off the baseball field get along and really intertwine with one another."

The rivalry was more like the Red Sox and Yankees before the last two seasons. It was slanted toward Fitzgerald in the win column over the last two decades and, then, with Buddy's first win in the series you would get the siren call for the 'Party at the Red Light.'

Bill graduated in 1992 so he knows what the game has meant over time.

"It's amazing- regardless of what was going on on that field- that there was something going on bigger that night," he says. "I talked to one of the opposing coaches after the game and all he told me was that he knew, when that spear stuck in the ground, that we were in trouble. It was just an amazing thing when you win that one."

"I don't know if Fitzgerald planned it or not," Irwin coach Drew Tankersley said. "You're aware there's white on white with white helmets. That's what their team did and that was pretty cool. Seeing Buddy throw that spear down that night was, I think, emotional for everybody. That was the last game that he coached, I guess, standing up- not from the podium." Tankersley also points out it was the first time Irwin beat Fitzgerald at the new version of the stadium in Ocilla. The 2018 win was at Jaycee Stadium to the north in Ben Hill County.

"I don't think you could have asked for a better game to beat them, though, for the first time on that field in front of everybody. That was pretty awesome." There would be some unexpected, added responsibility for Tankersley that would come in short order.

"I thought he was going to discontinue coaching," he continues. "I didn't know he was really going to miss the time he would later. I knew it was a serious deal, but I remember him calling me and after that missed game at Mount Paran, he said 'I want you to be calling the plays. You've been here with me.' I basically came in the same year and I was a little bit nervous. I've never done it for him and for him to say that to me...? I communicated with him as much as I could and I didn't want to let him down."

Tankersley wasn't the only one that felt that way.

"It was an amazing night. You've got 3,000-3,500 people all wearing white," Irwin coach Pete Snyder adds. "There are people over there I love. And, obviously, he lives over there. He has church over there and he never moved. There are so many people over there- just as many as he knows here. Boy, you talk about someone who always thinks the best of people... I mean, he will not say a bad word about anyone. He loves those he left from his coaching in Fitzgerald and there's a family back and forth here and there, really."

"Remember, Buddy said he didn't like the idea of planting the spear, initially," Irwin coach Troy Fletcher says. "But to walk out early before everybody else does and to see that stadium and it being fully white, it was a lot of love that showed. To see him plant the spear, we walked out and they all gave a standing ovation."

Fletcher still gets choked up thinking back... in his mind, all this happened yesterday.

"I think that that was a good example of really what these communities mean to each other in the people who are part of them."

"That was, I don't know, probably the last glimpse of Buddy you would see before it really started going downhill," Principal Scott Haskins admits. "But, you know, he was just so elated to plant the spear before the game. I think the reason was because he saw the outpouring of support.

"Think back to the golf cart with the Touchdown Club and everybody pitching in to do that. I think that that was just another one of those gestures that just reinforce the love that everybody had for the family. You know there were times when he just was hurting and he just could hardly do anything. That such a great gift from them and you know how well received by the family it was. The white out and the golf cart were great gestures in a season of them."

"Buddy saw that everyone there let the family know they loved them with the white out," Irwin Coach Luke Roberts says. "After the game, I remembered Tucker Pruitt was upset because he lost. But, of course, he and Buddy had a relationship as far back as anybody. It is respectful and loving from the time he was a pup. When you looked at the crowd that night, it wasn't people from Fitzgerald wearing purple and it wasn't folks from Irwin County wearing red. Everybody was wearing white in support of Buddy. As he fought cancer, you saw so much support and love for one man."

"I have to tell you this," Lloyd Stembridge says as he tried to describe the rivalry this time around. "Just before the war started, there was a peace treaty. In all the pain, we stood sharing what was going on. Some of us were crying, but it was a magical moment. The fact that everybody wore white- I mean it wasn't purple and red, it was a white out- and, I think, it symbolized the galvanizing of that area for getting behind Buddy. From there, it was the white out. It was the signs. It's 'We got your back, Bud.' It's stickers. It's going over to his house and all of that stuff.

"I think that it was just one of those galvanizing moments throwing the region's support around the family. In South Georgia, it's something bigger than 'Friday Night Football' and you know it. To see our community rise above football, it was a magical moment for us."

Lloyd is not wrong… and it would only grow from there…

Fitzgerald 8

Purple Hurricanes

Irwin County 35

Indians

1	2	3	4	F
0	0	8	0	8
6	8	21	0	35

Chapter 5

SEPTEMBER 6- JOHNSON CITY, LOSS 20-13

The West Florida football season would get its start on a Thursday night in Johnson City, Tennessee against traditional Division II power Carson-Newman. The Eagles, by design, will want to take as much of the clock with their running game as humanly possible.

And they did... a little over 35 minutes of possession by the time the game was done at Burke-Tarr Stadium in the season opener for both schools. About three-quarters of the total yards by Carson-Newman came on the ground and would give them a two touchdown lead going into the fourth quarter.

UWF would find their rhythm and put a touchdown on the board with 6:53 to go in regulation as Austin Reed threw a 9-yard score to Tate Lehtio in Reed's debut at quarterback for the Argos. UWF blocked a Carson-Newman field goal attempt – the first one of those in program history– with 31 seconds left to give them a fighting chance at a tying score. But Reed's Hail Mary attempt was turned into a sack before he could get rid of the ball. The Argos had their chance, but ran out of time.

You want those kinds of tests before you go into conference play- regardless of the division you're in for NCAA football.

But there were other things on Kaleb's mind- and the rest of the Nobles family, for that matter...

The weekend would bring its own set of challenges...

September 9th

We took Buddy to the ER in Tifton Saturday because of complications he developed. They determined that there was a hole in his stomach (either from the tumor or the procedure he had on Thursday). Tift Regional sent him by ambulance back to Emory where the procedure had been done. They are trying to get the hole in the stomach to close up by hitting it with antibiotics and TPN IV nutrition. He is not allowed anything to eat or drink to keep the stomach empty. The latest ct scan was unclear regarding the hole but they did not see air, which is a good thing. Once they are sure the hole has closed they are giving him his first dose of chemo at Emory.

We expect to be here for several days. Missing practice is killing him but he has been coordinating with all of his coaches and he knows they have everything under control. What a blessing the coaches and our school administrators have been.

September 10th

I am just getting to my phone.

The scope determined the hole in the stomach has sealed but the bleeding is coming from the tumor. It was too much to cauterize so they are hitting it with radiation starting tomorrow. The team will tell us tomorrow how much radiation and when chemo can start.

I watched God perform a miracle today because Buddy was close to dying and GOD listened to the many, many prayers

being prayed for Buddy. We have a long road ahead so please keep praying. Buddy will never ever quit. He is a fighter.

Thanks to all who prayed, visited, helped us with expenses and held our arms up as we were too tired to hold them up ourselves. And a very special thank you to Brian Cobb and Marty Roberts who helped us get Kenley's car to a Ford dealership up here because her power steering went out. Satan is trying us but GOD is bigger!!

September 11th would be Buddy's first radiation treatment... the first in a string of attempts to chase the cancer inside of him...

"It was tough for us," Pastor Lloyd Stembridge recalls. "Four years ago, we moved right behind them in Fitzgerald, and I became his Pastor and his friend. For me, it was very emotional and we never gave up that there wouldn't be a miracle for Buddy. Even in the tough times, I could go over to the house and we would just sit there and talk- and we would talk about a lot of things and remember the good old days. There were times where there were tears and concern, but we just, kind of, left it with God.

"I never gave up on it until Tammy would call me that one morning later on. He had Jesus Christ in every aspect of his life and you could measure it through those boys he coached. He let them know that Jesus is bigger than football. He, his wife, and his boys and daughter are part of our Church community and always will be. I think his legacy is that he brought Jesus Christ into his fight every day. They even taught me a lot about faith as we got to know each other."

WEST FLORIDA 13 (0-1)
vs CARSON-NEWMAN 20 (1-0)

1st	02:52	C-N–Antonio Wimbush 2 yd run (Nate Craft kick), 2 plays, 53 yards, TOP 0:37
2nd	07:19	UWF–Jervon Newton 2 yd run (Austin Williams kick failed), 7 plays, 56 yards, TOP 3:04
2nd	03:31	C-N–Nate Craft 20 yd field goal 7 plays, 55 yards, TOP 3:39
2nd	00:43	C-N–Nate Craft 35 yd field goal 8 plays, 31 yards, TOP 1:39
3rd	04:01	C-N–Derrick Evans 43 yd run (Nate Craft kick), 7 plays, 66 yards, TOP 2:43
4th	06:53	UWF–Tate Lehtio 9 yd pass from Austin Reed (Austin Williams kick) 8 plays, 79 yards, TOP 3:18

Chapter 6

SEPTEMBER 13- AT MT PARAN CHRISTIAN-
CANCELLED/SHORTER, WIN 42-14

The Carson-Newman game was in the books for West Florida. It was a tough game in a tough environment on an odd day of the week to kickoff the 2019 season. But there were a lot of lessons to take from it if you were associated with the Argos and headed back to Pensacola. Irwin was coming out of the bye week and was getting ready for a stern test against Mount Paran Christian.

But the Nobles family was getting to know Emory-St. Joseph's Hospital too well...

"Nothing happened before the Carson-Newman game," Kaleb recalls. "I got to be there and coach like normal. That game being on Thursday night probably helped a bunch because I had a little bit of time off on the weekend. Dad got taken to the hospital in Tifton Saturday night and then to Emory overnight so I took off to Emory early Sunday morning. Dad's condition wasn't great during that week so I wasn't in the office at all during the week of our Shorter game."

The life of a coach means you have to be able to work in whatever environment you're in. For Kasey, it meant staying in contact with folks in Ocilla. For Kaleb, he brought his laptop to Atlanta and was the night owl of the bunch. He would sit in the room with Buddy, getting in his viewing and prep for the game against the Hawks. There would be time, late in the week, where he would fall asleep in the chairs- laptop still playing plays.

He was still a part of meetings and would stay in touch with the quarterbacks on the phone as he thought the risk was too great to be far away from Atlanta. Kaleb still wanted to do his job, since he knew his dad would expect nothing less.

"There was one night, about 1:30-2:00 in the morning, I was up watching our film from that day while Mom and Dad were falling asleep," he says. "I'm sitting in the recliner in the hospital room right beside dad and I have my computer on the food tray as my makeshift desk. My chair's kind of parallel with Dad in the bed. I'm watching and our Tight End didn't do a good job of cutting a guy off on a play versus the Scout Team. I thought Dad was asleep but he wasn't, because he goes, 'Your tight end needs to get his head on the other side'. I started cracking up because I thought he was asleep but, little did I know, he's right there watching film with me. It was a very funny moment, but I wasn't surprised. We ended up just watching the film together for the next hour because neither one of us could sleep. I'm thinking, man, this is unbelievable. I'm still getting to do my job at the hospital- with my dad. It is little moments like that that I cherish from my dad.

"My Dad, of all people, when he's sitting in a hospital bed is still telling me to go to Pensacola and is telling me 'I'll be fine. Just stay there.' I told him, 'Dad, you're in the hospital. You're not fine right now. I'm right where I need to be and I'm not going anywhere.'"

The modern technology would work like this: Practice would end around 6:30 in Atlanta. It would take an hour for the film to load for Kaleb to view it. He would wait until his mom would fall asleep to watch it. There was no way he would be anywhere else than Atlanta.

"I don't think God has anything to do with the schedule of football games," he continues, "but it kind of worked out pretty good. Playing at Shorter in Rome, it's a little bit over an hour away from where we were at Emory."

He would meet the team in the team hotel and briefed head coach Pete Shinnick and the rest of the team on his dad's condition.

Kaleb first told the Argos during Fall Camp and he told his quarterbacks in a position meeting. He didn't want it to be something that pulled attention away from practice and game days. By his own admission, his mind was constantly on his dad while doing his job but Coach Shinnick and the rest of the staff couldn't have been more understanding.

"There was no mistaking it. Coach Shinnick is a big Christian-very firm in his faith- and he's not afraid to talk to us about that. There's no mistaking of what he is about and what he believes."

To give you an idea, Kaleb transferred into UWF to finish his college career. Coach Shinnick reminded him of his father-no cussing and, at the same time, someone who focuses on making his players the best husbands, fathers, employers, and employees that they could be. Guys on the team reached out to text Kaleb to show support with all the time away from campus. But Shinnick told Kaleb to take as much time as he needed to be with family. They both knew Kaleb would be away from campus for a while, but that didn't matter. He was told to take as much time as he needed as much as he hated to be away from UWF. To have that support was immeasurable and everyone would welcome him when he would return to campus.

"Something you never expected to have to do was game planning in the hospital," as Kasey tried to get his players ready for Mount Paran Christian. "We were all trying to be up there as much as possible as it was tough to balance being up there with him and still game planning. It was a little bit emotional throughout the week knowing that. He was trying to convince all his doctors up at Emory that it was a good idea if they let him out Friday just to go to the game and then come back to the hospital.

"That was his idea. They quickly put a stop to that and said, 'No, you have more serious things to worry about. You don't need to go to the game.' He was down about not being able to go to the game and, when we were warming up, I just remember feeling really, really weird. I was so used to being on the field with him walking around pregame and it kind of hit me there that, man, this season's going to be pretty crazy. It doesn't feel right being out here coaching and not having him on the sidelines."

Buddy would be keeping an eye from his hospital bed with Tammy at his side the entire time.

During the Indians bye weekend, Buddy had his first complication at the house. The family went straight to Tifton where doctors did a bunch of tests and x-rays. It was hard to keep track of everything, but they did find a perforation in his stomach-basically a hole in his stomach that had to be addressed and that had to be done at Emory. The family would go back and forth from home to Tifton, to Emory, and back for recovery and practice in Ocilla. Buddy wanted everybody to just focus on the team and the kids on a daily basis. Much like his conversations with Kaleb, Buddy wanted Kasey at practice at Irwin County.

"He didn't want the kids to lose anything in those days when he wasn't there," Kasey says. "I wasn't able to be a practice and Luke Roberts would be a big help aligning coaches to be able to do separate drills with Buddy in the Intensive Care Unit. Dad was still focused on the kids those two weeks leading up to the Mount Paran game-even with a lot of back-and-forth from the hospital. There's traveling during the day and going to practice when I can."

The game with Mt. Paran Christian still was on at their Kennesaw campus- about 45 minutes northwest of the city of Atlanta. From Chieftain Circle to the front door, it's 214 miles or 3:20- and that's without stretching your legs, having a walk-through, or grabbing a meal. Head Coach Mitch Jordan has built a program that has made a post-season appearance every season dating back to 2013 and includes a 14-0 title winning run in 2014. The Eagles had made a trip to Ocilla in the 2018 season and came up on the short end of a 40-20 decision. Both teams were ranked in the top five of their respective sections in Class-A.

"I got to know him that season and they were an incredible football team," Coach Jordan says. "I was impressed with how he built that program from the top down, Everything from their hospitality when we came to Ocilla to seeing there was no ego with Coach Nobles at all. I was taking mental notes all the time down there and I was also impressed with how their fans treated our team when we were there."

He took notes on how Buddy was having success at Irwin County- and not just on the field. It would be in the art of the detail, how they warmed up, how the middle school program was run, and even the effort and care the program put into their new weight room facility. Coach Jordan got to return the favor in 2019 (with those notes he took in a notebook all his own), but had to keep an eye on the skies and local meteorologists to see how dicey conditions would be all night long.

As the team was coming off the field from pregame warmups, every player stopped by a FaceTime video that was set up by Billy Stevens. He told all the kids he loved them and it was a pretty special moment for Buddy, while he wasn't there in person, that he got to interact with the kids, tell them he loved them, and told each other to fight.

"Buddy had his iPad in the hospital and Billy had his phone," Irwin assistant Troy Fletcher remembers. "We had it set up to where Buddy could be right there and could see the game with Billy. So, if he wants to tell me and the coaches anything (or whatever he wants to do), you can do it right there from the hospital. Our biggest concern was that we didn't want him getting upset. He's a coach with passion. He loves the game of football, loves it for the kids, and we didn't want him hit with any other setbacks."

The game itself had an opening kickoff and, with heavy rain and lightning in the area, everyone had to go back to their locker rooms. That's where they stayed. For hours… before the game was eventually cancelled.

"It sucked that we couldn't play," Kasey added. "We traveled all the way up here, spent all this money to come up to Atlanta and everyone had to turn right back around. At the same time, in my head, I was also thinking Dad doesn't have to miss any games. So, maybe he'll get out by the time we were going to play Clinch County."

"He was concerned about that," Fletcher adds. "Maybe, the good Lord blessed us in the end with us playing Clinch the following week. In a way, you almost got a double-bye week where no one got hurt. You had all this travel and, then, be involved in recovery from that. You have got one of your biggest rivalries in the state right out of the blocks when it comes to region play if he was not able to be there again. And it was a little bit of a diversion with adjustments for us to be as calm as possible through that time for the kids and try to do everything we could to keep the kids first.

"Nothing changes for a Friday game scheduled and it really gave the kids some time off."

When the game was over, the Nobles family would head back to Emory with all of the unknown. And the unknown was pretty bad.

"It was a long trip for us," Irwin assistant Pete Snyder said. "The people up there were just so nice and so kind. There was this outpouring of love and affection for Buddy and his family and everyone came over to see us. They were just so welcoming and they raised money for the family. It was the best game where we didn't actually play a game that could have ever happened, if that makes sense. That whole experience was a blessing up there."

"The coaching staff went to Atlanta to see him in the hospital," Irwin assistant Jared Luke said. "We didn't know what direction it was fixing to go, you know? We were concerned. We loved our brother. Buddy Stevens drove us up in the van, we came back to town, we went to practice, and would take the trip to Atlanta. Kasey and Coach Tankersley did a tremendous job preparing, studying, and getting ready for this game. And it was an example of those things where you knew you had a good leader in Buddy because of how prepared your other guys worked to get ready for a game that had only one play."

"Late Saturday night of the bye week, he was having some pretty serious complications," Snyder adds. "We got word early that Sunday morning from Kasey that they were just going to head to Emory right away. We all rode up there on Monday and were really expecting the worst at that point. Was he going to pass away even...? We all felt that we needed to go see him. So, we got up there and several other people were there as well- Buddy's pastor was one of them. We took turns in small groups going back there to see him. When I went in, he's up in the bed and he looked like he's got color and he was in pretty good spirits. We were talking and we were really surprised by it all. Tammy started crying. She was praying and everyone's praying with her and she just felt like God was not done with him yet.

"I told her 'I'm right there with you and He wasn't done with him yet.' It was really a miracle. It was really, really bad but he somehow made it through. It was just a really encouraging day, honestly, for us. Buddy was doing a little bit better even if we knew Buddy might be there for a while."

Drew Tankersley admitted that there was a bit of a running joke that if Buddy could get to Mount Paran Christian and be on the sidelines in a hospital bed, he would be there.

"You're just across town. You know, we love him but he wanted to be there. I would have loved to see that game continue on and it wasn't shocking to me a bit to see if he had shown up at some point."

Bill Barrs and Dr. Clayton were also part of the group that went to see Buddy at Emory. One thing stuck with him. "He kept telling us, 'Make sure my guys are taken care of... You make sure my guys are taken care of... Make sure that they get this. Make sure they get that...' He's in a hospital bed and you know what with the situation he was in... The first thing that comes to him is to make sure my guys are taken care of..."

"You had a lot of young men who had to grow up pretty quickly because of all of this with Buddy," Casey Soliday adds.

September 14th

One lesson I have learned this week is to not take anything for granted. This afternoon Kenley was sitting with Buddy as I jumped in the shower in his room. When I got out of the shower

I could hear them both through the door. Buddy was saying "Go baby, Go baby, Go!!!" I opened the door and saw that they were watching JD King make a run on the Ga Southern football game. I have heard him cheer about football games many times before but it sounded so much sweeter today!!

God is so much bigger!!

Buddy has had a good day. He has had several visitors today and loved every one. He is watching some football and resting, trying to regain some of the strength that radiation has zapped. We still have a long way to go but right now I am thankful for the little things!!

It was only a 90-minute drive for Kaleb to go from studying game film in the ICU Waiting Room at St. Joseph's. Anyone that made the trip to Barron Stadium, just outside of downtown Rome, Georgia got to see a special day for redshirt freshman Austin Reed. Shorter University made the jump to Division II and has had trouble transitioning to life in the Gulf South Conference.

Reed would be responsible for six touchdowns on the day to tie a record set by Kaleb back in the 2016 season. He ran for the first two and, after the home team tied it at 7 with a 65-yard run by Tupac Lanier and tied it at 14 on a TD pass (an uncharacteristic move by Shorter), the rest of the day was the Argos. Passes to Kevin Grant, Quentin Randolph, Ka'Ron Ashley, and Rodney Coates the day was a comfortable 42-14 win in the Gulf South.

Shorter only had 93 total yards of offense in the second half as well and their losing streak grew to 41 games. That streak would come to an end on the Hawks' Senior Night in November with a win over Allen University- after 48 straight losses. Virginia Lynchburg would head to Pensacola after the Argos conference opener. That Saturday afternoon would give Kaleb a bit of a mental break from a week of sleeping in chairs and staring at game film on a computer screen. His mind, though, was never far from the perimeter of the city of Atlanta.

"Ocilla is what south Georgia football is all about," Coach Jordan adds. "It really is. Only getting to play one play is disappointing in any situation where you'd like to play a game against any opponent. You would go your way in your schedule after that night and they would go the other way. I was a Buddy Nobles fan this past season, yes."

He would watch the championship game like a lot of other coaches that weekend in December- rooting for Irwin County. Being a head coach and Athletic Director at a Christian school, what Buddy would say later that afternoon would resonate with Coach Jordan.

"High School athletics are about how to do it the right way people. The question is: Are people still doing it the right way...? There are two approaches you could take. You could be in a world where things are being done exactly the right way, but if you don't win, you think that you can't win. You can also do things the right way for kids and do it with integrity. He is a great example of a role model for that way of doing things.

"Buddy was a good man."

WEST FLORIDA 42 (1-1 , 1-0)
-VS- SHORTER UNIVERSITY 14 (0-2 , 0-1)

1st	04:24	UWF–Austin Reed 1 yd run (Austin Williams kick), 13 plays, 78 yards, TOP 6:12	7	0
1st	03:06	SU–Tupac Lanier 65 yd run (Nicholas Pope kick), 5 plays, 80 yards, TOP 1:12	7	7
1st	00:51	UWF–Austin Reed 6 yd run (Austin Williams kick), 6 plays, 76 yards, TOP 2:06	14	7
2nd	13:05	SU–Andrew Warren 46 yd pass from Tyler Pullum (Nicholas Pope kick) 5 plays, 72 yards, TOP 2:40	14	14
3rd	12:45	UWF–Kevin Grant 8 yd pass from Austin Reed (Austin Williams kick) 5 plays, 71 yards, TOP 2:07	21	14
3rd	09:14	UWF–Q. Randolph 51 yd pass from Austin Reed (Austin Williams kick) 5 plays, 61 yards, TOP 2:04	28	14
3rd	04:02	UWF–Ka'Ron Ashley 16 yd pass from Austin Reed (Austin Williams kick) 7 plays, 55 yards, TOP 2:41	35	14
4th	11:06	UWF–Rodney Coates 20 yd pass from Austin Reed (Austin Williams kick) 9 plays, 79 yards, TOP 3:41	42	14

Chapter 7

SEPTEMBER 20- CLINCH, 14-0/ VA-LYNCHBURG, 69-0

A t first I was thinking that we might get kicked out tonight as we watch and cheer from the hospital room, but now I am thinking that Coach might have half the hospital in our room watching with us. You know he has told everybody about his Indians and has quite a few coming in the door saying "Go Indians"!!!

Don Tison, Junior is as much a part of the Clinch County fabric as anyone else in Homerville and the surrounding cities in the area. His dad, Don, Senior, coached the program from 1974-1993. In the years he was allowed, Don, Junior was a ballboy and got to patrol the sidelines with his dad. He would play, graduate, and eventually return to be an assistant for a high-powered offense under another legacy- Jim Dickerson. When Dickerson retired Don, Junior was given his chance to be the guy in charge. The Panthers were back-to-back champs in Single-A Public and ran a record of 25-3 over the last two seasons and, if you go back and look at Clinch's run of three titles in four years, the team went a collective 49-6. This would be a battle of Number One and Number Two. The team that was always in the way of the other in winning a region title and then the reverse would be true chasing a state title. Irwin County would always seem to get that first victory, but Charlie Brown could never get to kick the football when Lucy gave him the chance to go two-for-two...

In 2019, Clinch had beaten two other top-ten teams in Hebron Christian and Brooks County. Their third win of the year was a dominant 47-12 win in Vienna when Dooly County's Bobcats hosted Clinch, but this one started region play and could, for all intents and purposes, tell you who the top overall seed would be in the Single-A Public playoffs. One inside track could yield to another and mean that the winner here could even host all the way through a playoff run. The win, for either side, could be massive... and it was a game in late September

With Buddy undergoing treatment, Casey Soliday was taking over as interim head coach. That also meant Casey got to answer questions when the media came to cover practice. WALB-TV's Paige Dauer visited both teams and Casey talked gameplan.

"We practiced all week on being physical, so that's what we want to be. We know they're going to be physical, they're going to be athletic and fast, we just got to be able to match those kind of things," said Soliday. With a defense that had given up only 15 points in two games (and a kickoff), this made sense.

"It's a huge game because of the history that we've had with them, playing against them in the state championship game and before that we've got a long history. So, it's a very very competitive rivalry," Tison told Dauer later that week.

"I have to be honest," Kasey said, "our practices were smooth. Everything went well. Our kids were very mature about this whole process throughout the year. They said they knew it wasn't going to be normal, but they came out to practice every day with a focus that you normally don't see with high school kids. It's tough to get high school kids to be completely focused all the time, but I think due to the circumstances, they were pretty locked in throughout the year. We didn't didn't have to deal with the normal day-to-day drama that kids might get in trouble in school or anything like. Everything was pretty calm and focused on football."

Buddy had a script made up for the game plan against Clinch. He had the daily practice script with every play scripted. The team would film practice with those elements and upload it so Buddy could watch it at night in the hospital to be able to give feedback for the other coaches on staff for the following day.

"For him to be able to be involved without being at practice was nice," Kasey continues. "I know from talking to him that he was not happy that he wasn't going to be able to go to the game. Obviously, there's a huge history there and it's a big game. This was the first game, I think, Dad hadn't called offensively and I thought Drew Tankersley did a really good job calling plays that night."

The game itself had half-a-dozen turnovers and five of them were in the fourth quarter alone. Clinch was in control of most of the first quarter- so much so, in fact, that Irwin ran only three offensive plays in the first quarter. Period. The only scores came when an alert Gabriel Benyard scooped up an Eric Anderson fumble and ran it in for a score in the first half and on a defensive score by JyQuez Marshall in the fourth quarter.

The 14-0 final for Irwin was the first shutout of Clinch since a 30-0 loss to Eagle's Landing Christian Academy in September of 2013 and it was the third straight regular season win by Irwin County in the series.

"We didn't score as many points as we'd have liked," Kasey says, "but we were pretty good on defense. We were pleased with how the offensive line played and, obviously, pleased with the defense for the defensive touchdown. Things started to fall in place and we got little breaks here and there, so that was a good sign. A lot of times you can tell if you're going to have luck on your side for the season. I know that's a weird thing to say, but a lot of times that does play in the success of the season. We had the right breaks at the right time and I think that set us up for home-field advantage in the playoffs even though it was early in the season."

With Buddy being as sick as he was at the time and all the travel and appointments that took up time away from the normal day-to-day of a football season, getting a win like this against Clinch that could eventually win you a region title was just as important. You don't have to travel for football games every week, either.

"That's the second one of the three that you say you have to get every year," Marty Roberts adds. That regular-season win over Clinch was another one of those statement games. It put you a step ahead early in the season towards winning a region Championship. If you won that game you, basically, had a two-game lead in the region because you had to lose twice since you have the tiebreaker against them in case you lost one.

"They didn't have DJ (Lundy) that night since he was hurt and, with Buddy in the hospital, you could just see the team wasn't going to be denied- that night or that whole season. I have never seen a group come together like them. It was just one big family and they played their hearts out. I think Clinch crossed mid-field one time and, although it was 14-0, and we had two flukey touchdowns to beat them you just felt like the game was never in doubt."

September 21

A note from Coach Nobles:

I am so proud of Indian Nation. It was not the prettiest game but a good win. It was hard fought on both sides

I have the utmost respect for Clinch County. I have spoken several times with retired Coach Dickerson this week and exchanged several texts with Coach Tyson last night. Such an awesome program in Homerville. I have received many messages and calls from that way since my diagnosis. Seeing the white shirts last night joining our programs together in this fight that I am in was very humbling!! I am sure we will meet again down the road. Best of luck to y'all until we meet again.

Thank you Creekbox for airing the game. It allowed me to be part of the game. Our prayers are with y'all also, Coach Dickerson shared with me that one of yours was involved in a car accident yesterday. We will continue praying for her and her family.

Indian Nation I am so proud of our players, coaches and fans. You all rose to the occasion and came out victorious!! It was tough watching from the hospital and not being there but I am so very proud of all of you. You did not back down!! You have all covered my family and me with love, prayers, cards, calls, messages and donations. Thank you and GOD bless each of you. I am coming home this week and hope to see you all very soon. I love y'all and appreciate you

Virginia University-Lynchburg restarted football back in 2011. They were one of 16 schools to play in the NCCAA- the National Christian College Athletic Association. It's a loose grouping of schools that play schedules against NAIA and NCAA schools and they house themselves in either the NCCAA itself or will be in an NCAA division and play both ways in their year. The Dragons had been a willing opponent after UWF was having a hard time trying to fill out their 2019 schedule and had only scored 42 points in their three losses- half of those came the previous week in a loss to Savannah State.

It would be an even longer day in Pensacola...

The Argos scored 11 different times on the night at Blue Wahoos Stadium- with ten different scorers. It was only 7-0 after one quarter as Anthony Johnson ran in from two yards out. He would be followed by Jaden Gardner, Rodney Coates (through the air), Evan Mitchell, TJ Williams, and Kevin Grant in a 35-point second quarter. The third quarter would add an Austin Williams field goal and the second-string kicker, Alex Virgilio would start the fourth for a 48-0 lead. Marcus Clayton, Evan Williams, and Sam Vaughn would wrap up the 69-0 blowout to send VUL to 0-4 as West Florida would improve to 2-1.

The visitors were held to minus-12 yards rushing on the day and 127 total yards. The team would set three scoring records and had scores on offense, defense, and special teams for only the second time in school history.

Mississippi College would be just around the corner in Gulf South Conference play then Delta State would come visit to wrap up the three-game homestand…

"If we want to be the team we think we're capable of being, then we've got to take care of business at home," UWF Head Coach Pete Shinnick told Senior Writer Bill Vilona of goargos.com after the game. "I got a team that is receptive. We think we can get better and we look forward to getting after it this week (in practices)."

Shinnick knew what he was talking about and the rest of Division II would find out over time.

"I drove back to Pensacola on the 20th from Emory because we were making some good progress with Dad," Kaleb says. "I showed up to put our Friday schedule together. What we normally do is an offensive-defense meeting in the afternoon, and then we'll do a walk-through, and then do a quick team meeting. I wanted to get there just in time for a walk through. But I got there for the offensive meeting, walked in, and sat down in the back of the whole room just stood up and wanted to give me a hug.

"It was pretty cool to understand that my guys were all there for me. They had your back and they didn't have to do the things that they did and have done since I first told everyone at UWF. You could worry about being away because that can affect my job security. That can affect my job but it's never been a thought my mind the whole time because of how good our coaches are."

With everything going on off the field in Pensacola, it was good to have a game to focus on. The team thought that if they could get some momentum after the loss to Carson-Newman, they could gather some steam going into Gulf South Conference play.

"We knew we had a good chance to be good, but as we started putting wins together, it was pretty cool to see."

The plan going forward for Kaleb would be to coach through text and Facetime during the week, come back to the team (either in Pensacola or on the road) on Fridays, and be there on game days. He would, then, take off either after the game (if it was early enough in the day) or early Sunday to catch back up with family and be there with them and his dad. That timeline would repeat after Lynchburg.

But things would take a turn toward the end of the week as the Argos got ready for Mississippi College.

Clinch County 0

Panthers

Irwin County 14

Indians

1	2	3	4	F
0	0	0	0	0
6	0	0	8	14

VIRGINIA-LYNCHBURG 0 (1-4)
-VS- WEST FLORIDA 69 (2-1)

1st	08:05	UWF–Anthony Johnson 2 yd run (Austin Williams kick), 8 plays, 66 yards, TOP 3:51	0	7
2nd	14:16	UWF–Jaden Gardner 7 yd run (Austin Williams kick), 2 plays, 46 yards, TOP 0:35	0	14
2nd	08:37	UWF–Rodney Coates 2 yd pass from Austin Reed (Austin Williams kick) 10 plays, 70 yards, TOP 4:22	0	21
2nd	05:55	UWF–Evan Mitchell 22 yd pass from Austin Reed (Austin Williams kick) 2 plays, 48 yards, TOP 0:33	0	28
2nd	05:39	UWF–T.J. Williams 44 yd interception (Austin Williams kick)	0	35
2nd	00:44	UWF–Kevin Grant 29 yd pass from Austin Reed (Austin Williams kick) 9 plays, 78 yards, TOP 1:58	0	42
3rd	07:23	UWF–Austin Williams 37 yd field goal 6 plays, 15 yards, TOP 2:09	0	45
4th	12:02	UWF–Alex Virgilio 37 yd field goal 9 plays, 29 yards, TOP 3:05	0	48
4th	09:55	UWF–Marcus Clayton 3 yd blocked punt return (Alex Virgilio kick)	0	55
4th	07:32	UWF–Evan Mitchell 30 yd pass from J.C. Robles (Alex Virgilio kick) 2 plays, 37 yards, TOP 0:47	0	62
4th	02:51	UWF–Sam Vaughn 2 yd run (Alex Virgilio kick), 7 plays, 53 yards, TOP 3:13	0	69

Chapter 8

SEPTEMBER 27- TELFAIR COUNTY, 45-7/MISS COLLEGE, 27-21

There are moments in a season that crystallize what football means to the towns they represent, what people tied to those programs mean, and what everyone tied to those teams mean to each other. After ten rounds of radiation in Atlanta, Buddy came home on the 24th of September.

But there was something he didn't know. About 100 people were lining the street where he lives in Ben Hill County to guide their car that last little bit back into their driveway.

"It was pretty cool, man," Buddy said at the time. And the word "cool" got extended a few seconds and added some syllables. "I didn't know a thing about it."

He wanted to see the football team...

Much like the scenes in those stereotypical western movies when you see the hero in the white hat storming into town at the end ready for the gunfight at high noon, Buddy and Kaleb came riding up the dirt road that links the fieldhouse to the upper practice fields. Dust was kicking up behind the cart and announcing to the team that someone, and they couldn't figure it out at first, was coming to visit.

When you ask the coaches themselves, they can kind of agree that it was Jamorri Colson and "Big Bubba" that broke ranks first and realized it was Coach Nobles. QB Zach Smith, by his own admission, tried to tackle Jamorri and keep him on the ground so he could get to see Coach first, but it wasn't meant to be. An entire roster of 60 students broke ranks and left practice behind so they could see someone they loved very much return home after ten rounds of radiation.

"Everything came to a stop and all the kids came running," he said. "It was pretty cool there, too. When they came running, they circled the golf cart. Tell you something... I felt like the Pied Piper. I stayed for an hour during offense, team, and group. So, when it comes to going to practice, I'll just be in the golf cart for right now."

"Mom gave him strict orders to stay on the golf cart and not walk around much," Kaleb adds. "Dad being Dad though, he looked at me and said 'You think Mom can see us way out here?'

and proceeded to step off the cart and correct things he didn't like during their team session. It was true Buddy Nobles form."

"Mom sent me a video of him going to the practice field," Kenley says. "I could see Jamorri throw his helmet down and start running and then it all broke loose from there. I started crying while watching the video because I could tell how much he means to those guys. I know how much they mean to him, so just seeing them run up to him was emotional"

Buddy would hang for his first two periods, as was his current custom, and head home to the house ten minutes away in Fitzgerald.

"I went outside after we got settled and tried my best to speak to everyone who came to see us. After we got back inside, I went down and sat in my recliner for about an hour and, then, I went and lay down on my couch and slept like a baby for a while."

But before he conserved his energy that week, he talked about the rivalry game that his team took care of a couple of days before...

"Clinch played great, too," he admits. "But we capitalized on the mistakes. I just couldn't believe we shut them out. I was kind of shocked at that. But, you know what? Our kids are unbelievable."

There's another video out there Tammy shot that particular Tuesday afternoon as Buddy headed back to the high school practice field. He rode up to practice in his golf cart. Tammy was in the car behind.

"That whole day of him coming back and just being able to to be out there with the guys," Coach Snyder said, "was amazing. They love him. He's a tough guy. At practice every day, he demanded action and, in spite of him being tough on those guys, they absolutely loved him and would do anything for him."

Radio analyst Bill Barrs likened it to a holiday:

"It's kind of like: I'm going to see my child because I haven't seen him in so long. It's like Santa Claus and the kids when they first see him at the mall and everyone wants to sit in his lap. For him to actually get to walk up and talk to them face-to-face...? Those kids were excited."

"The golf cart was a big thing to help him out along the way," Coach Drew Tankersley admits. "I think that that speaks to how everybody loves somebody in the family down here in Ocilla. That's just a tribute to the booster club and people in Irwin County donating money. That's one good thing about Irwin County and then small communities and the businesses where people are always very generous and willing to give and willing to help one of their own- especially somebody like Buddy. When things are not going great or you need a pick-me-up or some help, doing something like that was special. When he was able to come back and the cart got him around and helped him move around the practice field that was big for him."

"He was able to come out for a little bit late during practices," assistant Troy Fletcher adds. "There would be times where he would look at the offense during scrimmage time during practice. Part of the time we talked to him and he would watch the scout team practice beforehand. He would be there for those periods and we told him that we can handle the rest. It was really exciting for him driving up and when the players saw him driving up, it was like little kids that ran straight to him. That was a very exciting day."

"To see that, I think, and if you didn't know the story or you weren't intimately connected to it, I think that that was another one of the personifications of the relationship of Buddy with not just the players but with the family and the school and Ocilla," Marty Roberts says. "And just what it meant to the fabric of that entire relationship."

When Buddy Nobles took over as head coach at Irwin, Marty says, everybody noticed the team lost the state championship. Then, they lost another one and, then, Irwin lost in the third round the third year. You heard a lot of people talking on the street and in businesses in the area that "that's he's the one that can't win the big one." Folks would say within earshot that while, yes, you have got to be good to win the state championship. But you've also got to be lucky and Irwin, for some reason, when it came to that last game just wasn't. Buddy and his staff would keep on their path, kept winning and kept winning, and fans and followers of Irwin County just kept loving Buddy more and more.

"In 2019, you didn't hear anything negative from the very first game," Marty continues. "Yes, at the time of the prognosis and it was out in public, it was just like everybody forgot the past and 'let's get with Coach.' What it did in that year for the community, brought it together- not that it wasn't together before- but it just got everybody together with a one hundred-percent connection."

Then, the added element of the signs on the street corners which you normally see for civic events or elections, meant not just Irwin and Ben Hill counties, but an entire region was "Nobles Strong" and "We Got Your Back, Bud" and went forward as one with all the peaks, valleys, and days in between.

And any chance Buddy got to tell his story, and had the strength to do it, he would...

To an author who would visit practice that week, as a matter of fact...

This long road that the Nobles family is travelling has some new stops involving doctor's appointments and chemotherapy in October for starters. But there are some shorter-term items that Buddy gets to look forward to — like the game with Telfair County on Friday night.

"I plan on being at the game Friday night," he said at the time. "I just don't know where I'm going to stand. I may be on the sideline, but I don't know how much energy I'll have. I may go up to the booth and call plays from up there, but it's a bit of a long walk. I might just sit in a chair on the sideline and call the plays from there, just where I can see the plays and do that. I'll be there and there won't be any difference."

But, even before that, there's something else ... two things, actually...

"Keep putting out the message that all coaches need to get checked out," he said. "If they feel one thing funny, that's why they have insurance and that's why they have good doctors. Just tell them to get checked out."

"You know what...?"

"What...?"

"I'm going to go take a shower and sleep in my own bed."

Telfair County had alternated their way through the first four games of their 2019 season- winning in Alamo against Wheeler County, losing in McRae against an improving Bleckley County team, winning in Alma against Bacon County, and losing their region opener at home against 8th-ranked Turner County, 27-24.

Matt Burleson was in his 8th year as head coach for the Trojans and he knew how tough an early season test this was going to be.

"Obviously, it's always a difficult game because he is or is at the upper echelon of not only our region in Class A, but also in the state. So it's always a big game and is always a measuring stick," Burleson says. "We're still trying to build our program to where we would like it but at a time you play someone like Irwin County, you always can use it as a measuring stick to the see where you're at and what you need to do and what you need to improve upon because that's who you're aiming for... several runners-up seasons in the state. Irwin really is the one that I use as a code to look at how you stack up against the big dogs to see where you're really at as a program."

Telfair placed stickers on their helmets as well, but Burleson had another reason for their acts of support that included him and his staff wearing t-shirts backing the Irwin family that they wore on the sidelines instead of their normal coaching polos.

"We did it in the color of the type of cancer he had and we wanted to do that just to lift Coach Nobles, his staff, and their community," Burleson adds. "We wanted to let them all know that we were thinking about him, praying for him, and loving them all outside of the actual game."

Having lost his dad to cancer, he wanted to share that he knew what everyone was going through, and he would be there if anyone needed to talk.

"It was kind of emotional for their kids that night because Coach Nobles was so loved over there. I hate that I didn't get to physically see him, but we had talked on the phone that week about everything. Coaching is a fraternity and it's a small world so we all know each other really well. We all talk to one another, some more than others, and we text back and forth during the year. With what was going on with Coach Nobles, we all stayed in touch with each other and would ask 'What's going on...? Have you talked to Coach Nobles or anyone in his family lately...? Let me know how it is going if you can't get a hold of them.'

"It was stuff like that just trying to see where he's at... see how the family is holding up... it was really good to see all the different things that the schools in our region and outside of a region were doing the show support for Coach Nobles."

"We told Buddy the entire time 'You stay at home and rest.' We were concerned of him getting sick again," Irwin assistant coach Jared Luke said. "We wanted him to get back healthy and be with Tammy. Going back to practice that week, there's a moving golf cart and here's your 60 kids running towards it just seeing who was in it. The way they embraced him in the way that they love him, man, it didn't surprise me one bit. You KNOW they were glad their leader was back. The funny part for me was Buddy was always tough on them, you know, he's always said he loved them. And he was on them, too- even at practice. But at that practice, when he came back it was a fist bump, shaking hands, and hugging, too. It was like the 'Same ol' Buddy' that always had been there and so that was something that was special to me with nothing changed.

"Those kids still had a standard they had to live up to... and it was amazing to watch them in the way they reacted to see their Chief back on the field."

In a game that would show the tenor of the Indians effort to come, Telfair would run 37 offensive plays on the night. They would net 71 total yards in a 45-7 Irwin win. Irwin would pick up 18 first downs to 3 for Telfair. Zach Smith needed to throw only 9 passes on the night, completing 8- 3 of them for scores to Gabriel Benyard and Jamorri Colson. 11 different players would run the ball on the night and another win was in the books.

"The funny thing, in looking at it now, and it didn't quite hit me until I looked at the schedule," Kasey says, "the touchdown Telfair scores were the last points anybody scored on the team in the regular season. That's ridiculous. This year was unbelievable and I know we're just a little Single-A school, but the starting defense didn't give up their first points until I think Chattahoochee County in the playoffs.Towards the end of the games, we're running in young kids in and out for those touchdowns."

In the 2019 season, the first-team defense would get on the second-teamers, good-naturedly of course, about giving up yards and scores. They wanted the string of shutouts that could be on the board and the coaching staff thought they could have more than they had. Running up the score, however, was an entirely different matter. There were times where Buddy had been where that opposing coach had been in his past. You don't want that spectre hanging over the program of a blowout and the lessons that could come from a scoreline that large.

If you're the team that ran up the score, what would that say about you and what you're teaching to your athletes in representing your community...? Would you want that done to you in the future...? And there are times where, if you're the team that gave up all those points, it would stay with young men and be a black cloud that you don't need for lesson-making. It was about showing respect for the opposing coach, their team, and that town you're hosting or traveling to for your Friday night.

As a rule, if things were out of hand, Buddy would give the starters one drive offensively and defensively in the third quarter. After that, the starters were done. It didn't matter if the other team was threatening a touchdown or an Irwin team wasn't moving the ball on offense. The greater plan was to get the young kids ready to play and rest the older kids.

Unfortunately, Buddy had to go back into the hospital on September 25th, just a day after returning home and was not able to be at the Telfair game. More serious health complications came with this hospital stay.

"Dad got out of the hospital that Tuesday, and he went to practice that same day," Kenley remembers. "But he went back to the ER the following day, and was taken back up to Emory in Atlanta. I talked to mom on Friday, and the doctor had told them that he might have been getting to go home that weekend. So I was going to stay and work Georgia Southern's game against Louisiana Lafayette on Saturday.

"Mom called around 1am Saturday morning, and that's when we had about a 3 hour phone call before my cousin, Emma, and I decided to take off for Atlanta. That was probably the worst drive because I was half asleep and just praying the whole time that I would get to talk to my dad again. Thankfully, he pulled through and was able to go home the next week. He watched Charlton and Lanier from home the next 2 weeks before getting back on the sideline against Wilcox."

"I helped Mom with getting Dad home from Emory on Tuesday and then I returned to Pensacola the next morning thinking that things were going to be fine for a little while," Kaleb adds. "I wasn't back in the office probably 30 minutes before Mom called and said Dad was having trouble again and they were taking him to the ER in Tifton. So, I ended up driving back to Tifton Wednesday and making it to the ER that evening. Dad's blood levels were pretty concerning so he was transported to Emory by ambulance at about 2 in the morning while Mom & I drove behind them. Once they got him stabilized in Emory, my plan was to drive to Pensacola on Friday for our game the next day and then return to Emory after the game. Mom got in touch with me at about 5 in the morning on Saturday and said I needed to get to Atlanta as quick as I could.

"I was driving to the hospital much faster than I should have been driving and made it just in time before the surgery. The surgery was very long so there was a lot of sitting around and waiting. I watched our game that night online on my computer and was able to communicate with our coaches and QB throughout the game. Of course, the game I couldn't be there for went to overtime so I almost was kicked out of the hospital for yelling in the waiting room when we scored to win it in overtime."

The Argos had Mississippi College at home and the Choctaws weren't intimidated by playing at Blue Wahoos Stadium in Pensacola. A scoreless first quarter combined with a sustained drive by the visitors and a pick-6 gave them a 14-0 lead before the Argos woke up. A Ken Channelle touchdown catch and an Austin Reed 1-yard run tied the game heading to the fourth quarter. Jervon Newton ran in from the 2 to give UWF a 21-14 lead, but Choctaws QB Detric Hawthorn would send the game to overtime as he ran in from the 5 as time expired.

The first overtime game in Argos history would end in the bottom of the frame as Austin Reed found Kevin Grant from the 18-yard line. UWF would improve to 3-1 on the year and head coach Pete Shinnick would get a Gatorade bath that would soak his clothes.

Back in Atlanta again with Buddy, Kaleb took to social media and didn't hold anything back in the process.

Rest assured, his opinions were NOT in the minority.

-Cancer sucks.

There have been people around us that have gone through it, but never this close to our family. We have seen the struggles that people have experienced from it, but you can't put into words how terrible of a disease it is. Some of the conversations we have had to unfortunately have the past few weeks are some words you never imagine having to hear or say and would never wish on your worst enemy. Through everything, the person that has been the most steady hand through it all is our Dad. We have had multiple times where (in football terms of course) it feels like we are backed up and there is 1 second left on the clock and our best game plan is a Hail Mary. Through everything, he just keeps plugging along and is always ready to tackle the next obstacle with an enthusiasm unknown to mankind. The Faith that he exhibits on a daily basis is amazing and does not surprise us at all.

-Never underestimate the value of impact.

For the past weeks, there has been an unbelievable amount of support and outreach more than we ever deserve. There have been countless people stop by, text, call. Many people we are close with and some we aren't and just want to see how he is doing. We are blessed to get to see and talk to Dad on a daily basis as a family. But what we have seen is the impact our Dad has had on people outside our family. Plenty of people have reached out that didn't have to but have because of something he has said or done, maybe even just one time. But they did, only because his ability to care for everyone and make them feel like they are family. Even in the last few weeks, he has become somewhat of a rockstar throughout Emory Hospital. People in the halls have stopped us countless times just to ask "How is Coach doing?". We have all at some point asked him "Do you know them?" And most the time his response is "Nope, just saw them in the hall the other day". We joke about it all the time as a family, but he could talk to anyone, and that has not changed one bit through

this all. Dad has a platform as a coach to impact people all over and His impact is something that cannot be put in words.

-God has a plan at all times.

We as a family would consider ourselves pretty lucky because we have not had to experience an overwhelming amount of heart-aches in the recent past. But during a rough patch at one point, Dad and I had a conversation about bad things happening and why certain things happen to great people. Our conclusion was that God does not wake up every morning and make decisions like we do. Each person's plan was set in motion long before we were born. God did not wake up one morning, snap his fingers, and make Dad sick. The Lord has, without us knowing, been pre-paring us for this for years. As a family, we have been placing our faith and hope in the Lord long before this was thrown our way. And we know that the Lord has already guided our steps through this battle. "Best News Ever" by Mercy Me says "What if I were the one to tell you, That the fight's already been won. What if I were the one to tell you, the work's already been done". This battle has already been won and we have our faith in that every single day!

Thank you to everyone who has reached out and are praying for our family. Continue to pray as this will be a long battle and we are prepared to hold his arms up every step of the way. Again, no intentions of bragging with this. Just wanting to explain how proud we are to have the best Dad in the world as our Dad!

September 28th

PLEASE BE PRAYING!! They are taking Buddy back for a interven-tion radiology procedure to try to repair an artery that has rup-tured. There are some complications that could occur as a result of the procedure but it is Buddy's choice to KEEP FIGHTING!

September 30

Buddy is still in CCU. His hemoglobin levels have been steady. He is still super tired but is having trouble resting. His body has been through a great deal over the past month and is just trying to keep up. He is a strong man and he won't back down.

I pray that he sleeps well tonight and that this evil disease is wiped from his body.

Thanks for prayers. Please continue. I can tell Buddy is tired and needs to be lifted up today.

Telfair would finish 4-6 with that initial stretch of losing their first four region games in Region 2. But, they would rebound nicely with wins in two of their last three before a season-ending loss to Clinch in McRae.

Coach Burleson thought about going to the championship game at the end of the season, but the conditions turned into a bit of a deterrent. He found a way to watch...

"I was going to go over to the stadium to watch, but it was cold and rainy and all that. But, I was glued to the TV watching it. It was so awesome to see Coach Nobles with the platform once again and that the GHSA allowed that to happen so that he could be out and sit down. It was great to see his daughter right there with him because I have a young daughter as well. I know that was special to see. It was just a great thing that he was the Marv Levy of high school football- and, for him, to go to finally get over the hump and get that Championship, I know it meant a lot to him and it meant a lot to his family.

"But for him to finally get that Championship as a head coach and share that special moment with his family, his players, and what looked like about the entire county of Irwin probably at that stage, it was a great thing to watch. You can feel how moving it was on TV and you can feel the emotion that was going through that stadium. You could tell that they were going to win.

"Just being able to see him hold that trophy... I know that's one special moment for now. And if you're just able to hold that trophy up and then, of course, you see the picture of him posted that night of them passed out with exhaustion... I'm sure from everything that he's gone through, sleeping with that trophy just shows you how much it meant to him to be able to finally be smiling when you want to take a picture to see that night."

Telfair County 7

Trojans

Irwin County 45

Indians

1	2	3	4	F
0	0	0	7	7
14	17	7	7	**45**

MISSISSIPPI COLLEGE 21 (2-2 , 1-1)
-VS- WEST FLORIDA 27 (3-1 , 2-0)

2nd	13:22	MC–Jordan Wright 22 yd run (Drake McCarter kick), 13 plays, 81 yards, TOP 7:39	7	0
2nd	11:32	MC–Derric Hawthorn 65 yd interception (Drake McCarter kick)	14	0
2nd	02:13	UWF–Ken. Channelle 32 yd pass from Austin Reed (Alex Virgilio kick) 5 plays, 66 yards, TOP 1:56	14	7
3rd	07:50	UWF–Austin Reed 1 yd run (Alex Virgilio kick), 9 plays, 38 yards, TOP 4:33	14	14
4th	14:54	UWF–Jervon Newton 2 yd run (Alex Virgilio kick), 10 plays, 63 yards, TOP 5:33	14	21
4th	00:00	MC–Detric Hawthorn 5 yd run (Drake McCarter kick), 19 plays, 0 yards, TOP 3:39	21	21
OT	15:00	UWF–Kevin Grant 18 yd pass from Austin Reed ( ) 5 plays, 25 yards, TOP 0:00	21	27

Chapter 9

OCTOBER BEGINS

On October 1, Tammy took to Facebook again... and it was a busy couple of days on social media...

What an unbelievable roller coaster ride

It is so hard to believe that it has been less than 2 months (August 7) since we discovered this evil tumor. Buddy has been through it during that time. His first stay at Emory St Joseph's lasted 16 days and then he was able to go home for 1 short day and right back up here again. This is day 6 of this stay at St Joseph's with no end in sight yet

It is levels up and levels down, good news, bad news. It has been a physical and emotional journey on Buddy and our family as well as so many of the Buddy Nobles fans far and wide who have been praying us through this journey and holding our arms up. Thank you all so much. We feel the love. Buddy is reading texts and comments and knows how very much he is loved

So far today he has had a level down followed by a level up scenario, but they haven't been below 7.5 which is good. They are talking about possibly sending him from CCU to a regular room today as long as he maintains levels and his blood

pressure is good. He got a really good nights sleep and is rested today

Buddy's faith in his LORD and SAVIOR JESUS CHRIST has never wavered!! He is sharing his faith with everyone that crosses his path. He knows that GOD is leading him every step of this journey. He wants everyone that is sending him love to know that he loves you right back!!

Our family also wants to say thank you to all for prayers, visits, texts, posts and donations. We love and appreciate all!!

Please continue praying GOD is listening and HE is so much bigger!!

October 2nd

Buddy has set some goals to get back on the sideline, coaching his boys and also to get back to church!! It may take a little while to get there but he is fighting to get there!! He won't back down. Thanks to all that are holding our arms up as we get tired!

October 3rd

Good news this morning!! Buddy is going home today. His levels have remained steady and the doctors feel he is ready. We are eager to get home but a little uneasy based on our last one day discharge

The Doctors want him to go home and rest and have told him to hold off visitors for a while to allow him to build up his strength. We know everyone is eager to see him but are going to ask that you call or face time until we feel he is ready. If you call or FaceTime we can pass it to him if it is a good time. We love and appreciate all of you and are so thankful for how much you all love Buddy. We are blessed!!

I will post updates as I can but please pray for a safe ride home and pray that Buddy's body continues to heal!!

October 4- At Folkston/Charlton, 56-0

In the off-season, Rich McWhorter left Charlton County for another job in northeast Georgia- Jackson County. He came down to the swamps from Illinois in 1990 and turned a small school into a destination for college coaches that, for starters, wanted to recruit an athlete with the last name of "Bailey."

288-79-2 in 29 seasons with four state titles and 15 region titles are always a part of the Charlton pedigree and, as McWhorter exits, his long-time assistant Russ Murray took over. Graduation decimated the 2019 team and Murray had a lot of freshmen playing against upperclassmen all season long. The opening win over Frederica Academy was the only one on the board to date as the Indians would lose to Brantley, Appling, Atkinson, and Turner with Irwin County coming to town for "Champ Bailey Night." The school was naming the field in his honor. He was getting a street named "Champ Bailey Way." And he would do all this wearing his Hall of Fame jacket that he was honored with in August in Canton, Ohio.

"We played a lot of young kids with everyone graduating," Charlton County head coach Russ Murray admits. "There was a lot of pressure on them and they got a lot of experience throughout the whole year. Against Irwin, short of their bus breaking down, it was tough going against them. I think they scored the first six times they had the ball. We did everything we could just to try and be the best we can be.

"Buddy wasn't able to come to our game because of his health. I talked to him a time or two with Miss Tammy leading in, but he wasn't able to do it. We all were just pulling for him, you know, because at that time last year, he was just like the rest of us. Then, he got sick. Football is football, but life is more precious than that. We were all concerned."

But the folks at Charlton did two things that stood out on a region game night in line with everyone else that Irwin County came in contact with in 2019. They painted a "BN" on the field at the 50 as a salute to Buddy Nobles on the Irwin sideline.

Russ wanted to do something else.

"I wanted to do something to, some way, honor him," he continues. "My mother is a cancer survivor and I know how expensive it is when you live in a rural town. You've got to go for treatment somewhere else. You have to drive every day, or at least once a week, and I know gas is pricey."

They passed the helmet around. And both sides of the stadium came up with $1,300 and presented it right to the family.

"It's just a small gesture," Murray says. "We did it to let them know we were caring for them."

"That was very cool," Marty Roberts admits. "Charlton County was selling bracelets. Atkinson would sell bracelets later in the year. But you'd go in and they'd ask if you want to buy a bracelet- even if I've already got an armful. It was just unbelievable to see the support that he had- even from everybody in our region and other schools that's not even in our region. It was like the whole of South Georgia just was behind Buddy Nobles and Irwin."

Marty and Buddy would shoot each other texts when Buddy couldn't be at games. Marty told him not to worry this time around since he was calling the plays in Folkston.

"I said they picked a bad night to honor Champ Bailey," he continues. "I said I'm just going to go and tell you up front, I'm calling the plays again tonight and I'm going to hang half a hundred on him tonight. He did text me back. He said that would be absolutely great if you can pull that off. As soon as the game was over, I shot him a text and I said 'I told you!'"

Irwin County would take care of business...

Each team had 38 plays from scrimmage on the night. Irwin had 294 total yards of offense to Charlton's 45. 12 different players ran the ball for Irwin and four different players scored, two special teams touchdowns, a defensive score, and a passing score from Zach Smith would make it 56-0 with a running clock. Smith would only throw two more passes on the night.

"It was 56 to nothing at halftime," Marty said. "And that's another thing that I admired about Buddy. We would be so far ahead at half-time and he'd maybe have the starters come out of the locker room and have one series- regardless of the score- maybe two series if that first series was sloppy. Buddy has said in the past he never liked to run up the score on other teams. He's been in that place of that other coach and knows how he feels. He knows how those other players feel. It was a sign of respect."

"We would watch Charlton and we knew they were really young this year," Kasey said. "With Dad, we didn't want him to push it and drive all the way over to Charlton County and just risk anything happening the day after getting out of the hospital.

"But with the Champ Bailey Night, we thought that being there was just the coolest thing. It's not often you get to see that jacket the Hall of Famers wear and Champ was out there wearing the jacket. We normally go in the locker room after warm up, but we told our kids they had to go take a knee at the goal-line. We wanted them to sit down, relax, and just watch the ceremony. This might be something you never get the chance to see for the rest of your life. You might not ever get to see, in-person, somebody wearing this jacket and we just tried to explain this to them. These kids were young and we tried to explain to them how special of a player Champ Bailey was.

"Then, we turned right around, and we were clicking off and clicking defensively. You could tell it was really going well at that point for us."

"They graduated a good bit and were playing about 80% freshman," Irwin assistant Troy Fletcher added. "Our defense was pretty stout and, I think, we scored 21 points with them alone. We went out on defense, got to stop Charlton and then in one or two plays, we'd be back out on defense. We almost went the whole first quarter like that and, then, we got to get a break from that for the rest of the night."

But the larger message came from the passing of the hat in the stands, the painting of the "BN" logo on a visitor's field, and the warmth from one county to another on a Football Friday.

"They were pretty doggone good," Coach Murray said. "They had all the tools. I watched the championship game and I'll tell you something...

"He's in a lot better shape than we are right now. He's not putting up with all the mess we're putting up with here on this Earth. He's up there in Heaven living his life His way and

God Is Bigger. I truly believe that. But he won the race and won the ball game."

October 5- Delta State, 48-3

Meanwhile, it was Homecoming in Pensacola…

West Florida came into the game with visiting Delta State with identical 3-1 records in the Gulf South Conference. Both teams had the same number of points in the "RV/Receiving Votes" category in the Division II poll. After the game was over, only one of those sides would be held in the same regard.

A crowd of just over 6,000 would see a consistent effort on the scoreboard. Demetri Burch would have a breakout game with a first quarter TD reception- and it wouldn't be his last. Anthony Johnson would score from 9 yards out and Rodney Coates would score with 16 seconds left in the half on a 47 yards throw and catch with Austin Reed. Ka'Ron Ashley would catch a pass for 34 yards and Burch would get his second on the day with Reed connecting from 34. Shomari Mason would run two in for the fourth quarter for the 48 points for UWF. Delta State's field goal half way through the quarter gave them their only points and, frankly, not much else to take from Pensacola.

Delta State only moved inside the Argos 20 twice and scored the fewest points on a game day in 16 years.

The story in Fitzgerald and Ocilla had some good news on the weekend as well...

October 7th

We have a game plan!

Buddy is scheduled to start chemo this Wednesday in Tifton! This week will be quite busy. He had an oncologist appointment in Tifton today. Wednesday he starts chemo. Thursday he has a follow up appointment at Emory. Friday back to oncologist in Tifton to get chemo pump off. Thank you God for these appointments!! After what Buddy has been through over the past month I am so thankful for the opportunity to have all of these appointments and to get chemo started!

We know we are by no means out of the woods but, we have a game plan!!

Buddy's story was spreading to eyes and ears that may not have had a chance to see the story to this point. Jorjanne Zorn Paulk wrote about the Nobles family for her Southern Mercantile Blog four days later:

"Before the Nobles family came to our little town, they actually spent several years in our rival town in the neighboring county. Usually, there's a lot of trash talk in the week leading up to the rivalry game. This year, though, the focus was planning a "White-out Cancer" night, where fans of both teams dressed in white to show their support of Coach Nobles. It was a beautiful sight!

"Y'all, I have to tell you the truth. I enjoy watching a football game, but I've never been a diehard football fan. So, I'm not writing all this because I love football. And, although Coach Nobles has been a great influence in our community, I can't say that I know him all that well. What I am hoping to point out here is the way our community–and communities all across our state!–have come together to show love and support during a crisis. That's just what we do here in the South. We may have our differences, but when someone is in need, differences are put aside, and we focus on what really matters."

Jorjanne is not wrong... and the family got some rest

October 12th

I am thankful to be spending the day resting and watching football with Buddy and Kenley

Buddy is doing ok. The first chemo treatment is done. Chemo pump was removed yesterday. He is still really tired. Hopefully his energy level will improve over time. We beat the streets almost every day last week going to appointments. As of right now we do not have any appointments this week so, hopefully he can rest and get some energy back

Thanks for all the well wishes, food, prayers and love that is still being sent our way. As this crazy journey continues we are so thankful to have so many folks hold our arms up for us when we get tired. Please continue to pray that God continues to give Buddy the strength to fight this and that this evil cancerous tumor disappears from Buddy's body!!

October 15th

We are doing pretty good. Buddy is still hibernating this week trying to rest and regain some strength. I was able to return to work yesterday. Buddy's mom is staying with us and hanging out with him during the day. We have no appointments this week so rest is the main priority

Some of his players FaceTimed with Coach earlier and it brightened his day!! He has the desire to get back on the field but still needs to regain some strength

Region play and conference play would continue under the pressure of the schedule off the field while, at the same time, the Nobles family would go forward as best they could trying to find answers for a heartless opponent attacking them head-on.

Irwin County 56

Indians

Charlton County 0

Indians

1	2	3	4	F
28	28	0	0	**56**
0	0	0	0	0

DELTA STATE 3 (3-2 , 2-1)
-VS- WEST FLORIDA 48 (4-1 , 3-0)

1st	13:10	UWF–Demetri Burch 32 yd pass from Austin Reed (Alex Virgilio kick) 4 plays, 43 yards, TOP 1:50	0	7
2nd	05:04	UWF–Anthony Johnson 9 yd run (Alex Virgilio kick), 10 plays, 70 yards, TOP 4:07	0	14
2nd	00:16	UWF–Rodney Coates 47 yd pass from Austin Reed (Alex Virgilio kick) 7 plays, 65 yards, TOP 1:45	0	21
3rd	10:33	UWF–Ka'Ron Ashley 34 yd pass from Austin Reed (Alex Virgilio kick) 6 plays, 53 yards, TOP 3:13	0	28
3rd	02:13	UWF–Demetri Burch 34 yd pass from Austin Reed (Alex Virgilio kick) 5 plays, 45 yards, TOP 2:12	0	35
4th	14:08	UWF–Shomari Mason 31 yd run (Alex Virgilio kick failed), 4 plays, 58 yards, TOP 1:38	0	41
4th	07:53	DSU–Taylor Crabtree 25 yd field goal 13 plays, 66 yards, TOP 6:15	3	41
4th	06:56	UWF–Shomari Mason 57 yd run (Alex Virgilio kick), 2 plays, 67 yards, TOP 0:49	3	48

Chapter 10

OCTOBER 18- AT LAKELAND/LANIER COUNTY, 41-0/AT WEST GEORGIA, 30-2

If you travel down Georgia 90 and Georgia 135 from Ocilla, it could take you close to 45 minutes to get from Irwin County High School to Lakeland and a matchup with Lanier County.

After the dominating performance against Charlton, the Indians would be entering another week as the top ranked team in Single-A Public. Head Coach Kurt Williams and Bulldogs came into the game at 2-4- losing three of their first four against Union County of Florida and Montgomery County. Their non-region schedule ended with a win over Hamilton County of Florida, 41-21, but they were 1-2 in early region play.

In a bit of a back-and-forth, Wilcox County, the 9th-ranked team at the time, shut them out 41-0. They would rebound in a win at home against Atkinson, 28-21, before losing a heart-breaker to another top-ten team in Turner County 34-33.

"In Single-A, I mean, it's knock down-drag out, every single week," Williams admits. "We all beat each other up pretty hard. This is my second year at Lanier and I know you have to be on your 'A' game every week. We had a little bit of momentum coming in to the game."

The home team knew they had to play a perfect game to have a chance against Irwin, but the Nobles family had more on their minds...

Tammy gave everyone an update going in:

Go Indians!

Coach Nobles and I really wish we could be with our Indians tonight!

We are cheering from home!

Indian Nation we love you!

Coach Nobles said let's get the job done and bring home the win.

Lanier, thank you from the Nobles family. Jennifer Marshall sent us a picture of your cheerleaders filling the helmets for Buddy Nobles. We are so humbled and appreciative! We may be competitors on the field but off the field we are brothers and sisters in Christ. We are thankful to have you praying for us and helping us financially! God bless you all and thank you so very much!

"We went over to Lanier, but Dad didn't come," Kasey says. "We convinced him not to but, that night, we weren't blocking very well off the ball and those kinds of things on the field weren't going well early.

"We were able to hang with them for about a quarter-and-a-half," Coach Williams says. "And then seeing Mr. D.J. Lundy and the rest of the guys that they have...???"

Williams laughs and he knows the rest...

Lundy scored twice on runs of 15 and 19 yards. Jamorri Colson caught two passes from Zach Smith from 42 and 36 yards. Kam

Ward scored from 20 yards out and Garland Benyard had an interception return for a score.

41 points in a hurry...

Lanier was held to 51 total yards on 50 offensive plays and only had 8 first downs on the night...

"I mean this, probably, was one of the best defenses we had. And it was, definitely, one of the best defenses I've seen," Williams says.

But Kasey and the staff saw some things on the field as the team chased perfection- in more ways than one...

"I know we won 41 to nothing," Kasey returns, "but, I mean, at that point we were trying to be perfectionists and we wanted things to be blocked up right. Even though we were scoring and we were doing some things right, we could tell some things offensively weren't clicking. So, after that game, we started going back to the basics blocking-wise. Not that we didn't change any blocking schemes or anything, but we went back to it with some drills that were really emphasizing just some of our simple plays. We weren't trying to get too cute. We just wanted to run our basic plays. We wanted to run the plays, like sweeps, so perfectly. So, that that week is when we really started the ramp up and try and get our kids playoff-ready."

But not before another round of Tom Petty's "I Won't Back Down" in the gym at Lanier County High School.

"Remember when Dad got out of the hospital for the Telfair County game and surprised the kids coming up in the golf cart?" Kasey asks. "That was just such a warm moment. The next day, he had some more complications and went right back to the hospital. After Charlton County, we had another bye week but he was still a little more involved. He could come out to some practices, I think, and just ride around in the golf cart for a few minutes. He was showing his face, but he was still trying to recover those weeks in between."

With another win in the books in Lakeland, the 4-1 Argos went to Carrollton, Georgia to take on 4-2 West Georgia after a bye week and the win over Delta State. The game was a meteorological mess. It was wet. It was muddy. And the UWF road white uniforms would, certainly, get more than a cycle through the washer and dryer to get used again later in the year.

"I think it worked out very well for me to get back and be able to do meetings and be at practice and all that during a bye week," Kaleb admits, "because, not having the hecticness of having to play a game on the road that upcoming Saturday, I think it kind of helped me and gave me some time to get back adjusted into the groove of things and trying to get back and just being around the team. It gave me a time limit to get back adjusted and not to know and not to worry about being in Atlanta. I'm FaceTiming, calling, and texting with the players or coaches all this time leading into the bye week. It couldn't have come at a better time, to be honest.

"It was miserable and they had made the playoffs the year before. I think we had a bit of a chip on our shoulder and we thought, with their scheme on defense, we could do something. We were playing pretty well throwing the ball so, of course, the night before the game it started pouring- from Friday morning to Sunday morning in Carrollton and they play on a grass field."

Tropical Storm Nestor would have his say, but so would UWF. West Georgia put up a safety in the first quarter and that's all they were able to do all day long against the Argos. The 24th ranked team in the country held the home team to 147 total yards. Jervon Newton rushed for 100 yards on 21 carries and Austin Reed had a very busy day. He threw a 23-yard pass to Kevin Grant, ran for 15 and 13-yard scores on his own. Jaden Gardner had a rushing score to add to his season tally and the defense matched the West Georgia safety with one of their own to close out the third quarter...

30-2 and the fourth quarter was more for making sure all four quarters were actually in the score sheets than having any stats along for the ride.

"It was raining and cold but that was probably one of the most fun games of the year because I think our defense forced six turnovers and our scoring 30," Kaleb continues. "It sounds weird coming from the quarterback coach, but I love running the football. We couldn't catch anything. It was in the rain and everybody's just soaking wet, but nobody cares."

If you're losing in a rainstorm, you may care a lot more how you feel than if you're winning. But UWF left with win number five on the year in one of the toughest conferences, on the road, in Division II. The Coastal Classic against Florida Tech was next on the schedule.

"What is unique by region," Coach Williams admits, "is our region is so competitive. But, at the same time, all the coaches respect each other. "It was truly a season to remember and you got to see how much everybody respected Coach Nobles.

"I thought it was an awesome and powerful moment when he got to say what he said after the last game of the year. It brought myself to tears and, being a fellow follower of Jesus Christ, just for him to be so close to winning a championship and have really good things over the years to finally get it...?

All he could think about was sharing the gospel with this powerful moment. To see someone in your field and see what kind of teacher or administrator he was... You see that they should just treat everybody with love and respect and that you're trying to make an impact and show the life of Jesus Christ in yourself to others..."

In addition to how Irwin County, on the whole, was showing itself to anyone they touched and came across in the 2019 football season there were those close to the program that wanted to do something more.

And they would...

"You have a small community within the big community all the time," Chris Paulk says. Paulk is the head of the Agriculture Department at the high school. And he would become part of an idea that would resonate with anyone who knew the Indians.

"A neighbor helping the neighbor is not a big deal to us, but you know we take pride in our school and the people affiliated with it. There's a lot of things over the years where people have really kicked in but, I'm going to say, the Nobles family really brought everybody together. If it's something that was needed, the need was met by so many different people in so many different forms. With what Buddy Nobles was trying to accomplish and what those boys were trying to accomplish, there was absolutely nothing that nobody can ask that couldn't be completed."

And Chris Paulk would be right...

Lanier County 0

Bulldogs

Irwin County 41

Indians

1	2	3	4	F
0	0	0	0	0
6	6	15	6	41

WEST FLORIDA 30 (5-1 , 4-0)
-VS- WEST GEORGIA 2 (4-3 , 2-2)

1st	10:00	UWG–TEAM 5 yd safety	0	2
2nd	04:16	UWF–Jaden Gardner 17 yd run (Austin Williams kick), 3 plays, 32 yards, TOP 1:06	7	2
2nd	01:10	UWF–Kevin Grant 23 yd pass from Austin Reed (Austin Williams kick) 3 plays, 16 yards, TOP 1:39	14	2
3rd	12:32	UWF–Austin Reed 15 yd run (Austin Williams kick), 3 plays, 25 yards, TOP 1:12	21	2
3rd	10:21	UWF–Austin Reed 13 yd run (Austin Williams kick), 4 plays, 34 yards, TOP 1:12	28	2
3rd	05:58	UWF–Ian Bush 6 yd safety	30	2

Chapter 11

OCTOBER 25- WILCOX, 16-0/
AT FLORIDA TECH, 38-14

R ob Stowe had Wilcox County in the top ten in Single-A Public the second they hit region play. The Patriots three wins were against Wilkinson County, Hawkinsville, and Berrien (two of those shutouts). Heavily-recruited two-way player Desmond Tisdol was leading the defense and the Patriots offense had cleared 48 points getting into Region 2.

A shutout over Lanier and a loss to Clinch, 28-22, actually gave the team a boost in the rankings- up to #7. Wins over Telfair in McRae and Charlton in Rochelle at Donnie Clack Stadium brought them to a 6-1 record as they headed to Ocilla. In his first year, Stowe had them up to Number 4- the school's highest ranking in the state since the 2011 year when Mark Ledford's team was #2 in the regular season.

Stowe knew the import of the eighth game of his season... and it was Homecoming on campus in Ocilla...

"It's always a big week, obviously," he admits. "This past year, it was an even bigger game because we happened to be the game for Coach Nobles where he was going to be able to make a return to the sidelines. We had heard about all that stuff and, of course, not being 30 minutes away from them, we would take a big crowd. It was a great game and, looking back on it, I felt like we played great defense that night. Our kids gave it all they had. Irwin played very hard, as usual, and they were playing with the added reason to win because Coach was back on the sidelines."

Buddy had a lot of help from a lot of folks who wanted to see him back...

"I think it was Buddy who first had said something to me about Hugh Freeze," Chris Paulk remembers, "and he had some issues up there at Liberty. He had to get through a staph infection and was wheelchair-bound. Eventually, he was able to come to games and, then, they had their stand for him that they had fabricated. The question was: What could we do...? Doctor Clayton showed me their picture and said, 'Do you think you can build that...?' I told him that it won't be out of that nice-looking metal. But, we can build a wooden platform. He said okay and wanted to know if we could really have it built.

"I told Dr. Clayton I thought by Friday we could have it done and had it completed. He didn't have any idea that it was the kid's idea to paint it and choose the color scheme. I picked out some plywood cut on a laser. We painted it using a stencil with the big 'BN' placed on it and the rest was history."

"I know that everybody kind of gravitates toward Des Tisdol when you talk about Wilcox, but that was another grinder," Kasey said. "That game decides home-field and that has, in recent history, decided a state champion. We knew, from watching Wilcox, they were the real deal and they proved it in the playoffs later on. We knew that game was just going to be a dogfight and they were really, really good defensively. We were really good defensively as well. But we were able to really start calling in on some things offensively and we got the job done."

But off the field, Kasey looks at the platform- as did a lot of folks in family and Ocilla. The Nobles family was trying to figure out ways for Buddy to be present and stay active in Irwin County's Football Fridays.

"He couldn't stand on the sidelines and we knew he wouldn't have the strength to stand for a whole game," Kasey continues. "We knew it was pretty dangerous for him and being there, I wouldn't have been focusing on the game. Luckily, we had Chris offer to do the build. Kaleb and my mom sent the picture of the Hugh Freeze stand and they just got rolling from there. The first game he was able to come back, that was a special moment- knowing that Chris and the entire community were completely behind it. Seeing him come out there and walk up the stand was very special.

"I think the kids enjoyed it as a certain energy with him being back out there and it was really important in getting him back out there. I think it was vital and to have someone get to sit next to him up there too with Kenley becoming his assistant again...?"

"I didn't realize that Chris and his students were actually doing it until mom sent a picture of it," Kenley said. "Everyone knew how determined he was to get back to the team, and it just showed how much he meant to this community and how willing anyone was to help us out."

"I'm going to tell you right now," Irwin coach Jared Luke says, "I work for the best school system. It did not surprise me one bit to watch the AG Department build that thing and put it on the field. Dr. Clayton said, 'Hey! We got to do something.' We talked about it because, if you go up in the Press Box, it was too far of a walk. It didn't surprise me because of the way the community comes together. At the school, everyone comes together for a common goal and they're always willing to help do anything."

"The stand went from Kaleb sending me a picture and saying this would be so helpful to Dad to becoming a reality in a week," Tammy says. "Dr. Clayton came to see me on a Monday, I shared the picture with him and he went straight to Chris Paulk and it was a done deal! The two of them took it from the thought stage to a reality in a week's time.

"That is one of many things that Dr. Clayton took care of. He was more than just Buddy's boss! He was his friend and his brother in Christ! His support and the support of the entire school system was unbelievable."

On the field, the game was the grinder that folks thought it would be...

A safety by Garland Benyard and two touchdown runs from Jamorri Colson (7 yards) and DJ Lundy (31 yards) were all the fans who went to Ocilla saw on the evening to move the scoreboard. Zach Smith would only complete three of nine passes against the Patriots defense and the Indians rushed for 182 yards. The defense of the home team was even more stout. Wilcox had 57 net yards on the night, four first downs, and went 1-for-11 on third down.

But 16-0 got Irwin County to 7-0...

Survive and advance...

"They had a really good football team," Marty Roberts said. "Buddy said after the first three or four series that Wilcox was not going to move the ball on our defense. So he wondered if he should call a conservative game. He said 'If we could get a couple of scores on the board, he just wanted to keep the ball from Wilcox's offense- maybe throw two of three passes and run the ball and get out of there.'"

"Buddy still wanted to be a part of everything, but it wasn't safe for him to go up and down the sidelines. Chris and the AG Department built the stand so Buddy could stay completely engaged the entire time. I ran into "Big Bubba" Marques Johnson, the big tackle, downtown a couple of weeks back and he said, 'You know... Mr. Chris is building it.' The more I talked to him he said, 'I would bring Coach Nobles up and down the stairs myself,' wherever he was. I asked him, 'You love Coach

Nobles, don't you?' He said, 'I love him like a father.' And it's because they may not have had father figures in other parts of their lives. He's not the only one, either."

"That was the next step in all of this... when he was able to be there, so he could be keeping an eye on things, still be on headset, and still be there," Irwin assistant Drew Tankersley said. "Kenley was right there with him."

When the AG Department started building the platform, Tankersley didn't know it was going to be as special as it turned out to be. "I didn't know they were going to make it as special as they did. They painted it red and it's got the big 'BN' on it- and it's completely painted with the "BN" logo on it."

Tankersley thought that was a special touch. Buddy still had the view he needed to coach...

Not that he didn't give the staff an ear full when he thought things needed to be said...

"He threatened to come down from it a few times," Drew said. "We can turn around and we're looking at him all the time. We did one thing he didn't like during the season and said if we did it again he was coming down out of the stand to the side-lines. Seriously, though, everyone did a great job on that plat-form. The whole student body did a lot of legwork- swinging hammers and putting nails in it. So, it was a special thing for the whole community that nobody will ever forget."

"When they built the platform, it was amazing to have that ready," Irwin assistant Pete Snyder adds. "It was just perfect. It could not have been any better. Buddy was in and out of practice early all of those weeks, depending on how he was feeling, he could put in the game plan and let us know what he wanted to do for the game. Putting his gameplan in for this game got us ready for that win. That shutout was a good thing for everyone that week."

"Buddy had gotten really weak at this point and he couldn't move very well," Irwin assistant Troy Fletcher said. "And it wasn't safe for him to stand on the sidelines. I mean, he wanted to be there so bad and everybody wanted him there, but we also were thinking more just about his safety. We had talked about having him in the Press Box, but that was pretty high and there was just no way he could get up there. So, they built the platform for him and he could look right at the benches on both sides.

"He could actually lean over and talk with the players he wanted to," he continued. "He called the Wilcox game himself. In any of the games that he was involved in running the offense, and for the practices, he would come home. When he couldn't be there, he was making the game scripts. He was doing everything that he always did as far as watching a film on other teams, putting together game plans, and putting together an offensive script. The dedication he had, in the end, with what he was going through- just showed his love and passion for the game for a job for Irwin County. He just was not going to let this situation affect everyone with so many people involved with the program."

"People were talking about doing a little platform for Buddy," Irwin assistant Chip Rankin adds, "and you know, in our mind, we're thinking a little platform- two or three feet off the ground... something just big enough for him to sit on. The next thing you know we see this huge undertaking that they had done and how awesome it was and that was just amazing to see."

"Of all of the things they did to help Buddy, that was unbelievable," Buddy's longtime friend, Steve Hoard said. "I mean people don't do that unless they love somebody."

"I think that was big for him," Irwin assistant Clayton Sirmans said. "He wanted to call plays and he was able to because he could sit- seeing and enjoying it. I think it was awesome and I was excited to see what he was able to experience. Being there and being in the game and able to call the plays, it was an emotional time and a game for those seniors who were going to play their last game at home. I think it took on extra meaning with the situation that Buddy was going through and then the seniors huddled around the platform. It was emotional and I think he appreciated, every day, what the guys wanted to do and what they meant to him. It was a season full of special, emotional moments."

Like having an entire crowd break out their singing voices to the tune of Tom Petty for another week...

"We're beat to a pulp right now," Buddy told everyone after the game. "But I'm gonna tell you right now. You guys started this journey a long time ago. We've got to have some new guys step up now. Defensively, you guys are bad to the bone now... I'm gonna do everything I can to be here next week. But, I'm gonna tell you... Men of character won this game tonight.

"I'm gonna tell you right now... to the community of Ocilla, I really appreciate what y'all have done for me. Not just during this time, but whenever it started, if I have my dates correct- March 8th, 2014. I looked a long time for a head coaching job and nobody would hire me. I always finished second or they wouldn't call me back. But, when this place called me, I knew it was a Godsend. Somebody asked me in my office after my first year if I was going to go ahead and leave. Why do I need to leave a place that's the best job in the state?

"You know what? It's all about the kids, the parents, the administration... it's all about that. Tell you something... When you drive past that red light, it oughta mean something to you. I love y'all and I appreciate y'all. I love y'all with all my heart..."

Buddy started to break down with Kenley in the driver's seats next to him...

"I'm going to fight as hard as I can... it's just hard, guys... it's just hard."

Casey Soliday would pick up the post-game speech at that point...

"Like 'Coach' said, we love y'all and we love the fight you had tonight. We have to have that fight every night and it comes from what he (Buddy) started. We just have to keep building on what he started."

It was time for the younger guys to learn from the older guys week in and week out for the rest of the season- however long that would end up being...

"There's only so few teams that are teams of destiny," Buddy said in his final words of the night to the team. "And you remember that... teams of destiny play hard, they get it done every Friday night, and they make it big. I got a 1-2-3 in me and you know what we say..."

1-2-3, PRIDE!!!

"I'm so super proud to be able to say I was able to coach in the game against Coach Nobles and I was able to spend some time with him after the game," Coach Stowe said. "And that might be the thing I remember more than anything else. Right after the game, at the 50-yard line, he came out on his golf cart as both teams came together. I think a lot of people from Ocilla and a lot of people from Rochelle were surrounding us all and he had a few words that he wanted to share. To the players, he was very encouraging about fighting and never giving up and always remembering what the real reason in life is- trying to have a relationship with the Lord.

"We were able to have a team prayer after the game. That was just very impactful to me and I'll always remember it."

At the end of every practice at Wilcox, one of Stowe's players would always want to say a prayer for Coach Nobles and the family. It reinforced the idea that while football can be impactful to towns like Rochelle and Ocilla, there are things in life bigger than football. What you can do, though, is use football for those larger platforms. You might want to beat each other on a Friday night, but at the end of the night, there is the knowledge that the experiences are shared, the love is shared, and you can lift one another up during your game week and after a game in a post-game prayer- even in the simple notion of putting a "BN" sticker on a helmet in colors that aren't your own..

"Football, especially, is so important that we learn to come together every day from all different kinds of backgrounds and socioeconomic status," Stowe continued. "It would be great if everybody would be able to come together in unity and work. It's about gathering and sacrificing your own personal gain for the benefit of the team. That showed this year with all of us and Coach Nobles."

Wilcox County did that and wore it proudly.

They would make it to the second round of the playoffs before losing to Pelham in a 41-36 back-and-forth affair. They would finish 9-3.

"The day of the title game, I remember it was a very rainy day the day before, so we just decided we'd sit there and watch it," Stowe recalls. "I was rooting hard for Irwin County to win the game being a fellow region mate. It was as exciting to be able to say that I was able to see it and to see him win the game in a convincing fashion. You know... you just know that God was smiling on him. And what he said on the platform...? There's bigger things in life and that's what it's all about."

For Kaleb, the Coastal Classic puts Florida Tech and West Florida against each other and, yes, there is a trophy involved...

The 20th-ranked Argos were heading to Melbourne at 5-1, 4-0 in the Gulf South Conference and the home team was 3-4 and 1-3. The game would take a while since Mother Nature got in the way with a lightning delay of just under an hour-and-a-half at Palm Bay High School late in the first quarter. But the first half, once it resumed, was one where West Florida got off to another hot start involving quarterback Austin Reed. A 4-yard TD catch by Tate Lehtio and a 1-yard keeper by Reed, combined with an Austin Williams 25-yard field goal gave the visitors a 17-7 lead at intermission.

A 61-yard TD run by Shomari Mason and a 65-yard catch by Kevin Grant from Reed gave some distance in the third quarter and an early fourth quarter run by Jaden Gardner put the win and the trophy to bed with a 38-14 win. The Argos tied a school record with their sixth straight win. Mason finished north of 100 yards on the day and Reed threw to 9 different receivers. Sadly, it would be the last trophy game as FIT dissolved their football program after the season concluded

It would be, however, a weekend of blessings across the board...

October 26th

Oh my goodness what a blessing it was to be at the football game last night. Thank you Dr Clayton and Chris Paulk for making a vision a reality, allowing Coach to be on the sideline and call the

game. Thank you Marty Roberts and the football boosters for providing the golf cart.

Everyone that has been following us on this journey knows that being there last night was a miracle straight from God. I will boldly say that I can see daily God answering prayers! Buddy and I both know that we still have a long way to go. His strength is still very low but we have faith that God is going to provide him the strength he needs. His faith and love for God was evident as he spoke to both teams after the game last night. His love for his coaches, players and all of Indian Nation is also evident in his post game speech. We both talk frequently about how blessed we are to have the support that we have. There is not a day goes by that we do not hear multiple offers of "if there is anything I can do"! We are truly thankful.

Coach has his 2nd chemo treatment on Monday. Please continue to pray that the treatments he is receiving is making that evil cancer go away. Coach has so much more to do and we pray for God's perfect will to be done in all of this but selfishly I pray that God allows Buddy a lot more time to work for HIM!! I stand on my faith that God Is Sooooo much bigger!! If anyone doubts that, just look at the pictures of Coach Nobles at the game last night!!

October 31ˢᵗ

Coach Nobles is ready for some football!!!

Coach is planning on going to Atco tomorrow night to Coach his Indians. His coaching stand is in place and ready!! Thanks again to all our Irwin and Atco folks who made that happen!!

Coach had a chemo treatment this week and has had minimal side effects so far. His energy level is still down and the Doc is trying a new medicine to help him eat and put some weight back on. Hopefully it will help him maintain or gain.

Everyone knows how social Coach is and he of course wants to meet and greet everyone because that is just him. Please keep in mind that Coach's immune system is down and he is susceptible to catch things that can cause him serious problems. It is flu season and his immune system could not handle that right now. One of his players was worried about Coach catching something after last weeks game and had his Grandma contact me (thanks DJ and Mrs. Virginia). Please remember Coach's compromised immune system and by all means talk to him and share your love with him but please, please do so without hugs etc. Being the social butterfly that Coach is he has dearly missed seeing everyone and loves being able to see and speak with you again. We look forward to seeing everyone tomorrow in Atco!! Go Indians!!!

Wilcox County 0

Patriots

Irwin County 16

Indians

1	2	3	4	F
0	0	0	0	0
2	7	0	7	16

WEST FLORIDA 38 (6-1 , 5-0)
-VS- FLORIDA TECH 14 (3-5 , 1-4)

1st	04:26	UWF–Tate Lehtio 4 yd pass from Austin Reed (Austin Williams kick) 6 plays, 14 yards, TOP 2:52	7	0
2nd	09:58	UWF–Austin Williams 25 yd field goal 7 plays, 9 yards, TOP 3:23	10	0
2nd	09:02	TECH–Mike Diliello 91 yd run (T. Schaneville kick), 2 plays, 91 yards, TOP 0:56	10	7
2nd	04:30	UWF–Austin Reed 1 yd run (Austin Williams kick), 6 plays, 33 yards, TOP 3:15	17	7
3rd	14:16	UWF–Shomari Mason 61 yd run (Austin Williams kick), 2 plays, 72 yards, TOP 0:00	24	7
3rd	11:48	UWF–Kevin Grant 65 yd pass from Austin Reed (Austin Williams kick) 5 plays, 78 yards, TOP 1:18	31	7
3rd	05:50	TECH–Kenny Hiteman 7 yd pass from Mike Diliello (T. Schaneville kick) 15 plays, 82 yards, TOP 5:53	31	14
4th	14:54	UWF–Jaden Gardner 2 yd run (Austin Williams kick), 14 plays, 75 yards, TOP 5:56	38	14

Chapter 12

NOVEMBER 1- AT PEARSON/ ATKINSON, 52-0/NORTH GREENVILLE, 17-14

It was a long season for Atkinson County leading into their ninth game of the season...

After a season-opening win against Montgomery County at home, the next two non-region games were losses to Berrien in a shootout and an improving Brantley County team under Geoff Cannon. Region play started with a win over Charlton

County, losses to Lanier and Clinch, a win over Telfair and a 7-point loss to top-ten Turner County. At 3-5, head coach Carl McGowan was having a young team continue to mature on the field but was able to have just as important a teaching moment on the field for the first day of November.

"We were just worried about Buddy and his family and helping them in any way we could to get him through the difficult times they were going through when it came to support," McGowan admits. "We all know that we're lucky to do what we do for a living and we were all supportive of Buddy. We just wanted to wish him and his family the best and I don't think anybody was turning a blind eye to the situation that he was going through. Playing for a couple of state championships and coming up short and, then all of a sudden, he's going to be right back in the mix and then this cancer thing jumped on him.

"The timing of everything was just kind of crazy. Getting ready for the game itself, we had been getting information from other teams and also we knew that Buddy hadn't really taken a backseat, but he was doing less of a role. We, probably, didn't have as good a handle on what they were going to try to do because he was not probably going to be calling the plays like he had in the past. We wanted to just make sure we were prepared for everything possible."

That preparation, eventually, would include the idea of hosting the platform that was built by Chris Paulk and his students-once they figured out it could be packed up and put back together on the spot...

They had it down to a science like a NASCAR pitstop...

"I thought that was absolutely amazing," McGowan said. "The teacher that runs our AG Department is friends with Chris at Irwin. They had called and they talked about what they were building for Buddy and how we can do it, too. The way our stadium is set up with a track, we let him know that if he wanted to bring that over here and set it up to give him a vantage point that we would have no problem making the accommodations to make that happen. You could tell it was built for Buddy and filled with love."

The weather would be one of the colder nights to date during the 2019 football season. Everyone around both programs were concerned about what to do for Buddy outside of having the platform commute from Irwin County High School to Pearson- about 40 miles each way from Chieftain Circle to Rebel Lane. So, they created a little duck blind with a tent curtain around the platform that made it look like a very large blind out of a "Duck Dynasty" episode.

"I actually went over to him during pregame and crawled up in there with him. I gave him a hug," McGowan said, "and so it was one of those situations where we were happy to see him. But we're doing it with a little bit of a heavy heart because of the situation he was in."

"I wasn't sure just and how feasible it would be for them to carry the platform around to the different schools," Kasey said. "We weren't even sure whether the schools would let us bring it out there on their field because, a lot of times, people don't want you sitting stuff on the field. Starting with Atkinson, though, they were very supportive and they were 100% on board with us bringing the stand. So, seeing them rip apart the stand real quick and be able to put it back together...??? Coming to Atkinson, and seeing a stand already on the field, that was so nice. Inside the blind, they even had a heater in there."

"At first, though," Luke Roberts adds, "he couldn't see everything with the blind up. So, they had to work at it a bit. He was really happy to be up there coaching, but if you ask everyone. The first thing they'll say is that it was a COLD night."

The game in Pearson was one-sided…

An early Garland Benyard touchdown catch was the only score through the air on the night. The other 7 scores were on the ground from Jamorri Colson from 75 and 71 yards out, Gabriel Benyard from 69, Kam Ward, Eric Anderson, Bernard Herring, and Matthew Payne from 53. Atkinson was held to 143 yards total offense- 138 of that on the ground. The Region 2-A title was heading back to Ocilla and the banner was ready to go for anyone and everyone that wanted to take a picture of a team that had accomplished so much to date, but still had accomplish a lot more in their own minds- for their team, their town, their county, and for their coach that they love with all their collective hearts. There's nothing like winning a region title with your dad in a duck blind on a stand that traveled from home to make the trip to add to the story.

"Mom, Kasey, Kenley and I basically got the idea for some kind of help for dad," Kaleb said. "Mom and I were talking about it with Dad on the phone the day after our Carson Newman game, so that was the basis for the platform. Because, when you go to research it, Hugh Freeze at Liberty had some medical issues. For a couple games, he was up in the Press Box nicely sitting in a hospital bed watching the game and coaching. If you Google it, it was a couple of weeks before dad would be home for a while. We did a little exploring through Twitter and I saw the platform. We all thought 'that's actually not a bad idea,' so Mom took it to Doctor Clayton.

"I mean how fast they built it was awesome in the fact they actually built a platform so he could be at every game and call plays and still be contributing on a Friday night. Obviously, it enabled him to do what he loves while he was going through what he was going through in his life and Kenley was right there. When she was in high school, she took care of things and set things up. She would come down from school when she could this past season and it made perfect sense for her to be there when she could. For them to build it for him to call plays and then for us to use it as his funeral really was full circle."

There were a few other ideas before the blind came together as a lot of folks put on their collective thinking caps about how they could get Buddy to a place that would be safe and a place where he could still do a job he loved

"I talked to the principal about it," Bill Barrs said. "We had several conversations and we were thinking that, maybe, we can get the local EMC to get a bucket truck there to help. But that was an amazing thing to see Chris and them come up with to give him the access to see what's going on but also to keep him out of harm's way. We did a little and then we did a little maintenance work around the boat trailer to get it ready to travel. I'm not going to lie about it. It was cool and it was just great to see Buddy to be a part of it."

"I didn't know how, with what they were planning, on building something to code initially," Irwin coach Troy Fletcher said. "We have that glass in the weight room that looks out over the football field. I looked out and they're taking the stand down to take with us. I think Buddy was sitting in a condo up there."

Fletcher laughs at that observation...

"I think that the platform speaks to the level of- and I'll just go and use the word- 'love' that everyone had. I made the comment that somebody had brought to my attention before the game had started that their cheerleaders we're going to take buckets into their home stands- for love."

"I thought it was pretty cool," Coach Casey Soliday admitted. "It's not every day that something gets packed up in pieces, gets driven 30 miles each way so it can be a part of everything. I'm thinking of all the things people wanted to do for Buddy and that platform was incredible. Every single time I can think of, people were stepping up to do things for Buddy and the family."

"They dismantled it and stuck it on the trailer, took it down to Atkinson, took it back down again and brought it home," coach Pete Snyder said. "It was really amazing. That thing was not small. It was just pretty amazing that they were able to do that and get it all done in the right time frame and have it all go back. Buddy and I joked about all the different things we would do with it- with the duck blind over the top of it."

"Their bleachers are so low to the ground, at AtCo, that if you're not sitting about halfway up you can't even see the whole football field," Irwin booster Eddie Giddens said. "You know what...? I never heard one person complaining about not being able to see with the platform there for Coach. Everyone was so proud that he was sitting in that thing and able to watch a football game, but it was great. The fact that Chris Paulk and everyone that was involved did what they did, it makes me be proud to be an Irwin County Indian."

"Everybody loves that coach here in town," Irwin Coach Tim Talton adds. "And then to show the family the love they do all the time... Add the platform in to all of this- and the fact that that thing packs up and goes and it made its way to Atkinson County...? That was surprising. I heard they were going to carry that thing down there. And when I got down there, it was already set up. Everybody says that blind is for duck hunting... for me, you could have used it for bear hunting."

"Irwin had a big lead at half time," Marty Roberts said. "I had loaned them a car that week from the dealership since their car was in the shop. Buddy was able to get in a golf cart and go back to the car at halftime to stay warm instead of having to walk to the parking lot. Normally, he would be back earlier than he was this game at the half, but when he did come back in the golf cart, everybody would give him a standing ovation, you know, and he would get up in the stand. You know what this is all about.

"When you get to know how much everybody was behind the platform being in Pearson, and how they supported everything, it made me feel good in that way. Right after the game he said: 'Have you got the banner?' I said I had it because I've always done a banner every time they win the region championship. I know the game that we're going to win the region, traditionally, so I keep it loaded up in my car. I've got it in the stands with me and I had it stuck behind my back before the kids saw it and unveiled it.

The kids tried to pry it out of Marty's hands for a few minute before Buddy got to speak from his golf cart about what they had accomplished to that point:

"Make sure you give Coach Fletcher your size by Monday," he said, referencing another t-shirt the kids could add to their clothing line of Irwin County Indian gear. "Where's Coach Soliday at...? I'm very proud of our coaching staff and our kids tonight.Guys, that's 5 out of 6 regions we've won in the last six years. Next week, Turner County, they're a tough team. Come to practice ready. This is for the number one seed in the playoffs. You get #1? We got it! Does everybody understand that...?"

Coach Soliday reminded everyone around the cart about the phrase "act like it." And that's what Irwin did, by his own thought in the game in Pearson.

"Guys, there's now a level that we want to get to... and we have to start acting like it. Practice, in school- so you don't hurt your teammates by not being able to play- take care of your grades... all of those things... Coach has been saying all year that you are a team of destiny.

"ACT LIKE IT! Then, we take care of our business..."

"That means who you hang with... that means what you're doing in public," Buddy continued. "People know who you are. When you walk into a restaurant, or you walk into a business. Those people know who you are. Carry yourself with class. I've told you before, there's only one thing your mom and dad give you that you can ruin. That's your name... mom and dad gave it to you. Carry it proud."

Marty pulled the rubber band from around the region title banner and mentioned a little bit of history that had been achieved- the 20th straight region win for the program. The seniors were 25-2 and they could be the all-time winningest team for a class if they won out.

When you focus on Buddy after the banner was unfurled, all he could do was shake his head in wonder from the driver's seat

Buddy told the team that he would see them one day the following week, the team was led in prayer, and they had their pictures taken under a goalpost.

To that point in his career at Irwin, Buddy Nobles was 43-4 in region play. And there was one region game to go before the regular season was concluded. The Indians could rest… after next week… If you get through Turner County, you can heal up a little bit. There would be a group of seniors who would be having a bunch of "last times" from this weekend forward.

It's the last home game… the last region title… the last practice… the last road trip… all of these "lasts" that would, hopefully, lead to something in the last game of the year.

"We all had hope that it was going to get better," Roberts continues, "but I think a lot of them deep down I knew were thinking Buddy was just hanging on- basically trying to get through to get them through their senior season. That's what's so heartbreaking. It just tears me up because you can see it develop the whole year. From July, to the diagnosis, or basically to August I think Buddy lost 30 pounds by then. When I came back before senior night, he was obviously a lot skinnier then because of all the trips to the hospital since he couldn't eat from the treatments. He couldn't keep anything down and it was just so hard to watch him."

Marty had seen it with his family. In front of him once more was someone he loved and a family he cared about deeply going through those same steps- literally and figuratively. Buddy was trying his best to climb steps that were built so he could keep doing what he loved. If he missed a game, it wasn't because Buddy didn't want to take a week off during a football season. It didn't matter if the steps the Nobles family were taking were up to a platform to coach or, simply, one in front of the other to go through your day. There were multiple communities there to lift a family up to help their stride.

That was only a small part of the love, in the form of many different things along the way, that helped the situation…

You have to eat, right...???

"I don't think my mom had to cook a meal from the time my dad went to the hospital the first time," Kasey remembers. "There were people at the church that were constantly cooking food and just coming into the house to leave it. And it wasn't just from Ocilla but from Fitzgerald, too. They were doing all the little things that you don't think about the help out. And we needed to get another fridge because of it."

By Kaleb's own admission, North Greenville had really improved as a program since their initial NAIA days. On Hall of Fame Weekend at Blue Wahoos Stadium, the visitors didn't look like the 3-5 record they brought into the stadium.

It was the Argos first home game in a month and, after an Austin Reed pass turned into a pick-6, they were down 7-0. A fumble on the next drive and a fumble on a punt return two series later didn't help matters. The only first half points for the home team came on a 30-yard Austin Williams field goal.

After a missed North Greenville field goal in the third, a time-consuming drive yielded a one-yard run by Jervon Newton to give UWF the lead they wouldn't relinquish. A 99-yard drive ended in a 38-yard pitch-and-catch with Reed and Ka'Ron Ashley in the fourth. But it would be enough in the end as a TD pass by the visitors would draw them to 17-14, but no closer. It was the seventh straight win for the Argos- a school record- as they improved to 7-1 and tied with Valdosta State for the top of the Gulf South Conference heading for the match-up between the two the following week.

The win wasn't pretty, but sometimes that's what you get...

"It was, kind of, a Backyard Brawl. And we did not play very well on offense," Kaleb admits. "Our quarterback did not have a great game- mostly because they were doing some really good things on defense. It's pretty similar to what our defense does and it causes some chaos a little bit. But I think that game kind of showed our guys, even as we were looking like we could have a good year, we may have been reminded that maybe we're not as good as we think. You still have to put in the same work to win all those games. Having a tight 17-14 game and having a game that was a lot closer than what we should have was important."

Kaleb was still doing his fair share of weekend multi-tasking from Pensacola or on the road in the Gulf Coast Conference. On Fridays, Tammy would text during games, keeping him updated on scores and such as the Argos were going through their walk-throughs. If the Irwin game was a large enough margin, he could get back to his game planning. But there were still those weeks of concern when his dad would be at home instead of coaching on the sidelines. On the road, he can pull Irwin games up on the computer or on his iPad, but his mind was truly in two places at the same time.

Talking and texting with family can only fill so much of that space...

Coach McGowan didn't make it to the Single-A title game this time around. Like most, the weather kept him from Georgia State Stadium.

"It was close early," he remembers. "Marion County didn't flinch after the first couple scores on the board. But, then, in the second half there was all their depth at Irwin. You knew it would take a real special football team to have to be there at the end with them. Buddy was still holding his head high, putting that big smile on his face, and getting up there with his kids. I just don't think you could have made a better ending any way possible. When he was up on the stage, there was the 'Ocilla, we did it' moment, but at the same time- right up front- it was discussing his love for Jesus Christ. For somebody to be put in that situation and not to not to be playing the blame game with 'why me,' but being gracious and being thankful for what the Lord has given him and the opportunity...? I just think that was probably one of those special moments I've ever seen.

"None of us, other than Buddy himself, knows exactly the effort that it took for him to be there and I can only imagine. It's just such a shining example of what it takes to go forward in times of trial and turmoil and negativity. Being able to go through that and hold your head high and still thank the Lord for the day that he had, I just think it's a message that no matter how bad things are, we go to work. We all want to sit around and sulk in the you-know-what at times even though you should really be thankful and grateful for the time that you're given." McGowan has always been impressed with Buddy as a man as well. "There would be region meetings that would take up a lot of time and coaches can't get back to work as soon as they can. Buddy was always discussing his love for his family- always saying something positive about his kids or about Tammy.

"He would just say how proud he was of his daughter, Kenley, for being on the sidelines with doing everything she was doing and how, when she graduated, he didn't know what he was going to do because she was the best in-game person to help him prep and also keep stats for him right there. He really appreciated those that were around him."

Irwin County 52

Indians

Atkinson County 0

Rebels

1	2	3	4	F
25	14	0	13	**52**
0	0	0	0	0

NORTH GREENVILLE 14 (3-6 , 2-5)
-VS- WEST FLORIDA 17 (7-1 , 6-0)

1st	14:44	NGU–A. Watson 32 yd interception (M. Gravely kick)	7	0
1st	01:04	UWF–Austin Williams 30 yd field goal 10 plays, 67 yards, TOP 4:53	7	3
3rd	02:22	UWF–Jervon Newton 1 yd run (Austin Williams kick), 12 plays, 80 yards, TOP 6:13	7	10
4th	11:45	UWF–Ka'Ron Ashley 38 yd pass from Austin Reed (Austin Williams kick) 9 plays, 99 yards, TOP 3:51	7	17
4th	02:12	NGU–L. Catalfomo 25 yd pass from D. Baker (M. Gravely kick) 12 plays, 81 yards, TOP 4:54	14	17

Chapter 13

NOVEMBER 8- TURNER COUNTY, 49-0/ AT VALDOSTA STATE, 26-21 (CONFERENCE CHAMPIONSHIP) AND WEST ALABAMA, 48-37

Before Senior night, Buddy got another round of visits from television stations on Monday and Tuesday of game week. He was keeping true to his schedule- hanging out watching the offense go through their paces. Tammy was in their car diligently waiting to take him home as the Indians were heading into the 2019 playoffs with one game left on the regular season board- Turner County.

"I'm doing all right," Buddy admitted from his golf cart that week. "I'm just weak from the chemo treatments but, you know what...? I'm still getting up every morning and that's the great thing about it. God's blessed me with another day and I come out to watch practice on Mondays and Tuesdays so I'm doing okay. I get to see my kids and I've been to the last two games, so that's what I love."

He got to share the story about two of the elements that showed a community's love for their head coach all over again as well...

"Our Booster Club bought me a golf cart when I first got sick and I could sit on it at practice because even the coaches were on me about sitting on our John Deere Gator. I was losing energy at practice so they bought me this and then Chris Paulk in our shop class built the platform so it's just been a community effort and it's really been a community fight. So I'm proud of what they've done for me and all the signs that you see you know praying for buddy we got your back bud and all that kind of stuff..."

Buddy admitted seeing the "We Got Your Back, Bud..." signs gave him hope in what he and the Nobles family were going through. It also gave him hope to see the players present themselves publicly in the way they were as young men. He was also quick to compliment his coaching staff, top to bottom, for what they were doing on a weekly basis in one of the toughest regions in the state.

"It doesn't matter who the head coach is at Irwin County," he said. "These kids are gonna play hard and they're gonna get the job done, so Friday night will be just like any other thing kids are gonna play on."

The first year Buddy was head coach, the seniors of 2020 were in seventh grade and Tammy was teaching them all math. Over time, whenever they would come talk to Buddy, it wasn't always about the plays on the field, practice, or even football in the general sense. It could be about life. It could be about school. It could be about studies and difficulties. One story stuck with him:

"One of my players came to me, very emotional, and said 'thank you' and, really, I hadn't done anything. But he got into the college of his choice. and he said: 'Coach, I got there because of your letter recommendation.' Well, really, he got there on his own but just being a part of stuff like that really makes me know then, it's more than what football is."

Four months into this treatment hamster wheel, Buddy would wake up about 6 o'clock in the morning. But Buddy wanted Tammy to get back in the classroom. His mom would come and stay with him at the house in Fitzgerald. He would watch game film at the house and check emails to have some sense of normalcy. If you asked, he would also admit he would try to eat as much as he can, but it's hard with the tubes in his stomach. The chemotherapy doesn't give you much taste. When it came to attending practice, that was on Mondays and Tuesdays- on purpose. He would go on Mondays and Tuesdays to see the early implementation of the game plan for that week, but he would conserve his energy for the rest of the time in the hope he could be a part of Friday night.

When he got to reflect on the week before and the win over Atkinson County- and the platform making the road trip with the team- he came up with a very common adjective...

"It was pretty cool," he said. "It's pretty cool to sit up there and, then, when they put the 'Duck Dynasty' blind up there...? I thought that was so awesome to be up there, but it kind of shows what Chris and all of them have done you know to haul it over there and and to be able to do things like that and have a heater in there...? They were taking care of me.

"It felt good. I can see. I'm elevated and I'm not in danger. I want to stay involved in the program and make sure I'm getting everything done I can. Coach Soliday is kind of taking over the day-to-day program, but I try to make sure I'm helping and doing this and doing that so that way I can still be involved."

"We could really tell, offensively, that we were kind of a well-oiled machine," Kasey said. "And, then, coming out that Friday night for the Turner game we knew we were starting to get on a roll. As a coach, you want to start to get on a roll in the last couple games of the regular season. Defensively, the guys were just dominant all year, but you want to go in being the top seed to get the bye week in the first round of the playoffs. That way, you didn't have to worry about it for a while, we would get to rest up. I think I'm like everyone in that having the extra week gives you a chance to heal. We love having that by week getting to prepare for the playoffs."

Turner County was trying to find a way into the Single-A Public playoffs. For those unfamiliar, there's math involved for the 2019 season. It has to do with region standings, regular season record, and power rankings based on quality of competition. So, even if YOUR math may give you the idea you're in the playoffs, you have to wait on the official results from the GHSA leading into the post-season that you want to be a part of to keep your season going. And, even after YOUR math, there's an appeals process that can be a part of the discussion before the top 24 teams proceed.

Nick Hayes' Rebels had been ranked top-ten all season long outside of week one. Heading into the season finale in Ocilla, they had lost two of their last three- a 25-point loss to Clinch in Homerville and a 15-point loss at home to Wilcox. At 6-3, the visitors had run through most of the rough part of their schedule, but the toughest test remained for the last game of their regular season. The Turner helmets had stickers on them to show their support for Buddy Nobles, the family, and Irwin County as well. The idea came about from a conversation with Wilcox Head Coach Rob Stowe and the Rebels had a part of their Monday meeting during game week set aside to discuss why the players were doing this for the opposition.

The Turner coaching staff told their team about what their act of kindness would mean and what kind of legacy Coach Nobles has. Hayes thought his players needed to know how successful he was, who he was, and what he stood for as a coach.

"It was one of the colder nights we had," Hayes recalls. "Coach Nobles and I talked earlier in the week on the phone and he said he would catch up with me afterwards as well. I told him I'd love to come together no matter what. I wanted to pray for him, pray for his team, and his family. I just remember it was a great game."

There was balance in the scoring for Irwin as Jamorri Colson caught a touchdown pass from Zach Smith for 45 yards. DJ Lundy had runs of 8 and 62 yards, Eric Anderson, Kam Ward, and Garland Benyard also scored on the ground and DJ Searcy wrapped up the scoring with a 5-yard catch from Cody Soliday on their way to a 49-0 final score on Senior Night.

Turner was held to 114 total yards- 101 of those through the air. Irwin had 404 of their 500 on the ground on the night and 14 different players carried the ball. The defense forced 5 Turner turnovers.

And Buddy was there for Senior Night- watching from a platform that continued to symbolize the love a community has for a family and a man who had made an impact on those 7th graders now playing their final games in the program. They've all been a part of successes and growth and got to go out on top of the region in the regular season- heading into a playoffs where only one goal would make the year a success...

That ever-elusive title... and he got to do it in front of friends and family even if it was a struggle...

"A couple of times we were on the phone during the season like we always do, and we had a bye week so some of us went over to watch," Coffee Head Coach Robby Pruit said. "I looked over and there was Kenley and Buddy was standing next to her. I barely recognized him at first. I didn't know who it was and he was a fraction of who we knew. I have to be honest. We almost broke down and I didn't go over there at first. Just to see how he lost all his weight..."

And Robby gets emotional just starting to talk about it...

"I can say it was just like my brother being ripped from you. A few years before he's 21. Then, he's the head coach at Union County. Then, he was with me on my coaching staffs. But, other than that a couple years here and there, we're talking like 25-26 years together one way or the other.

"He was going to tackle this like a coach. You find the obstacle, figure out what we're going to do that day, get past that obstacle, and go to the next. That was just how he was wired the first time that he was up to Emory, he was super weak but he would tell you 'I'm not dying in the hospital.' He was worried about his family who knows that he's not going. 'I'm not going to do that Tammy' and feeling that for all of his family."

"The platform has obviously enabled him to do what he loves while he was going through what he was going through in his life," Kaleb admits. "Kenley was right there with him-even when she was in high school. She took care of things, but she didn't do the same things with Dad on the sidelines.

Buddy and Tammy got to the stadium a little more than an hour before kickoff. If Irwin could take care of business as they had in all the weeks before, they could control anything and everything in the post-season in front of them. The coaching staff also got to see this group of 7th graders from their beginnings and see them take the field one last time in a regular season. Their work was far from done, but it was a bit of a curtain call.

"It was an emotional night," QB coach Drew Tankersley said. "I was happy that Buddy was able to be there with the guys that night. When he came in, those guys were 7th graders and his wife taught a lot of them. It was like that was THE group and you know that when they were in Middle School. It was really the group that we thought eventually would win one or two and you know they had never been beat- on any level. When they were 8th graders, they won the Middle School Conference Championship. We had some really good players in this group of seniors that we had- DJ, Jamorri, Jacquez and Bubba... they're all the same age. I think it meant a lot to them and to Buddy just for him to be able to be there in person."

"It was just a blessing for him to be there and be able to participate in this," Irwin assistant and Middle School Coach Pete Snyder adds. "Not that any other senior class was not important to him because they were all important. But, I think this particular senior class from their time as 7th graders, they have been right there with him the whole time. He was constantly in Tammy's classroom. He got to know these guys early, saw them grow up, and saw them perform. They were outstanding in middle school and just to see them grow up and be a part of their senior night was great- especially in these circumstances.

"I get chill bumps just thinking about it. It's unheard of... I get to be there when they're young and help develop them. Sometimes, we change positions of players at the Middle School level. Sometimes they end up playing that same position for the rest of their career. But we take a lot of pride in getting them where they're supposed to be. The development of the program that we have is because of Buddy."

"I coached the same group in 8th grade when the Middle School coaches had their championship on the backs of guys like DJ Lundy, Eric Anderson, Jamal Paulk, and Zach Smith that have all played for us," Jared Luke said. "Their accomplishments and their goals come full circle. Buddy was making these kids into good fathers and employees later in their lives as well. That was how he embraced them and how all the coaches embraced the players. We knew something special was going on."

"It just amazes me," Linebackers Coach Clayton Sirmans said. "Because we didn't put in a lot of work as far as schematically figuring things. You've got to give those players the credit, but we played, about, 15 guys on defense for the majority of the time we played in 2019. They were awesome and a very special, special group that worked hard and really understood the defense. We changed defenses about 3 or 4 years ago. The majority of the older guys have been in it, understood it, and played faster over time. But to look back and see what they accomplished was absolutely amazing."

So, with the game put to bed, Senior Night the celebration that everyone hoped it would be, and an eye on the third season, one of the men who was part of the hiring of Buddy Nobles-elevating him to a head coach position in the state of Georgia-reflected on the season to that moment and what the town and community he is a part of has done through one of the hardest seasons anyone can remember.

"It's just a small family atmosphere," Irwin Principal Scott Haskins said. "People love one another and they want to do for one another and recognize, not only for our fans but most people in the state, what people mean to one another in a time like this. They understand what Buddy was going through was bigger than the game. They recognize that we can do some things that were a little out of the ordinary, like build the platform. But, at the same time, if it causes a lot of people to sit back, look, and recognize that it is all about the family and community to tell someone like Buddy how much you love them, you can be especially supportive when someone is going through a rough time."

"Even as the scoreboard didn't go the way we wanted, it felt like we did a great job of preparing and having a game plan," Turner County Head Coach Nick Hayes said. "You tip your hat to those guys over at Irwin. You really do. They do what they do very well and they beat us, but I was so proud of our kids that never stopped fighting in the game. I was really proud of the way our kids fought to the buzzer.

"The horn went off and it was just a feeling of togetherness and it's a feeling I'll cherish for a long time. I kind of spoke first and let Coach know that we congratulated them on the win and, then, we just talked about his legacy. I reminded everyone around us that I called him earlier in the week and that he didn't want to talk about himself. He wanted to ask about me and then complimented me and told me that he was hearing good things coming out of Turner County.

"I just remember thinking to myself: 'Wow, you know, what a testimony. How humble that is.' I wanted to kiss him and I wanted his family to know how appreciative I was. He spoke back to our kids and complimented them for the sportsmanship and how hard they played- telling them that it's going to keep working for them. He could tell that they were probably turning the corner as a team a little bit, too."

So, on the field, Irwin ran the table in the regular season and would be the Number 1 seed in the post-season in Single-A

Public. They would get the week off and get to watch everyone else from team 9-24 sort it out amongst themselves.

November 11

Coach had a full weekend. A Friday night victory, dancing in the locker room, and a Saturday night game at VSU (Kaleb's UWF team was playing at VSU). Great weekend but he was worn out.

We had an oncologist appointment at 8:15 today followed by chemo treatment #3 (we thought). Once they did his labs, they cancelled chemo because his white cell counts were too low (they say this is very common). They rescheduled chemo for next Monday and sent us home. About the time we got in the door and unloaded, the Dr called and asked us to come back because Coach's potassium levels were very low and they wanted him to get an IV. So back we went and are currently getting an IV, which will take about 4 hours.

We are thankful that Dr Shah and his team are on top of all of this and praying his potassium and white blood cell levels go up and this evil tumor goes away!!

While we were getting labs, a Turner County momma who works in the lab asked coach why he let his Indians beat them so bad?? Our Indian lab technician took up for us though and said she thought it was a great game. She did fuss at Coach about the dancing. LOL

"People in the South, especially people in south Georgia, care about each other even outside of football," Coffee High Principal Rowland Cummings admits. "We all have our differences. We all have our own little issues to deal with, but when it comes to caring about people that's something we do well in South Georgia. You add football to that mix obviously in Georgia and when you look around the country, where the biggest start talking conversation every day is: What kind of football are we going to have football this spring…? From the NFL to here in South Georgia it is a rallying point for everybody in the community. Friday nights in south Georgia are special at Irwin County and in Douglas, it's much the same. It's very, very important to those of us who live here and it's for the entire community."

College coaches are never too far away from high school coaches, too. Clemson's national championship head coach, Dabo Swinney, has ties to the family from his days with Kasey playing in the upstate. So, he kept tabs on the family when he could…

Families and fraternities may look like they're spread out far and wide. But, really, it's a lot closer than you would think...

"I called Buddy and had a couple really good conversations," Dabo recalls. "When I hung up the phone with him, I remember he was just unbelievably strong and so focused at work and very hopeful in his will to fight. He was so excited that Kasey was there working with him and, certainly, with what Kaleb was doing down there at UWF with his coaching career and that he was just in a really good place.

"Again, it was pretty devastating news and he said it just took the sails out of him for about two days and then he, I think, realized the platform he had and wanted to use it to the fullest. I think it's just amazing the impact that he had on so many people's fates with this challenge he was facing."

For Kaleb, it was a chance to take on the top-ranked team in Division II, and it was only a small drive to Valdosta to take on the VSU Blazers.

And if you want to see where you are as a team, there's no better metric than taking on the top dog.

The 20th-ranked team in the country traveled to Valdosta to take on the top-ranked team in Division II in the Blazers. But when you spot the home team a 20-0 lead in the second quarter, it's all uphill. The Argos would score twice in the third as Shomari Mason went in from 4 yards out and Austin Reed connected with Quentin Randolph to draw within 6. But Valdosta State would widen their lead and take the win, 26-21. The Argos would drop to 7-2, 6-1 in the Gulf South while VSU would improve to 9-0, 7-0 in conference.

"Most weekends," Kaleb says, "you'd want to do a boomerang-go from Irwin to Pensacola or wherever and back home. With Dad's health being what it was, being an hour from Valdosta for our game Saturday, I wanted them to come. Marty McGhin, team chaplain and Director of Football Operations at VSU, made a huge Christian impact on my life in my time there as a player and is still someone I talk to frequently. I called him a few weeks before and we, kind, of set it up for Mom to park right behind our team buses. They picked him up in a golf cart and basically drove him up to where he was sitting because he couldn't walk as far and it was too much of a toll on his body. It was so cool because it allowed him to be at the game. At the time, I obviously wasn't thinking about it, but it was actually the last game of mine that he was at and I am so thankful he was able to make it.

"I hadn't seen him in a few weeks because his treatments had been going well and we had a few road games. So, when he came in on the golf cart, I was able to leave the field before warmups to go see him. I have hugged him a lot in my life but that hug was one of the most special ones because a gap between seeing him at that point felt like an eternity. It was great to sit on the cart and talk with him for a while before he made his way to the stands."

The Argos would learn a lot about themselves at Bazemore-Hyder Stadium as well...

"We didn't play very well as a whole team in the first half and we came up short," he continues. 'I think that game kind of gave our guys confidence to go: 'All right, well, if that's the number one team in the country that we just played, we didn't play even close to our best, and lost to them by 5 points, What's our potential...?' So that means that if we play with them when we're at our best, we can play with anyone. Our guys know from our head coach all the time that 'Our Best is Good Enough.'"

They would return home for the regular season finale against West Alabama for another test. The back and forth between UWF and UWA would finish with a game that had 85 points, 62 first downs, 1,091 total yards to ensure a playoff berth.

Austin Reed would throw for 443 yards and 5 TD's in a 48-37 win. The Argos would make it to the playoffs for the second time in the team's four-year history. The win was also the school's first-ever regular season win over West Alabama.

They would find out who their first round opponent would be the following afternoon and it would be a run the Argos would remember on multiple fronts. The team could have their end of the regular season banquet and not worry about "if" there would be an Argos post-season, just wonder about travel plans.

Turner County's season would end in the second round of the 2019 playoffs. After knocking off the 19-seed Macon County in Ashburn, 31-12, they would fall to Mitchell County 36-7 to the Number 3 or 4-ranked team in the state depending on the poll. They would finish 7-5 and give the program their fifth straight winning season in region 2.

Nick Hayes was actually in Atlanta with his wife watching the Single-A championship game on an iPad in their hotel room.

The weather was so bad the night before and so cold the next morning that he stayed indoors.

"I was just jacked up for him when he won," Hayes said after the season. "To give the Lord credit and not just talk about it...? He definitely lived it. What an inspiration it was to me as a young head coach of the time. It was a blessing to see what he said and for him to use the platform of his sickness and, probably, get a thousand people watching online and all the people in the stadium to see it...?

"I thought it was perfect. If I ever have to go through something like that, I hope I do as gracefully as he did. He handled it so well..."

Turner County 0

Rebels

Irwin County 49

Indians

1	2	3	4	F
0	0	0	0	0
20	17	12	0	49

WEST FLORIDA 21 (7-2 , 6-1)
-VS- VALDOSTA STATE 26 (9-0 , 7-0)

1st	09:56	VSU–Seth McGill 2 yd run (F. Ramirez kick), 10 plays, 76 yards, TOP 5:04	0	7
2nd	13:27	VSU–Jamar Thompkins 22 yd pass from Rogan Wells (F. Ramirez kick) 8 plays, 67 yards, TOP 3:52	0	14
2nd	05:30	VSU–F. Ramirez 19 yd field goal 13 plays, 84 yards, TOP 5:45	0	17
2nd	00:10	VSU–F. Ramirez 20 yd field goal 8 plays, 87 yards, TOP 1:42	0	20
3rd	09:46	UWF–Shomari Mason 4 yd run (Austin Williams kick), 10 plays, 79 yards, TOP 5:06	7	20
3rd	04:19	UWF–Q. Randolph 8 yd pass from Austin Reed (Austin Williams kick) 6 plays, 59 yards, TOP 2:42	14	20
4th	12:25	VSU–Seth McGill 4 yd run (Rogan Wells pass failed), 11 plays, 62 yards, TOP 6:46	14	26
4th	05:53	UWF–Shomari Mason 6 yd run (Austin Williams kick), 10 plays, 67 yards, TOP 3:39	21	26
			21	**26**

WEST ALABAMA 37 (6-5 , 3-5)
-VS- WEST FLORIDA 48 (8-2 , 7-1)

1st	11:07	UWF–Q. Randolph 27 yd pass from Austin Reed (Austin Williams kick) 7 plays, 66 yards, TOP 3:53	0	7
1st	08:27	UWA–C Saulsberry 19 yd pass from Jack McDaniels (Tre Jackson kick) 8 plays, 75 yards, TOP 2:40	7	7
1st	04:11	UWF–Samuel Antoine 0 yd fumble recovery (Austin Williams kick)	7	14
2nd	14:55	UWA–Tre Jackson 26 yd field goal 12 plays, 71 yards, TOP 4:16	10	14
2nd	10:30	UWA–D Battle 1 yd run (Tre Jackson kick), 7 plays, 68 yards, TOP 2:35	17	14
2nd	07:59	UWF–Q. Randolph 17 yd pass from Austin Reed (Austin Williams kick) 5 plays, 79 yards, TOP 2:31	17	21
2nd	05:36	UWA–Tyriq Martin 45 yd pass from Jack McDaniels (Tre Jackson kick) 6 plays, 70 yards, TOP 2:23	24	21
2nd	03:06	UWF–Ken. Channelle 8 yd pass from Austin Reed (Austin Williams kick fail) 7 plays/79 yards/TOP 2:30	24	27
3rd	10:05	UWA–Tre Jackson 22 yd field goal 12 plays, 58 yards, TOP 4:55	27	27
3rd	05:09	UWF–Rodney Coates 13 yd pass from Austin Reed (Austin Williams kick) 12 plays, 75 yards, TOP 4:56	27	34
4th	13:50	UWA–D Battle 2 yd run (Tre Jackson kick), 3 plays, 9 yards, TOP 1:01	34	34
4th	12:26	UWF–Q. Randolph 50 yd pass from Austin Reed (Austin Williams kick) 4 plays, 65 yards, TOP 1:24	34	41

4th	06:08	UWA–Tre Jackson 39 yd field goal 16 plays, 62 yards, TOP 6:18	37	41
4th	01:34	UWF–Anthony Johnson 9 yd run (Austin Williams kick), 8 plays, 75 yards, TOP 4:34	37	48

Chapter 14

NOVEMBER 22- CHATTCO, 47-22/ AT WINGATE, 38-17

Chattahoochee County would be an interesting test for Irwin. The Cougars came out of a stacked Region 1- Pelham, Mitchell County, Terrell County, ChattCo, and Seminole all made the postseason.

Head Coach Jody Allen had a rough start in 2019- losing to Terrell, Marion, and Mitchell before finding their stride winning six of their last seven to finish the regular season. Their only loss was to Pelham, so all four regular season losses were against playoff teams. The defense would register three shutouts and the "Notre Dame Box" was the offense that would confuse teams in southwest Georgia. As is the case when teams face offenses like the veer, triple option, or wishbone, it's not something you can effectively simulate in practice and takes a lot of discipline to keep in check.

Their first-round playoff match-up was a win against Washington-Wilkes in eastern Georgia which set up this match-up against the top-ranked team in the state. But Coach Allen's history went further back than a second-round game in 2019.

"I was an assistant coach at Florida State and recruited the state of Florida as a part of my duties at FSU," Allen says. "Part of my recruiting for years included Lake Butler. So, I tried to get CJ Spiller to Tallahassee. That's how far back our relationship went.

"For a really long time, I didn't stay in touch with him," he says. "I had heard details that it was a somewhat dire situation for Buddy. But, when we talked during the week of the game, it wasn't all about football. It was good to reconnect with him, though."

Coach Allen had also recruited Kasey at the same time he was keeping an eye on CJ. The unorthodox offense at ChattCo was one like the triple option. If your defense wasn't disciplined from the beginning of every play, they could break long ones on you all night long.

"They had some good athletes in the backfield," Kasey said, "so if we let one of them slip early, they were out the gate. Defensively, considering what they're playing against I thought they played really well."

But this was no normal football season- on multiple fronts...

Marty Roberts was with Buddy in his golf cart before the game started. Drew Tankersley walked up to talk a little shop.

"He came up to coach before the game and he said: 'Coach, we were thinking about putting in a fake punt with a pass this week. It's there to call it if you want to call it.' He looked at us and said, "Let me tell you something... Up to this point, in my coaching career, I'm 16-for-18 I think with fake punts.' He said the two times that he failed, one of those we passed. His memory, even to this point of his health, was amazing."

There were plenty of Buddy's players he coached at Lake Butler that came up for the game. But there was another special moment that happened before the game as well. And it involved the spear in the pre-game.

"Buddy didn't know what was going on," Marty continues, "and when the team came on the field, they ran through the tunnel. I had Tammy and Kenley plant the spear that night. That was really special for him to see his wife and daughter plant the spear that night. When the players come through the banner in the endzone and onto the field, they normally run on the field. They just start jumping around getting excited for the game. This time, they go over and completely encircle the stand that he and Kenley are sitting in.

"Tammy and the players from Lake Butler come up, too, and they start singing Buddy's theme song as it's playing over the loud-speaker. The fans and the whole team finished singing that song and Buddy teared up. He couldn't hold it back. Then, he says 'All right, let's go play ball.'

The game was off to a hot start as Zach Smith needed only three passes to get Irwin into the endzone. Gabriel Benyard would score twice and DJ Lundy would power into the endzone for a

19-0 lead 13 seconds into the second quarter. In that emotional week for the Benyard family where Garland had been shot accidentally, he and his mother would be in the family truck in the endzone watching Gabriel score and keep scoring. Garland was on oxygen watching all this happen in front of him and after the first long touchdown run, his brother would point at the sky, point at his family with his hand over his heart and keep producing for the both of them. Five more touchdowns would go up on the scoreboard in the next nine minutes...

Four of them by Irwin... You read that right...

Chattahoochee County scored on the first-team defense of Irwin County- on a 90-yard kickoff return. But, before ChattCo could catch its breath, Irwin went into the endzone again... and again-leading 40-6 at the half. The visitors would score twice on a running clock and the final would end up 47-22. The run of wins for Irwin continued and they would wait for the winner of Manchester and Johnson County.

Chip Rankin knew something else was going to happen after the game was over, too... and leave it to a Gainesville, Florida rock-and-roll hall-of-famer to play a part in a south Georgia storyline. Tom Petty's "I Won't Back Down" would become part of the Irwin County fabric going forward.

"I'm sitting up in the Press Box and I see the whole thing," as he knew the celebration around the platform was about to happen after the final whistle. "Everyone circled around Buddy and Kenley. When we beat Fitzgerald at their place two years ago, that was the song that he played in the locker room. Then again, when we beat them this year, for them to do that was pretty awesome."

The crowd would hit their notes one more time after a win... and for another week, no Indian backed down... on the field or off...

Interim Head Coach Casey Soliday undersold the efforts of the team he watched for the first 11 games of their season after another big win.

"If you have time to step back and sit there, you go 'Wow, our defense was more than okay.' That's pretty impressive what those guys were able to do in the season to that point. We thought there were games we could have played a lot better- like the time we played Clinch in the regular season. But you could see they all had the confidence to take care of business that season."

Irwin assistant Troy Fletcher looked at the other side of the ball as the Indians put up another effort in the 40's by the end of the evening:

"It was amazing what they did offensively. Because, if you think about it, there were some issues to work through early in the season. There were only a few adjustments that had to be made, but you knew once they were made, then it'll be just fine. Chattahoochee County came into town and were a lot better football team than people gave them credit for coming in that week."

"I mean... the football team was amazing," Mike Posey said as he watched the team from Florida. "How they carried them-selves...? That's what he instilled in them and that's how they played football out there." He would find his way to the ChattCo game and one of the first things he did was give as many folks hugs as he could find. "Seeing Buddy's Mom sitting in the corner, we would just talk and I still saw that they were still having faith in their future. The hope and prayer that something will change was still there, but they never let on to anything if something was up. And if they didn't bring it up, I wasn't going to bring it up.

"I wish we just got to keep 'Free Spirit Buddy' sitting in that locker room or in his coach's office. Me during this time...? I'd be going nuts. How he can hold himself together, worry about who they were playing that night, and what they were going to do...? I mean, you can see it in his eyes every once in a while, but the family carried themselves so well, I don't know how they did it."

"The biggest lesson for me about this season is perseverance after reconnecting with Buddy and seeing Irwin County," Jody Allen recommends. "When you're working on fighting things in front of you, there's also the need to do things right. The Nobles do that."

The post-season road for UWF started in Wingate, North Carolina against the #4-seed in the Division II playoffs. There really isn't a direct way to get from Pensacola to Wingate, since it's a 50-minute drive from Charlotte-Douglas International Airport to the southeast, and there had to be a lot of coordination during the week to figure out just when everyone was leaving and what the itinerary had to be.

Kaleb had Wingate to prepare for in the Division II playoffs, so his time was in Pensacola to start...

"The team was going to fly on Thursday to get there, so we can be in the hotel all day Friday. We had played at Wingate in 2017 in the first round of the playoffs and we shut them out back then (31-0). We, kind of, knew what was looming if we won that game. If we take care of business, like we know we can, then we're probably going back to Valdosta to play again."

"The character of this team is going to win this game on a weekly basis," Kaleb thought. "If both teams are talented whoever has the most character, and takes care of the little things the entire game is going to win this game."

A chip-shot field goal got Wingate on the board first, but UWF went on one of those offensive rolls they were known for in 2019. A field goal would tie it by the end of the first quarter, but familiar names would get four straight scores on the board and get the Argos to the fourth quarter and it was a the familiar names that got the visitors the distance they needed- Austin Reed would only complete 8 passes on the day and three of them were for scores. Two went to Quentin Randolph and the other to Tate Lehtio. Anthony Johnson would rush for 109 yards on the day and worked his way into the endzone from five yards out.

It was 31-3 after three and a Jaden Gardner run would give the Argos another score on their way to a 38-17 win to wrap the Bulldogs season at 10-2.

That character would be on display again as the rematch with the top-ranked Valdosta State Blazers would be on the board just around the corner.

Chattahoochee County 22

Panthers

Irwin County 47

Indians

1	2	3	4	F
0	6	16	0	22
12	28	7	0	47

WEST FLORIDA 38 (9-2)
-VS- WINGATE 17 (10-2)

1st	08:23	WU–M. Robertson 24 yd field goal 9 plays, 61 yards, TOP 4:11	0	3
1st	05:27	UWF–Austin Williams 37 yd field goal 4 plays, 0 yards, TOP 0:56	3	3
2nd	12:47	UWF–Q. Randolph 56 yd pass from Austin Reed (Austin Williams kick) 2 plays, 65 yards, TOP 0:37	10	3
2nd	00:20	UWF–Anthony Johnson 5 yd run (Austin Williams kick), 9 plays, 60 yards, TOP 1:56	17	3
3rd	13:11	UWF–Tate Lehtio 13 yd pass from Austin Reed (Austin Williams kick) 2 plays, 13 yards, TOP 0:40	24	3
3rd	04:11	UWF–Q. Randolph 7 yd pass from Austin Reed (Austin Williams kick) 15 plays, 69 yards, TOP 7:51	31	3
4th	14:11	WU–Nijere Peoples 1 yd run (M. Robertson kick), 13 plays, 75 yards, TOP 5:00	31	10
4th	06:18	UWF–Jaden Gardner 16 yd run (Austin Williams kick), 4 plays, 34 yards, TOP 2:14	38	10
4th	01:11	WU–Kalen Clark 3 yd run (M. Robertson kick), 3 plays, 23 yards, TOP 1:03	38	17

Chapter 15

NOVEMBER 29- MANCHESTER, 54-12/
NOVEMBER 30- AT VALDOSTA STATE, 38-35

As a coach, player, or team that has a fall and winter schedule you want to be practicing Thanksgiving Week.

The capitalization is intentional...

It's one of those markers on the calendar where, if you're still playing, you can see the end of the schedule and the possibility of playing for a title. If you're part of a team that is sleeping later, not going to school or practice, and watching everyone else- it's a lost opportunity that you wish you were a part of going forward.

For Irwin, it was a part of the schedule that they wanted to be a part of all season long. They expected to be there. They expected to play next week. They expected to play a few more games. Period. They expected to be in Atlanta playing for a title. End. Of. Discussion.

For Tammy, Buddy, Kasey, Kaleb, and Kenley it meant two games after an important holiday where they gave nothing but thanks on multiple fronts...

Even if the beginning of the week was a rough one...

Coach had a chemo treatment on Monday and it really has caused him problems this week. He was nauseous from Monday through Wednesday then got a sore throat. With all that going on he has not been able to eat much so he is very weak. We were hesitant about coming to the game tonight but Coach was determined to go.

During the game he began feeling weaker. It took a little encouraging from me but I convinced him to leave since he was not feeling well.

We are at home now and he is resting. I tried to convince him to go to the hospital but he did not want to go.

Thank you to everyone that has checked on him and is praying for him. We are learning on this journey that even though he has the desire and determination to do things, he has physical limitations. Unfortunately last night his body was not strong enough to make the entire game. He was upset that he had to leave during the 2nd qtr. He loves to call plays and watch his

Indians play. He loves to communicate with his Coaches before during and after the game. He loves to celebrate after a victory with his team and Indian nation. His body did not allow that last night and he is upset that he was robbed of that last night. Please share your celebration photos today so he can be a part of the celebration.

The first thing he said this morning after he ate some breakfast is "I am going to be at next weeks game! You can count on that"! The desire and determination is there, please pray that he can eat well this week and have the physical strength to be there. He also said "Guess what Tammy, we are practicing on Thanksgiving and I will be there"! Practicing on thanksgiving is an honor! If you are practicing on Thanksgiving that means you are still winning!! Nice job Indians!!

The pregame song was so awesome! Thanks to all who worked hard to put it together. From the sign about not backing down to the players surrounding Coach to the entire stadium singing "Won't Back Down" it was amazing.

We appreciate all the well wishes and prayers. We love and appreciate all of you. Please continue to pray for Coach this week. He is fighting hard. We pray that his body's strength will catch up with his desire and determination. If it does then there is no limit!! We know that the powerful GOD we serve has no limits and are praying that GOD continues to strengthen Buddy!

GOD is bigger!!

November 24 (Kenley)

Such an awesome experience getting to plant the spear with my mom on Friday. She is a super woman if I have ever seen one! Someone recently said that I am the one they always see by my dad's side. While that is true, I definitely would not get that opportunity if she did not do what she does. She has always been

a behind the scenes type of person not wanting to make things about herself. This journey has definitely not been easy, but she has been the strongest person throughout. I cannot even put into words how much she amazes me daily dealing with everything from getting Dad to appointments to going to school and getting her teaching done. There is no way to express how thankful we are for her!

Thanksgiving

The Nobles have so much to be thankful for!!

We have had a good week. Buddy has rested all week and was able to make it to the game Friday night. His Indians took care of business! Garland was released from the hospital and was able to watch Gabe put on a show!! Love those Indians!

Indian Nation showed up and supported their team and coaches. Coach and I hear the crowd cheer each time he comes on or off the field. Those moments mean so much to both of us. We love and appreciate each of you!!

Coach had several of his former Indian players home from college that came to visit him. Coach loves you guys!

Coach Nobles had several out of town visitors at the game too. The purple lettermen jackets on the field was another group of young men who played for Coach back in Union County (CJ, Jeremy (aka Thunder and lightening), Willie & Mike Oliver). Thank you guys for coming. Coach loves seeing and talking to you guys. In addition to the players, Coach Dettor, Coach Hoard and several friends made that long drive. Chrystal, Savannah and Ciara Woodall, Storm and Kaleb Davis, Bonnie and Eddie Cavin, Greg Box and his partners and probably others that I am unintentionally leaving off. Thanks to all of you for coming.

Greg Box, Mike Oliver and even one of our officials all gave Coach some words of encouragement. All have been through similar battles as Coach and are all doing very well right now. All told Coach to keep fighting, praying and have faith!! Those words of encouragement help Coach continue his fight!! Thanks to each of you for taking the time to share, love on and encourage Coach. It means more then you will ever know.

We also had a very full house of family members over the Thanksgiving week. You all mean so much to us. Thank you all for traveling far and near to make this Thanksgiving very special. (Kasey, Kaleb, Kenley, Katy, Grandma, Kevin, Debbie, Emma, Josh, Jessie, Jake, Uncle Bill, Aunt Susan). We love each of you.

Coach is scheduled for his next chemo treatment on Monday. Please pray that these treatments are destroying the tumor and that he does not have any bad side effects this time. We have a big week ahead and Coach has work to do!!

GOD is Bigger and Coach Nobles will never back down!!!

"Thanksgiving was weird, but it was also a time we really got to sit and spend time with each other and just reminisce on everything from growing up through our childhoods and football from years back," Kasey says. "That's one thing Dad had. He had a memory that was just unreal. We were talking about memories and he would pull something out of his head. He would know the exact place and exact scores of games from 20-25 years ago. So, that week was really just enjoying each other's company. It was nice."

"I was excited for Thanksgiving this year," Kenley adds. "The years before, it was just another holiday. But for this year, we got another holiday with Dad, and we didn't want to take it for granted. We have to practice on Thanksgiving week because our lives revolve around football. And if we're not having practice on Thanksgiving week, it's not a good Thanksgiving. Dad and I convinced mom to stay home to start cooking while I drove him to the morning practice. I didn't let him see, but I cried a little on the way to the school. I wasn't sure how many moments like this we would have left, so I just wanted to take it all in."

Admittedly, it's tough to get the whole family together for a holiday during football season...

Manchester was next to make the trip to Ocilla for the quarterfinals. The Blue Devils were the Number 9 seed in the Single-A Public bracket and had little problem with the 24-seed Taylor County in an opening round regular season rematch, winning 40-0, and taking care of 8-seed Johnson County in Wrightsville 36-20. At 10-2, it took a two-touchdown effort in the fourth quarter to get that distance between themselves and the Trojans.

RB Anthony Ferguson and LB Tylan Hollis were the focal points for Evan Hochstetler's team that had been a top-ten team all regular season long- save the opening week of the year. A decisive win over Taylor County had them on everyone's radar. Their only losses, coming in, were in a non-region 56-6 loss to Northeast and a region loss to Brookstone in a 28-27 heart-breaker.

"I've always had a lot of respect for Coach Nobles," Hochstetler says. "Thanksgiving week is a week that you always want to be practicing in the morning. You put the food you're eating later in the oven and attack the day. It's that little bit different in your week than you do when you're not in school. Irwin County did get to the state championship game last two or three years prior to the 2019 season.

"They were born into a battle," he admits, " and you can tell they're playing up for their coach and, then, that this is one of the games people were talking about more than any other playoff game that week. We knew we were going somewhere special."

"We were where we were hitting our stride consistently," Kasey admits, "and we could tell almost what's up in this game like we could during the Charlton County game. Everything that could go right when we tried it in that first half we had it. It was just a lot of points against a really good team. I think they had beaten Marion County pretty bad earlier in the year (43-14). They were full of talent and you could see they had some young kids playing, too."

Two Gabriel Benyard touchdowns- a 50-yard TD pass from Zach Smith and a 49-yard run combined with a Jamorri Colson touchdown made it 21-0 before anyone could get settled in their seats. Manchester scored to make it 21-6. But, then, it was DJ Lundy's turn. Runs of 65, 24, 27, and 41 yards, with a JyQuez Marshall pick-6 sandwiched in there, made it 54-6 on the Indians' way to a 54-12 win.

It was a rare, post-season opportunity for the entire family to be together on a holiday. And it was one that Kaleb wouldn't trade for anything...

"I wasn't able to be there on Thanksgiving day with everyone because of our practice schedule for the game. With us playing Valdosta again in Valdosta the next day, I worked it out to make it to Dad's game Friday night and then head to the team hotel after the game. He actually didn't know Katy and I were coming to the game so we got to surprise him in his office about an hour before the game. Of course he had a huge smile and immediately looked at Mom and said 'You knew they were coming the whole time didn't you?' which gave everybody a good laugh. Those little moments were the best while we were going through what we went through."

"I don't know that I've ever seen a first half like that with the Irwin offense going at full throttle," Kaleb said as he prepped for the West Florida game in Valdosta against VSU the following day. "Because Dad was on the platform that whole game, or the first half for that game, and when Irwin was up it was in a hurry. Dad let the other coaches call plays in the second half and, in the end, it ended up working out awesome for us because he and I sat on his golf cart with mom, Katy, Uncle Kevin and a bunch of people around us. We found the golf cart in the end zone for the whole second half and told dad, 'Hey, you don't have to call plays. You can take a nap if you're not feeling good. If you have got to go home, go home.' But he didn't want to go.

"Getting all the family together for hugs and watching Kasey coach...??? It was great to just stand there and just hang out. That was pretty cool to be there to be able to sit and talk with Dad."

And, if folks that were tight with the program had doubts about getting to the last game of the year again- and winning this time around- those were falling away...

"You go into all these playoff games nothing-nothing and, you know, I talked to somebody after the game and we noticed in the first half Manchester just couldn't catch Irwin and couldn't catch a break that they needed," Bill Barrs admitted from his spot in the booth. "I thought our defense played pretty well against them and it all came together the second half. Of course, it was an amazing performance where DJ had a big game and it just felt like it did it earlier in the year. Destiny is something you, kind of, believe it but you didn't until that game. Then, it was like: You know what...? This is meant to be this year..."

"We're sitting together after the game," Marty Roberts recalls, "and Buddy has gathered everyone around. He's talking to the other team just like he always does and he just looks at them and he says that this was just a ballgame. Buddy said that if this is the worst thing that ever happens to you in your life, he said you're going to live a pretty good life. Coach Hochstetler just said 'Amen! Yes sir!' You know...? Like, hey, this is just a ball game fellas. From Buddy's perspective, it's '...look what I'm fighting you know...?' If this loss tonight is the worst thing that ever happens to you, you'll have a pretty good life..."

The following afternoon, West Florida was an hour or so down the road at Bazemore-Hyder Stadium to take on the Blazers in, ironically, another rematch from the regular season.

From a full three weeks prior...

The Argos and Blazers were cagey out of the blocks and it took a quarter for the visitors to take the lead heading into the intermission. Anthony Johnson crashed in from the one-yard line and Ka'Ron Ashley caught a 33-yard touchdown pass from Austin Reed to take a 17-7 lead. The third quarter was a chance for West Florida to gain a little distance with touchdown runs from Jervon Newton and Johnson again as VSU tried to counter with a Seth McGill run on their side.

The fourth quarter, inasmuch there were ideas of absolute character and destiny in Ocilla, showed it might be the same in Pensacola. Three VSU scores on a 64-yard TD pass and short runs by McGill and Jamar Thompkins gave the home team a 35-31 lead with 2:12 to play. Austin Reed and the school's all-time leading receiver Tate Lehtio started with four straight pitch-and-catch moments including a conversion on a 4th-and-8. They would combine again to get the ball to the one-inch line of Valdosta. With six seconds left, Johnson crashed in for the game-winner in a 38-35 classic.

"I had a quick, little flashback of all the time in Emory Hospital, all the stays, and Dad not being at certain games this season and thinking: 'Right... this is it, Lord, we've been through a lot this year.' And you're thinking, 'Well, our season comes down to one play.' We scored and everything our guys had worked for helped get it done. What an ending it was."

UWF would go to 10-2, 6-0 in road playoff games all-time. The Argos would also stop VSU's 25-game winning streak and their 13-game home winning streak. The Number One team in the country in Division II ended their season at 10-1.

"We had a phenomenal week of practice and played with a huge confidence on both sides of the ball. Our guys executed the game plan that we put together about as good as they could. It obviously came down to the wire but our guys knew if we were at our best, we could finish the job. There was definitely a little more prep time and film watched for that one. Kasey and Katy were able to be at the game. To celebrate with them after the game made the victory even sweeter and then to get on FaceTime with Mom Dad and Kenley was awesome."

Next up for the Indians was a familiar opponent from Homerville as Kaleb and the Argos would head to Hickory, North Carolina for the Super Region 2 title game against 6th-ranked and 13-0 Lenoir-Rhyne.

Manchester 12

Blue Devils

Irwin County 54

Indians

1	2	3	4	F
6	0	6	0	12
34	14	6	0	**54**

WEST FLORIDA 38 (10-2)
-VS- VALDOSTA STATE 35 (10-1)

1st	09:32	UWF–Austin Williams 27 yd field goal 12 plays, 49 yards, TOP 5:28	3	0
1st	08:07	VSU–L. Gallimore 69 yd pass from Rogan Wells (F. Ramirez kick) 4 plays, 81 yards, TOP 1:18	3	7
2nd	12:11	UWF–Anthony Johnson 1 yd run (Austin Williams kick), 14 plays, 80 yards, TOP 6:30	10	7
2nd	00:12	UWF–Ka'Ron Ashley 33 yd pass from Austin Reed (Austin Williams kick) 12 plays, 85 yards, TOP 5:07	17	7
3rd	07:54	UWF–Jervon Newton 2 yd run (Austin Williams kick), 7 plays, 22 yards, TOP 3:18	24	7
3rd	03:49	VSU–Seth McGill 12 yd run (F. Ramirez kick), 11 plays, 75 yards, TOP 4:05	24	14
3rd	00:10	UWF–Anthony Johnson 4 yd run (Austin Williams kick), 8 plays, 75 yards, TOP 3:39	31	14
4th	14:24	VSU–L. Gallimore 64 yd pass from Rogan Wells (F. Ramirez kick) 3 plays, 75 yards, TOP 0:46	31	21
4th	08:03	VSU–Seth McGill 2 yd run (F. Ramirez kick), 8 plays, 81 yards, TOP 2:48	31	28
4th	02:12	VSU–Jamar Thompkins 1 yd run (F. Ramirez kick), 12 plays, 81 yards, TOP 3:38	31	35
4th	00:06	UWF–Anthony Johnson 1 yd run (Austin Williams kick), 11 plays, 75 yards, TOP 2:06	38	35

Chapter 16

DECEMBER 6- CLINCH, 36-0/
AT LENOIR-RHYNE, 43-38

C lint Thompson of the Valdosta Daily Times caught up with Clinch County head coach Don Tison, Junior during the week of the semi-final. He asked what it's like going against Irwin County on the football field.

"It's like fighting your brother. I didn't have a brother but I know brothers fight and they fight a lot and make each other tougher. I really think that we can give some credit to Irwin for the success that we've had because we know that we've got to come to work and really work extra hard to compete with them because we know the type of program that they have."

"Obviously, when we see the brackets come out, you see that potential matchup. You just have the vision of how much fun and how big of a game that would be but then you fall back to take it one game at a time."

"It's just a great environment, whether you're playing Homerville or you're playing in Ocilla. It's just a great environment to be in. It's going to be like a state championship environment."

Becky Taylor, over at the Tifton Gazette newspaper, broke down the numbers:

"...46th meeting between the schools. Ocilla first picked up a football in 1922. Clinch was a late bloomer, waiting until 1952. They first met that year, the Panthers' ninth ever game. Irwin won, 42-6. The Indians were dominant then, Clinch not so much. The Indians won every meeting, 10 of them, until Clinch mustered a tie in 1980. The Panthers won their first in 1981.

"The series soon tilted to Clinch's favor and the Indians went nearly a decade without a win. It's evened back up again and the Sept. 20 win tilted the series to 23-22-1 for Irwin."

Clinch beat a surprising Warren County team in the quarterfinals, 38-16. Tyler Morehead had 151 rush yards and Michael Walker was right behind him with 78.

Buddy told Becky during the week that Morehead "...is somebody special" as the Panthers came into the game with an eight-game win streak. He also admitted something else:

"We're going to have to play a perfect game."

"We knew we got them at home in the game to go to the state championship," Kasey admits. "I know history hadn't been kind to us in the second playing of Clinch in a year, but something felt different. We just felt like it was our time. It was our year with everything that was going on. Our kids practiced and were laser-focused. We had a great week of practice and, then coming out that night, we already had the situation with Garland and he wasn't playing.

"So, we were without a wingback and without an outside linebacker. I want to say within the first six or seven plays our other wingback, Eric Anderson, tore his ACL. That kind of threw us for a loop in the first half. We couldn't figure out anything. We couldn't get anything going offensively. We didn't have a wingback. We were just trying to keep our head above water."

Usually, Buddy gets to rest and gather his energy for the second half at half time. Not against Clinch in the semi. As soon as the team made it to the locker room, Buddy had Kasey pull a chair into the player's locker room. He started writing on the dry erase board to get the team ready for the second half. There were adjustments for the missing wingback on offense and figuring out the best way to win the rematch that had, so many times in the past, not gone their way.

"He's a phenomenal halftime adjustment guy," Kasey continued, "but that night just watching him get up, work on that board, and seeing things kind of come together...? Then, coming out of the locker room we had just a tunnel of people surround us. Half the crowd was lined up outside the locker room, the siren was blaring, and it just felt really different walking out there after halftime.

"Early in the half, we put together a pretty long drive. We were just running the ball well, hitting them right in the mouth, and driving it right down their throat to score. You could just kind of feel the weight lifted off our back because we knew, at that moment, that it was about to be good."

The play of the year for Irwin happened on the next drive, and you can hunt it down on YouTube fairly easily. Gabriel Benyard reached up, back, and behind himself to pull in a Clinch pass for an interception. In the end, Irwin scored 36 as the rout was on as the defense came together to help turn it on for the win.

"Knowing where we were with Buddy and how important it was to him, this game just had a different feeling to it," Andy Paulk says. "Watching Buddy during that game, I doubt I will ever experience anything like that night ever again."

"That was probably the sweetest win for Buddy throughout the whole year not discounting the state championship," Marty Roberts says. "I don't know when the last time was that Clinch got shut out. But I know they've never been shut out twice in the same year. They would have another laser-focused week after that and they were just absolutely determined they were going to go to Atlanta, we're going to take care of business, and we're going to come back so we can have a party at the red light."

"To have one of our best players, Eric Anderson, tear his ACL in the first half that game," Drew Tankersley says, "we had a ton for him in that game plan. We were down to our number 3 wing back and it just threw everything off. We were just in survival mode trying to get to half-time. Nobody said it, but being in the locker room with Garland hurt and, then, Eric hurt I think there was some worry in there."

But the coaches scrapped the game plan and put together another one. DJ Lundy had a lot of good runs on the evening and Irwin even ended up scoring on a play on the goal line where the coaching staff was trying to call a timeout. Drew was running down the sideline trying to get an official's attention, but the ball was snapped and Irwin scored despite themselves.

"It was just a relief to win," Drew says. "It was like a monkey was off our back. We can finally say we did it twice in a year. I think everybody was just so anxious to get there to play for a championship."

The team wouldn't do a lot differently going forward. There would be FaceTimes with Buddy to come and a game plan to prepare and one more hurdle to clear.

"We went out that second half and our kids were not stressed about anything," Irwin assistant Troy Fletcher admits. "They knew that they wouldn't be stopped. We kicked off and got them down inside the 20. Then, we got the turnover and scored and went up by two scores. I'll be honest. They were hungry and I wanted that one badly myself."

As was the custom after home games, Buddy and Kenley would drive the golf cart to the area near the fieldhouse. With as many people as could fit around them, Buddy had a few words to tell everyone...

"GIMME AN 'A'!"

"GIMME A 'T'!"

"WE GOIN' TO THE A-T-L, BABY!"

Amongst the cheers and cowbells, he continued: "My man Orgeron at LSU, he said it best..."

"WE COMING!"

"Defense... you played your butt off. Special teams... You played your butt off... Offense, I thought last week's first half was awesome. That was unbelievable, guys... Go out there and celebrate, but be classy to Clinch."

He then was given a red marker to check off the second of three boxes on a sign. The first check mark was when the team finished the regular season undefeated. The second one was for beating Clinch (again). The third had to do with their next appointment.

"I told you guys before the game," he continued, "I hope you love each other. Because I'm going to tell you. We got no color on this. I hope you love the color of a man right here."

Buddy tugged at his black polar coat that had the "IC" logo on it.

"I taught you to dream. Let's finish our dream this year."

"After halftime, they just found another gear and they got us," Clinch Head Coach Don Tison said. "They were a great team and they deserved it. It was just unreal how good their defense was."

Coach Tison knew Marion County was a good team- having played them in the semifinals the year before. Most of that team had returned for another year for that last game of the year. But seeing a rival and a friend, all at the same time, summon the strength to talk when asked afterwards gives the range of emotions you would expect.

"It was hard because I've known him for several years and just to see you know what that cancer had done... it was tough watching him. But, man, you can just tell you how much he loved everybody. With him getting out there and having that opportunity to talk about Jesus and his love for Jesus Christ and how, if you don't have that, you don't have anything in your life. In a way, it's almost like the Lord let him live long enough for him to get there. It was good to give him that opportunity because he knew then how bad it was. He would take advantage of that moment and, man, he was just a great person."

When asked about what Buddy and his legacy are, Coach Tison was resolute in his answer:

"If you want to be worth anything in what you're doing, whatever your profession, you have to love people around you, you have to bring people together, you have to love them, you have to respect them, and at the same time you have to demand a certain level of excellence. You can attain it and get there, but you can also be respected and love each other at the same time.

"You don't make plans and you don't sit there looking five years down the road. Because you're not promised that. You need to do everything you can today and, then the next day, you do everything you can to be the best person that you can be and influence as many people as you can. Coach Nobles died in the way he did life every day because who knows what's next, you know?

"If I get news that I've got six months left, I don't want to waste any time. Because nobody knows when that clock is going to run out. You don't want to waste time with days you can't get back. Coaches are people where you know you're influential. You're around kids and you have a chance where you can change somebody's life for the better. When you have that opportunity each day, and if you don't take advantage of that opportunity in that platform in one way or the other, that's one last day that you have.

"All of my days are numbered, too. We just don't know how many days you have, so you do the best you can while you're here. Love God and love people, too."

The third round of the playoffs would send West Florida on the road again to take on Lenoir-Rhyne in a battle of #20 and

#6. Getting to Hickory, North Carolina isn't easy. It's in the mountains about an hour north-northwest of Charlotte and the Bears made it difficult for all of their opponents in 2019. They went 8-0 in the South Atlantic Conference and only 2 of those wins were less than double-digits. They took care of Miles in Round One and #25 Carson Newman to get to the game against the Argos.

10-2 vs. 13-0 and their 15-game home winning streak...

Pick your analogy as the game went about as back-and-forth as a game can get...

The Bears would muff a punt in the first quarter and it would lead to an Ian Bush safety for a 2-0 lead while Ka'Ron Ashley would combine with Austin Reed from 15 yards out for a 9-0 lead. Lenoir-Rhyne QB Grayson Willingham would close the margin to 9-7 after a touchdown run to close out the first. Both teams would combine for 31 points in the second as Reed would throw two more scores to Quentin Randolph and Rodney Coates, but a Jace Jordan rush for the home team would close the gap to 26-21 at the break.

The Argos lead would increase to nine by the end of the third off a 75-yard Marcus Clayton kickoff return, but the visitors would expand and hold on to a lead all in a 15-minute period on the football field. Anthony Johnson would run in from 8-yards out on the first play of the fourth to make the lead 40-24. But two scores by the Bears in a little over two minutes would draw them to within two at 40-38 with 11 minutes to play. An Austin Williams field goal with 2:11 left would give the final margin to UWF, 43-38. But a Willingham pass had to be picked off by D'Anthony Bell at the Argos 5-yard line before they could exhale and get ready for a national semi-final.

Both teams would rack up a total of 892 yards of offense and Austin Reed would throw for 360 yards and three scores.

"Unbelievable play there to end that thing," UWF head coach Pete Shinnick told Eric J. Wallace of the Pensacola News Journal after the game. "I'll tell you what, just a great team effort. Lenoir-Rhyne is extremely well coached and did so many good things.

"That's a heckuva football game. Two weeks in a row. I don't know if I can handle this much more."

"I knew we had a special group at the beginning of the year," UWF center Devin Gibson told Wallace as well. "We took that tough loss to Carson-Newman, but now we've found our groove and we're just playing really well. We're playing complete, 60-minute football."

And they would have to do it one more time on the road to make it to a championship game... something Irwin didn't have to worry about...

Clinch County 0

Panthers

Irwin County 36

Indians

1	2	3	4	F
0	0	0	0	0
0	0	23	13	36

WEST FLORIDA 43 (11-2)
-VS- LENOIR-RHYNE 38 (13-1)

1st	09:52	UWF–Matthew Gotel 1 yd safety	2	0
1st	06:57	UWF–Ka'Ron Ashley 15 yd pass from Austin Reed (Austin Williams kick) 7 plays, 52 yards, TOP 2:50	9	0
1st	02:30	LR–G. Willingham 2 yd run (Chase Allbaugh kick), 12 plays, 75 yards, TOP 4:27	9	7
2nd	14:54	UWF–Q. Randolph 4 yd pass from Austin Reed (Austin Williams kick) 5 plays, 73 yards, TOP 2:31	16	7
2nd	09:30	UWF–Austin Williams 23 yd field goal 8 plays, 71 yards, TOP 3:34	19	7
2nd	04:44	LR–Dareke Young 19 yd pass from G. Willingham (Chase Allbaugh kick) 11 plays, 75 yards, TOP 4:46	19	14
2nd	02:31	UWF–Rodney Coates 47 yd pass from Austin Reed (Austin Williams kick) 7 plays, 78 yards, TOP 2:06	26	14
2nd	00:44	LR–Jace Jordan 6 yd run (Chase Allbaugh kick), 5 plays, 54 yards, TOP 1:40	26	21
3rd	09:41	LR–Chase Allbaugh 20 yd field goal 12 plays, 76 yards, TOP 5:14	26	24
3rd	09:30	UWF–Marcus Clayton 75 yd kickoff return (Austin Williams kick)	33	24
4th	14:54	UWF–Anthony Johnson 8 yd run (Austin Williams kick), 13 plays, 80 yards, TOP 6:07	40	24

4th	13:26	LR–Ryan Carter 4 yd run (Jaquay Mitchell pass), 4 plays, 75 yards, TOP 1:22	40	32
4th	11:11	LR–Ryan Carter 2 yd run (G. Willingham pass failed), 4 plays, 16 yards, TOP 1:19	40	38
4th	02:11	UWF–Austin Williams 33 yd field goal 4 plays, -1 yards, TOP 0:23	43	38

Chapter 17

DECEMBER 14- GA STATE, MARION COUNTY, 56-14/ AT FERRIS STATE, 28-14

December 11, 2018 stuck with GPB-TV's Wiley Ballard...

"It wasn't just my first State Final with Georgia Public Broadcasting; it was my first time ever being on TV! Granted nowadays the distinction between *television* and *online streaming* becomes less clear with each passing Netflix series, not to mention I bet we had more viewers on _GPB. org_ that morning then on traditional TV sets, but that didn't alter my mood one bit. I couldn't believe it. The 2018 State Championship between Irwin County and Clinch County was on _local television_ and I had a role to play.

"On a day best described as a dream come true, my fondest memory was my halftime interview with Coach Nobles. His Indians trailed 10-7 and the offense was sputtering. They'd squandered multiple red zone opportunities and hadn't taken care of the ball. Naturally I asked what adjustments the Irwin County offense could make in the second half. His wry reply was one for the books.

"Score!"

"It's often said in the world of television that the best say more with less. At halftime Coach Nobles had said it all with just one word."

Then, there would be times shortly thereafter that a talk would mean just as much as half time adjustments told to Wiley on television.

Buddy and Tammy came to Georgia State Stadium ready for a title game. He was brought in with a wheelchair with a big smile on his face...

"It was almost like he knew it was fixing to happen, you know?" Drew Tankersley said...

In the four seasons Chris Kirksey coached Marion County in Buena Vista, the Eagles had done increasingly better in the post-season. From a first-round appearance to a second, a semifinal, and now a final, his electric offense and solid defense had them close to the top of the Single-A Public rankings all season long. QB Trice McCammon was getting a lot of notice on teams of the year and was leading an offense that averaged over 30-points a game. LB Kendrick Hawkins was the focus of a defense that registered two shutouts in their first three games and would be a part of the discussion in Region 4.

Marion beat Schley, Lincoln, and Pelham- all at home- before making their way to Georgia State.

"It was a first for me," Kirksey admitted. "In my 25 years, I haven't been in a championship finals one time. So it was very exciting. The guys were very focused and we had a really good week of practice- even though it didn't show up on game day. We had guys who never backed down from a challenge all season long last year and it showed early on."

"Irwin left on Friday morning," Marty Roberts remembers. "They always do something at the high school with the student body and then go over to the elementary school. I'm an emotional person and I said I'm going to do something different this year for the send-off. So, in a really good rain, mind you, we went through town. The kids were just laser focused all week long. They told me, once they got to Atlanta, they were all business."

Mike Posey made a point to watch every title game on television when he could. His allegiances were with Buddy- and it didn't matter the color of the jersey. Their school disbanded in the mid-1980's, so Irwin had become his school, too. There was no way he would miss this ending in 2019.

Casey Soliday had to focus on coaching for one more game and all the stuff that goes with it... from travel to logistics to television commitments.

"I was just constantly thinking about something we needed to do to take care of that week. It's almost, at that point, a lot of the X's and O's stuff is taken care of. It becomes planning and preparing for the trip, getting there, and then all the things that people are going to do. That week really just blew by for me."

"Championship week was exciting, man," Kasey says. "We had already gotten the heavyweight of Clinch off our back. We had to practice well, but we've watched the film on Marion County by then. We know they are a really talented team. But, I think, that if there was ever a chance for us to win it- it was in practice. They were locked in. We had a great week of practice. The kids were all ready for the trip up to Atlanta. It went smoothly and everything just went well."

"It was almost surreal," Irwin assistant Jared Luke recalls. "I just felt like all week that this is the Dream Season. It was crazy, of course, because you have to plan all this stuff out- all the people at the Board of Education office getting hotel schedules, getting meals taken care of, and things like that. At practice all week, it felt like it was all fixing to come full circle. I just felt like we couldn't be beat. I didn't care who we played that week, I felt like we weren't going to be beat. DJ Lundy came to me early in the year and told me this was the year and that nobody was beating us. It wasn't going to happen on his watch.

"I felt that same way that entire week of the state championship game. We still prepared the same way. We wanted to include Buddy as much as he could and we wanted to stick to his game plan."

"I think, just getting Buddy to Atlanta," Irwin assistant Pete Snyder recalls, "some folks thought that someone had offered to let him use their private plane to fly up there to Atlanta. But the weather was so bad that he couldn't do that. I had to drive up to Atlanta for this game as well, but the situation was not good for Buddy. It took him a while to get up there and it was late when they got there and it wasn't easy. Nothing was easy about that trip for them.

"In the playoffs, we practice at 6:30 on Thursday mornings. But Buddy would still be there. Tammy drove up and he got out. He was on his golf cart. The message for the guys was the same as always: 'This is a really good team. We're going to play well...'"- those kinds of things. But it was a morale-booster just to see him there for the kids. He had one early morning practice since he had been in the hospital. So, that was big."

There was an initial concern about Buddy being on his platform. Since the AG Department had proven it during the regular season with the trip to Atkinson County, the school and the school system would have had no problem disassembling and reassembling what they had made for the program at Georgia State Stadium. But, after some back and forth discussions, the GHSA came up with a smaller one for Buddy and Kenley to perch on for the game. It wasn't as steep a climb- about a half-dozen steps. And it was about the size of a small conference table. To a man, everyone on the staff and everyone associated with the program couldn't have been more grateful to the GHSA and to Georgia State University to give him some kind of on-field presence. It would have taken too long in transit to have him up on the press level- although Irwin had prepared for that if that had been the eventuality. And for someone who was as integral to the program as Buddy is, to just have him on the field meant so much to an entire community.

Buddy came into the locker room and he was there the entire pregame. He sat on the couch provided in the space and he would alternate from sitting to lying down and resting before the game.

"He just, honestly, looked very tired," Pete continues. "We were kind of worried. We were all worried and wondered: Is he going to be able to do this?"

"The guys were ready to go that day," Coach Troy Fletcher says. "When they're ready to play, they felt like they were not going to be denied. They locked it in in film studying the Marion County quarterback, Trice McCammon, and what we needed to do. They put a great game plan together defensively. It was a fun and a good week with no distractions, really. But nobody really understood what Buddy's body was going through. He literally laid on that red couch to conserve as much energy as possible."

"Nothing against Marion County," Irwin assistant Drew Tankersley said, "but we were as confident as we had ever been on our team. Everybody was ready to get there because we felt like it was going to be a really good day and it turned out to be one."

Buddy didn't make the travel timetable to Atlanta with the team. He and Tammy took an extra couple of hours to get to Atlanta. They stayed at the Marriott Marquis with the team and had a tremendous view of the city beneath them.

Irwin Superintendent Dr. Thad Clayton was part of the logistics army that made sure an entire team and the community that would follow would get there as seamlessly as possible.

"You see these things and you have folks who don't think twice about it. Literally, they ask 'What does it mean…? What does he need to do his job…? What does he need to do his job the way that he wants to do it…?' What can we do to make sure that he's safe, but can still do what he wants to do…? We will build the stand up again if we need to, but it's those kinds of pitching-in things that add to the greater tale.

"The facilities guys at Georgia State and everybody else were aware of the story. It wasn't a 'No, we can't do it.' It was 'What do you need? We'll do it.' We were concerned that the forecast was not great for the stadium that weekend because of the storms. So, GSU was offering us alternate plans. We had an on the field plan. We had an 'In the Coaches Press Box' plan. They had a golf cart plan. We had a wheelchair plan.

"Georgia State and the GHSA had to approve everything, but their approach was an incredibly uplifting part of the season. For me, that story further galvanized what's good about people. When there was a need for Irwin County and for Buddy Nobles' family, there was no request that was denied all year."

Tommy Palmer got to share the thoughts of an entire state on his state-wide "High School Scoreboard Show" all season long as everyone tracked Irwin County and the Nobles story. It was more than 50 radio stations that got to let everyone know from one end of the state to the other what was going on.

"I got so many different opinions from coaches and from fans who were eager to be on the show," he remembers. "Buddy was loved by a lot of people and we really had a lot of people praying for him and pulling for him and Irwin. It was good to have a diverse audience on the show with us and I had several different people make mention of Buddy in his situation. They were praying for him and we were all following it."

"That morning walking out on the field it was really emotional," Kasey said. "I had seen how Dad progressed throughout the year and you want to keep that hope that he's going to be okay. But seeing the things we've seen, I kind of knew that that was the last game for him."

"Doctor Clayton and everybody else in the community did everything humanly possible to make it easy on Mom and Dad for his trip up to Atlanta. It was a weird one because, normally, he's coming right up there with the team. It was weird not having him up there with us immediately. We were stressing trying to get all the kids settled because we got there and they didn't have all the room keys ready for us at the hotel."

But, by the time Buddy arrived that night, Irwin was ready to play. A lot of Buddy's talks during the season were just telling the kids how much he loved them, talking about the year the team had, everything they had been through, and how the game with Marion County was just the next step. There was one more goal to accomplish Saturday morning, but he also told them, no matter what happened he wanted everybody to know that he loved them all and appreciated all the support. There was also an internal concern about Buddy and having that place to be where he could coach.

"We were trying to figure that out during the week," Kasey continued, "and the GHSA said not to bring up the stand. They would build one like his own platform, and then it was perfect. it didn't have railings on the side, so at first we were a little worried because he wasn't that strong. He needed help walking, so we didn't want him to fall off."

But Kenley was up there to be another assistant coach for a championship game sitting right next to him the entire time- the best caretaker you could have.

"I came home, I think, Wednesday afternoon," Kenley says. "Dad was so weak at that point. A lot of people don't realize how much it took for him to be able to travel to Atlanta and be at the game." She had taken photos during the season and was reminded to take one more. Tammy told her to get a good shot of her father and she found one. Buddy had risen out of his wheelchair and was standing, ready to enter the arena one more time.

Tommy got to share his television duties with Larry Smith for GPB.

"Championship week is always hectic," Larry said. "What viewers see at home is a smooth production with everyone – announcers, camera operators, audio technicians, directors, producers, engineers, and countless support staff – all working in unison to capture a developing story live and record the moment for the ages. People will say "I remember where I was when..." and for 48 hours every year, we are well aware that we are the center of the universe for football fans throughout the state of Georgia. We wear it as a badge of honor and celebrate both those who emerge victorious as well as those who gave it their all but came up just short.

"The Irwin County-Marion County game in December 2019 had a different feel than most. We knew the situation long before we dialed into the conference call earlier in the week with interim coach Casey Soliday. Legendary coach Buddy Nobles was battling cancer. He had been diagnosed in late summer and his condition worsened a couple of games into the season, forcing him to give up much of the work to Soliday and his staff. But Buddy was still present nearly every day – in a golf cart on the sidelines during practice and on a specially-built platform behind the bench on game nights. Nobody said it, but the thought silently throbbed in the back of each of our minds: this could be Buddy's last game. One last chance."

"It was a little hectic on the defensive side for us," Irwin assistant Clayton Sirmans says. "They like to spread it out and the quarterback was pretty athletic. Just kind of getting everybody mentally ready and all the other things that go into it and putting everything into four loading trailers was the challenge-making sure we had everything. Coach Nobles was not able to be at every one of the meetings. Trying to plan for the meals and and all of the other things behind the scenes was definitely hectic.

"Over the last few weeks, you didn't know if Buddy still had the strength to be there. So definitely every time you see him, and that you know he's there, it was special."

"You know both these teams very well," Larry Smith said in his back-and-forth with Tommy Palmer on Georgia Public Broadcasting...

"Marion County throws the ball all over the place and Irwin County has 7 or 8 guys that run the ball very well. Jamorri Colson is just one of 4 or 5 who have been over 600 yards and 65 carries. They spread the ball around and they're not greedy.

"You have to control DJ Lundy. He's played 6 or 7 games since the injury," Tommy said in his Keys to the Game.

"Just be business as usual. They have been just a holy terror to everyone they've played. They have to pay attention to the secondary. They're very young back there."

"When I arrived at Georgia State Stadium Saturday morning, there it was," Larry adds. "A platform to lift its occupants six feet in the air, well above his charges. If you didn't know better, you might think it was a pedestal fit for a king...and no one would argue with you! Buddy's resume in football was well known. A six-time champion as an assistant in Florida, he'd ventured to southwestern Georgia with dreams of winning gold. Four times in five seasons he came close, guiding his team to the title match in Atlanta each December. But that crown had eluded him.

"The numbers on the pregame clock grew smaller as the stadium crowd grew larger. Players from both teams were warming up as a cart carrying Buddy emerged from the bowels of the venue. This storied edifice had etched indelible moments on our hearts and minds over the years – Muhammad Ali lighting the torch at its baptism, Michael Johnson and his gold shoes making Olympic history, Sammy Sosa's bat wowing an All-Star Game crowd, the World Series thrillers, and future baseball Hall of Famers throwing and swinging their way into immortality. And perhaps, today, Buddy would join them. A moment we would never forget.

"Buddy was escorted onto the platform and took his steps gingerly to get into a familiar place for the last time in the 2019 season. Kasey made sure he was settled and Kenley joined in her co-pilot seat one more time.

"Dad loves being a part of this and we loved what the GHSA has done in building this platform," she said.

"The physical toll of Coach Nobles' cancer was painfully obvious," Wiley said. "His trademark rosy complexion and full cheeks had faded to pale tones and a slender jawline. Instead of his easy stride up and down the sideline, he needed a wheelchair just to reach midfield.

"There was one thing that hadn't changed though: the gleam in his eyes. That was the first thing I noticed when I first saw him an hour before kickoff on that damp, overcast morning. And why wouldn't his eyes be sparkling? It was a State Final after all. And if you're a high school football coach in Georgia, there's nothing that gets your juices going like playing in the season's final game.

"Buddy called the entire game," Pete Snyder remembers. "And it was like he got out there on that platform and he was so focused and into it. He basically called the first play and when he told us what the first play was going to be he said, 'Guys, we're probably going to score on this play.' Honestly, that wasn't uncommon. It was not a far reach for him to say 'we might score on this' and then we actually do.

"Sure enough, we run that play and Gabriel Benyard goes some crazy number of yards to the house and that set the tone," Luke Roberts said.

"Just over five minutes into the first quarter Irwin County jumped out to a 14-0 lead thanks to a long run and pick six," Wiley said. "They brought that two-score advantage into the locker room at halftime up 28-14. And less than five minutes into the second half they doubled it, ahead 42-14. By then it was clear. Irwin County was going to give Buddy Nobles a state championship in his final game.

"I watched from my perch in the announcer's booth as Buddy was welcomed by a host of well-wishers upon approaching midfield," Larry added. "Smiles and laughs and pats on the back accentuated the chatter that was audible from high above. If you didn't know the story, you would never think that anything was amiss. Here was the veteran coach, arriving to take aim again at a title. It was a gorgeous morning. A storm from the previous day had blown through and the clouds had departed to leave the sky all alone for a perfect southern sun to dominate. Buddy escaped the crowd and slowly made his way to the stairs of the platform, gingerly making his way to the top. He surveyed the field and his players. His face glowed with anticipation; a perfect earthly companion to the ambient light from above. His daughter joined him as he settled into his chair and donned his headset with ease. The two shared a moment. Pride. Love. Honor. Excitement. Game time was here."

And Irwin County wanted to jump out to another early lead...

"Irwin County had a penchant for grabbing big leads early and this was no exception," Smith said. "On the first play from scrimmage, the Indians scored a 77-yard touchdown. On Marion County's next possession, Jordan Payne returned an interception for another score.

Andy Paulk, Kelly Wynn, and Bill Barrs were in the booth for "The Rocket..."

"They're gonna drop back... They're gonna throw the ball..."

"OH... INTERCEPTED!!! TOUCHDOWN, IRWIN! NUMBER THREE, JORDAN PAYNE!

"WOW!"

"NUMBER THREE, JORDAN PAYNE!"

"HE CUT HIM OFF! WOW! 13-NOTHING!"

"He jumped that route, Andy! I didn't see it coming. Jordan Payne and he walks in to the endzone...

"He read that route..."

"Yeah, he did..."

"28-yard interception return... and it's 13-nothing."

Irwin County had a 14-0 lead just minutes into the game. The TV cameras found Buddy often. His eyes intense as his Indians maintained that two touchdown advantage into halftime.

"But the Irwin County faithful knew any celebration would be premature. Fate had not been kind to their beloved coach and his hard-working program. Just like that prankster Lucy eternally pulling the football away just as Charlie Brown uncoiled his leg for the kick, Irwin had endured those trips to the championship game only to come away empty too many times.

"Coach Kirksey had really set up Marion County with their offense and he had them up pretty good all year with the slot receivers," Palmer says. "McCammon missed a couple of early throws that he should have gotten and they also had a couple of drops. When you fall behind 21-7, there's a heck of a lot of difference between being behind 14-7. When it got there, it's almost like you're thinking in the back of your mind it's really an uphill situation.

"Number 12, he's going to get wide again..."

"Touchdown, Benyard!"

"Gabriel Benyard, that's #2 for him today, Andy!"

"9-yard scamper around to the left, yep..."

"Watch Lundy, he's leading that block right there!"

"BOOM!"

"BOOM"

"And then there was that 'boom, boom, boom' that would come..."

Right out of a TV timeout...

"Irwin County takes the ball and hands it to Lundy up the middle and breaks through..."

"He's across to the left... to the 40, the 50, to the 30... TOUCHDOWN, DJ Lundy!

"They almost got him at the 1... Straight down the field..."

"Big Lundy all the way down..."

"Man!"

"WOOO! You gotta like that..."

"Hey, Bill! Watch the replay... That's one advantage we got..."

"That's one good thing about being here..."

"I missed the play, we'll watch it..."

'58-Smith, Watch him right here..."

"BOOM! Right up the gut..."

"Right over Smith's butt, the kick to the left and there he goes. He's off to the races... they almost catch him on the one..."

"He had a good angle, but you're not going to push him out of bounds..."

"Evan Ross with the PAT. it's up and good. Irwin County takes the lead, 28-0..."

"28-7!"

"May as well... 28-7... I'm just used to doing that..."

The misspeak in the booth got a good laugh, but the call meant just as much...

Wiley caught Casey Soliday on the way to the locker room and asked him about one Benyard and his first half:

"Gabriel...? He's just a phenomenal athlete. Key guy for our team and our defensive side. We just have to tackle better and I think we'll be alright"

"I think it's gonna be speed, speed, speed in the second half."

The Irwin County fans were also concerned over the Jordan Payne injury that caused a hushed tone in the western stands that were filled, but there was another half to play for a title as everyone tried to get word he would be okay.

"We had a good half offensively. Defensively, we were playing well. We just can't give up any big plays and we had to execute in the third-quarter. This third quarter is about to be really important."

"It was pretty tight at the half and I know that there were some opportunities that were kind of missed," Irwin assistant Drew Tankersley admits. "There wasn't any panic, but there was a little bit of feeling we missed those opportunities. What we were doing was working and we felt like if we came out and just stuck to our guns, our defense was going to play well.

"I felt good at halftime even being down two scores," Marion Head Coach Chris Kirksey said, "and then when the third quarter hit and our quarterback, Trice McCannon, went down and he didn't come back in the game we knew that was that was going to be uphill battle even more so than what we were already facing without him. From that point on, it just seemed like once the snowball got rolling against us it never got any better and just got worse and worse.

"Everything changed when Trice went out because he's the leader of our football team. I had said about Irwin County that those kids really had a lot to fight for with a chip on their shoulder- and they did all year. Their defense was, probably, one of the best defenses I've ever played against in my entire career. We knew that it was going to be a very tough challenge.

"They had all the tools. They had the size up front with the big guys. They had size and quickness with very athletic linebackers and then, even on the back, a lot of speed and athleticism on the backside of the defense. There wasn't a weak link and, of course, as a coach you always want to try to pick out a weak link on the defense or attack and there just wasn't a weak link."

Dr. Clayton, as a part of his responsibilities on game day, was on transportation detail to make sure Buddy could get from the locker room to the field- or any place else he needed to be at Georgia State Stadium. Getting to the field for the second half turned into a bit of an adventure.

"We had a wheelchair plan and we had a separate wheelchair plan to get him from the locker room where the team was going to run out on the field. Every year that we have played for a state championship Buddy was always there leading his team onto the battlefield. This year, I was attached to get him from the locker room to where they ran out.

"I could roll the wheelchair from the locker room where the team ran out on the field in about a minute and forty seconds. We're in the locker room and he's doing what you can to coach the team. We're keeping up with the amount of time until we go back onto the field and we get to about 2 minutes before time to return to the field and I'm thinking 'Okay, I'm going to have Buddy put in the wheelchair probably in the next 30 seconds.

"Buddy starts breaking out into the half-time motivational-win one for the Gipper kind of speech. We're now under two minutes to go and I'm thinking how I'm not going to be able to wheel him to the field before kickoff for the second half. At about 35 seconds, literally, I am wheeling him around the other side of the stadium. Before the game, I was shown a shortcut to get him to the field and I tell Buddy we're going to take it. There's a side door, basically behind the homestand. We get about 15 feet out on the turf and, all the sudden, we find a washout in the turf and I dump Buddy out of the wheelchair and onto the turf.

"Buddy is laying on the turf and his daughter, Kenley, is jumping up and down. Do you know the Santa Claus image where Santa

Claus' hair goes from brown to gray in, like, 10 seconds...? My hair could have gone completely gray in about two seconds. I'm freaking out and I'm looking down, bending over to get Buddy up and back in the chair."

Buddy would play the moment out in "Classic Buddy" fashion. He put his hand on his head as two more people came around the corner to help. Dr. Clayton had a sense of dread that the stadium cameras would capture Buddy on the turf with everyone around him trying to get him back in the wheelchair.

"He's like, 'Well, that woke me up.' His brother-in-law comes up to it and starts brushing off all the pellets off his face and said, 'Well, now you look like you played the game.'"

"The remaining 24 minutes would be an eternity," Larry Smith said. "Would this time be different? Can the boys finish up strong and win one for Buddy?

"Sometimes the script is too good to be true. If the events of that late fall morning ever make it to the big screen, moviegoers will probably mutter "they made that second half a little TOO much, ya know?" on their way out.

"But it really happened. Hollywood couldn't have done it better.

"Early in the third quarter, Marion County fumbled the ball and Irwin County recovered. On the next play, Jamorri Colson ran 45 yards to the end zone. 35-14 Indians."

"He would run over to Buddy and shake his hand the second he came off the field to celebrate.

"Full sprint...

"On the next possession, another Eagles fumble and another Irwin County recovery. One play later, the Indians scored again on a halfback pass from Gabriel Benyard to Colson. 42-14 Indians.

"Moments later, Irwin County's defense struck again, intercepting a tipped pass. That led to another touchdown. 49-14 Indians with time running out in the third quarter! The Irwin County faithful rose up and applauded as reality ebbed into view. Maybe this time Lucy wouldn't prank them. Maybe this was the year!"

"Within a couple minutes we had scored three touchdowns in the third quarter," Kasey said. "Just looking up at the score, looking in the crowd, and looking around at all the kids you kind of knew everything would happen this year. But the entire time we had been there to a title game again. People had been saying 'They're not getting it done.' And they're not getting it done multiple times. Finally, in Dad's last game, they we're about to get the job done.

"From that point of the third quarter all the way through the end of the game, it was just a joy with everybody talking and joking with each other over the headsets. I think, in this moment, in the context of how the season went and how everything went I thought it was pretty fitting that we got to take a quarter to just enjoy it and let our hair down and not be stressed about it.

Kasey would drop by the platform every now and then to see his dad and his sister. Kaleb's girlfriend, Katy, was on the field as well. She had been there for a lot of the season and had Kaleb on FaceTime as he was in Michigan preparing for a national semi-final.

But he wasn't THAT far away from downtown Atlanta...

"I enjoyed a lot of the fourth quarter," Coach Tankersley said. "I remember going up and shaking Buddy's hand. I remember him saying something along the lines of,'Hey!' And he pointed his finger saying we were about to get a big one.

"I do remember this: On the goal line, we got down there towards the end and I can't remember what play Buddy called. But I went against him one time. I said that we had to get his quarterback a touchdown. He had never scored a touchdown and he said go for it. He scored his first-ever rushing TD for us. I'm running over and giving Buddy a high-five and he gives me a high-five and gives all the other coaches a high-five. That was cool. When you have got that big a lead, there's no pressure at that point. So you really were able to hug each other and laugh and joke.

"It is kind of cool that all that work you put in all those days means you get 12 good minutes to enjoy it."

"As the minutes waned off the game clock, the pulse of the Irwin County sideline and its fans accelerated," Wiley Ballard admits. "I will never forget the sights and sounds of that second half because what unfolded next was the richest and most loving outpour of emotion I've ever experienced.

"With just over nine minutes remaining in the fourth quarter, Irwin County's quarterback Zach Smith scored the Indians eighth and final touchdown giving his team a 56-14 lead. After a few replays and the point after, we broke for commercial. Then a most amazing thing happened.

"The dark clouds which had blanketed the stadium since our arrival relented. Sunshine flooded the Irwin County sideline through an empty pocket in the sky's gray canopy. This ray of light triggered an eruption of cheers from the Indian faithful. The joyous commotion peaked just as our broadcast returned and our viewers saw Coach Nobles himself, seated beside his daughter, Kenley, raising his palms upward towards the sun celebrating the serendipitous intersection of sunshine and victory in what had been a season full of adversity.

"Next came my sideline talk on Coach Nobles' wife, Tammy. A middle school math teacher in Ocilla, Tammy was the first person with whom Buddy shared his dire prognosis. From that moment forward she walked with him every step of the way. Through appointments, chemotherapy, and rehabilitation, Tammy was there. Buddy lovingly called her his "Director of Cancer Operations" during his exhausting fight against the disease."

"All the way, Buddy coached on through smiles," Larry said. "He glanced at the scoreboard often, surely thinking "can this clock tick faster?!"

"The answer was yes. The lopsided score meant the mercy rule was in effect and the fourth quarter clock would run without stopping. With the outcome in hand, the game itself quickly became a backdrop to Buddy. His wife was being interviewed live on GPB and the stadium control room put her up on the giant scoreboard. The crowd roared its approval at the larger than life image and the cheering rose to a crescendo as she was replaced on the screen by Buddy himself. His daughter showed him something on her phone and together they smiled. It was finally going to happen. Buddy Nobles and the Irwin County Indians...moments away from that elusive state championship."

"As I told the story on-air our camera crew captured Tammy stationed quietly behind the Irwin County benches observing her husband and daughter coaching from their elevated platform," Wiley said. "She wore dark sunglasses with her lips quivering overcome with the raw emotion of it all. The culmination of her husband's decades-long career, the months-long fight for his life and their 34 years of marriage. It must have been nearly impossible to process.

"Then, suddenly she heard it. A loud roaring crescendo from the Irwin County fans behind her. A cacophony of cheers, applause and noise shakers. Her gaze drifted up and to the right towards the towering videoboard and that's when she knew that it was all for her. The videoboard's live feed of our broadcast displayed her proudly in front of the entire stadium and each seat instantaneously emptied as she received a standing ovation. She returned the applause with the most authentic gesture. Unclasping her hands from beneath her chin and raising them triumphantly in the air while humbly saying "Thank you" over and over again.

"Then our director cut back to Coach Nobles and daughter Kenley, their eyes welling up with tears and their faces overcome with love. Then back again to Tammy before returning to Buddy and Kenley. I've never seen a family's raw emotion captured so poignantly over the air.

"It was a breath-taking moment. I just remember desperately trying to articulate this emotionally gargantuan scene over the air. I felt so overwhelmed by it all. I suppose we all were. It was like our play-by-play announcer Larry Smith said shortly afterwards, 'if that doesn't give you a lump in your throat, I don't know what will.'"

"I've got 6:21 to still be a coach's wife, but then I'll be alright," Tammy said on the field.

"I thought that was cool. I mean that was awesome," Luke Roberts said. "That was just an emotional moment for everybody. I know I can remember Kenley crying when she saw her mom on the big screen. I didn't know that she was going to be on or anything, but when I finally saw her on the field obviously I wanted everyone to catch up with her."

A Marion County fumble made the margin 42-14 on the next Irwin possession. Two more scores meant the margin would go from 49 to 56 in short order. Three touchdowns in three-plus minutes led to that 12 minutes of running clock and simultaneous celebration.

"When things go awry, they go awry," Tommy said on GPB

"Talk about coach Nobles, winningest coach in Irwin history- this close to a championship.

That moment where Kaleb wasn't that far away from downtown Atlanta even as he's prepping for Ferris State...? In that same time frame where the video of Tammy was shown on the big screen at Georgia State, Kenley let out a loud cheer through her tears and raw emotion of the moment.

"Mom has always kind of been a behind-the-scenes person that never wanted recognition for anything," Kenley admits. "She never has been. She's done so much behind the scenes. She's given so much of her life to it. Dad has football and seeing her get some recognition on the board was so exciting. Dad was so excited about seeing people just cheer for her."

The other moment that stuck with anyone attached to Georgia high school football was that time when the cameras caught Kenley and Buddy looking into an iPhone and giving a thumbs up- sharing some smiles as the clock ticked down.

"Yeah, that was me on FaceTime with them," Kaleb admitted.

"He was watching the game on the team bus on the stream and then FaceTiming at the same time," Kenley said. "So, there's that secret now being told. It all came together at that moment."

"The game went into halftime and I was on pins and needles hoping they would keep on keepin' on. Mom and Dad would have killed me if I had gone to the Irwin game and not coached in mine," Kaleb adds. 'It was very emotional and it was tough to not be there but we had a big game I had to be there for as well. It was such a great moment to see my Dad get over the hump after all he had gone through the last couple months."

"It was important for him to be there," Kasey says, "so that was the best way possible that we could figure out for him to be there. Being able to interact with me, my dad, and my mom and sister I thought was pretty special. We wouldn't want him not to be a part of it so that was great that FaceTime was able to happen. For Kaleb to be able to experience that joy with us was special."

"Those of us in the booth are taught to "lay out" in those championship moments. In simple terms, shut up! Let the pictures and the sound tell the story," Larry Smith admits. "Let the emotions be heard. There will be time for talk later. I wish I could tell you that I laid up early because I'm such a good professional and a fair to middlin' play-by-play guy. But I would be lying to you. I thought about Buddy and all of the young men whose lives he'd touched. And the communities he'd impacted. And the sacrifice of all that time away from family. The thousands of hours in practice and studying film and in locker rooms and on sidelines and on buses. A lifetime and a career full of passion... to get to this place in time. Cancer had racked his body, but it wasn't going to steal this moment. His moment. I stood silently and, with a lump in my throat, cheerfully ceded the moment to Buddy and his family. Never have I rooted for one team over another in my long career, but I don't know how anyone could not tip their hat at this hour. Both teams shared school colors of red and white, so I suspect there were a few Marion County folks paying their respects as well in the waning moments."

People were walking up to the platform to get a few words with Buddy and Kenley as time was winding down. The crowd that had traveled from Ocilla and Irwin County started their traditional war chant and Buddy delivered the tomahawk chop from the podium. For Casey Soliday, he would get another special moment as his son, Cody,would even get reps at QB.

"I actually had a chance to talk on the headset to the other coaches in the fourth quarter," Jared Luke said. "It wasn't like we quit coaching because you have got to finish the minutes out 'til the buzzer sounds. But we're at a point we knew we pretty much had it sealed up and we all got to enjoy it."

The final quarter had twelve minutes on the clock and it took that long to end the season. Marion County had a few moments where Irwin County took advantage of mistakes and distanced themselves from the #2 seed in a 42-point win. With 21 seconds left, Buddy was helped from the podium and taken to his wheel-chair to make a final walk up a flight of stairs.

Andy and Kelly had their moment, too. The chance to tell everyone back home, listening on whatever device they had, that Irwin was bringing the title home to Ocilla.

A lot of folks wondered if Buddy would take the walk up a handful of steps to the top of the GHSA platform.

There was no disputing, if you knew Buddy Nobles- the man and the coach- that he would make his way up those steps to take hold of the championship trophy. The GHSA had it covered either way for the first time since 1975 that Irwin would win their last game of the year:

"Let's be honest. He's not going to miss this for anything," Larry Smith said on state-wide television. "How long and hard he has worked for this trophy

"Nor should he..." Tommy would add...

"It was just very emotional and if you listen at that particular time, Larry and I are kind of laying out for a little bit," Tommy said after the game. "It was more pictures than it was conversation. That was the thought by us and everyone in the production truck. It was an unbelievable feeling."

"Pete Snyder and I were up in the Press Box," Irwin Assistant Chip Rankin said, "and I think we were, maybe, up 42-14 at the end of the third quarter. I told him I think that we need to get down to the field because I didn't want to miss out on that celebration. As long as we've been waiting for it...?" To be honest, that was one of the best feelings I've had ever. If anybody deserves to be up on the stage at the end, it was Buddy."

"You knew that God was doing something in his life and you knew that he was a man of God," Irwin Assistant Dwayne Vickers said. "I was dead in the middle of the field with my iPhone and to see him up there in God's mercy and His grace. He said if you don't have God in this world, you can receive Him. The team believed in what Buddy said and the coaches were all going to be speaking the same message he said all the time."

"I was, pretty much, watching him, his wife, and his family after the game," Irwin assistant Tim Talton said. "Just watching the emotion that came over Tammy after all these years and seeing that we finally did it...? It was well deserved for all of them."

"I was fortunate to work that game with my friend and Georgia sports radio legend Tommy Palmer, who added his own brand of charm and wisdom to the moment like no one else could," Larry Smith said. "The clock struck zero and the celebration officially began. We talked only as much as we had to, making sure we didn't trample on this special moment.

"After a few moments, Irwin County made it to the stage and Jon Nelson – a Georgia sports broadcast legend in his own right – made the trophy presentation. Another indelible moment. With fate smiling down, Buddy Nobles hoisted a state championship trophy. One for the ages and maybe, one day, for Hollywood."

Everyone who had made the trip from south Georgia started their almost-weekly chant for "Buddy!"

Larry and Tommy continued...

"This is his football team. Coach Soliday and the assistants have done such a wonderful job with this group of young men...

"We asked Coach Soliday 'Who gets credit for these wins...?' Without hesitation... Coach Nobles..."

"Certainly, this day belongs to Irwin County," GHSA Executive Director Dr. Robin Hines said over the public address. "What a season it's been. You've been right at the doorstep, for quite a while now, now you've made it happen. This, certainly, makes us feel great to see the whole county coming to show up to represent Irwin County. To these outstanding players: Great job! That is a great job. Certainly, Coach Nobles, you are an inspiration to us all.

"I don't think there's anybody within the state of Georgia that isn't pulling for you! There's no question about that. We love you and you are an inspiration not only to Irwin County, but to football players and football coaches and communities all around this state. Thank you for being what you are!"

Buddy would hoist the trophy from the chair he was in center-stage. And it was truly a family affair with Tammy and Kenley joining Kasey and stars of the game on the platform. He would take the microphone to deliver a message to everyone who has been along for this ride. And it would be a message no one would ever forget...

The emotion of the moment was felt by an entire state. Buddy was confident in his delivery no matter how weak he was and how much fighting he had done through a season. The end result, winning in the last game of the year, gave everyone the ending they thought was just.

"Tell you what... what a platform that I've got to share Jesus Christ. Let me tell you something, without Jesus you got nothing in this world. But I will say this... Ocilla, we did it! I've had people call me, text me, send letters, stop by the house and just every-thing. It's just been something... To our players... I'm just going to tell you right now. And I'm always careful how I say things, but I think we were a team of destiny. And if there's a better Class A team in Georgia football, I want to see them."

He addressed his team- some with him on high, but most sharing the moment with one another.

"Hey, guys. We're going to the locker room with the big, black speaker now... Got a new song, too. Got a new song, too. Marion County has a class program. Love y'all! Thank you, thank you, Irwin. Party at the red light!"

It took a while for everyone to clear the field for the next championship game that was a part of the 8-game weekend at Georgia State Stadium. There were photos and interviews for television. And another round. And another round. But, the GHSA let it go for a while before everyone in an Irwin County color made it back to the room with the big, black speaker.

"We were always the first team up there to get the trophy," Kenley says. "That was a terrible feeling. It was Dad every year. We walked back to the locker room and the team and dad would be off on the side. He would be upset with how everything went down. I would hear and see things posted online after the game each year where folks were saying things about things they didn't understand, about people they didn't know, people that hadn't been a part of everything, and saying things about my dad they just didn't realize that we would see.

Kenley got to see her father give a speech about who he was as a person. All those years of coming close with all those years of people saying their piece about a team and a family that hadn't won the last game of the year finally had a moment they'll never forget.

"For Buddy to get up there and share that speech... Who knows...? That might save someone someday, so it was a good day," Drew Tankersley says. "Listen... to get him on that stage getting a trophy... I'm glad he got the opportunity to do it. You know it's heartbreaking. You know that it might end up being his last game, but what a testament!"

"Irwin County had secured its first State Championship since 1975 and it seemed as if this day were as close to perfect as any of us might ever see in our lives. And fittingly Jon Nelson crafted a perfect postgame interview," Wiley added.

"Coach Nobles addressed his players, his coaches, his team-mates, his community and his faith. He praised Marion County and expressed his gratitude to all of those who had supported him in his time of need. And in the end, the defining shot of the entire 2019 State Championship weekend was Coach Nobles eyes lighting up when he finally put his hands on the State Championship trophy.

"All of a sudden it was over. We signed off and our crew began working hastily on preparing for the second game of our qua-druple header. It felt so odd, so flippant. An hour-long march to this emotionally climactic peak only to have our attention instantly diverted to the next game.

"I vividly recall grappling with the sequence's abrupt finality as I walked up the stairs to the press box with Jon. We didn't say much as we ascended the lower level of seating. Each of us just processing the gravity of the moment. Then as we reached the concourse and prepared to climb the stairs I asked Jon what it was like to interview Coach Nobles on the championship podium, knowing it'd likely be the last time he ever interviewed his friend on a football field.

"His answer gave me peace. It epitomized what many including myself call the human condition, the communal bond we share by virtue of our very existence.

"'It's funny, you know," he smiled. "Many people came up to me when I was walking down the podium saying, 'That must have been the most difficult interview of your life.' And I told them, 'No. He's a dear friend and I love him. I knew exactly what I wanted to say. It was actually the easiest.'

"With everything he's been through, it was just a magical moment," Irwin assistant Luke Roberts recognized. "One of those feelings is elation, but it was just a whole bunch of emotions right there. He has always been huge in his faith in God and Jesus Christ- always steadfast in that. But he was his own man and if you didn't like it 'Sorry, not sorry.' That's one thing I love and also when he said 'If you ain't got Jesus in your heart, you ain't got nothing.' I believe that and, then, he said 'Ocilla, we did it!' I do remember all of that. You know, we're really lucky, Brother."

"It just goes back to just how strong of a Christian he is," Chip Rankin said. "The first thing he said 'If you don't have Jesus you don't have nothing in this world.' It was awesome and even in his situation that's still how he felt."

"Him giving credit to God and trusting Jesus through the whole thing just so much, it just poured out on everybody that day," Pete Snyder said.

Troy Fletcher got to share the field with his family- another moment you don't forget in a season of moments you don't forget, but he expected Buddy to make it up the stairs.

"I said there was no way that Buddy wasn't going to make it up that platform to get that trophy. You were not keeping him off of that stage. There was no way he wasn't going on that platform.

I can guarantee you that- kicking and screaming- it wasn't any secret he was going to be up there."

"Buddy's body was just deteriorating," Steve Hoard said. "Everybody knew that would probably be the last game he would call. But to see all Buddy's former players see the presentation and his joy afterwards...? I was brokenhearted, at the same time, you know...? Everybody was around and you know what's coming. But I'll say this... those last words he spoke on the stage were all about the destiny of that season. I'm telling you... those kids bought into everything and they did an amazing job keeping it together."

"I go there and it was more of a celebration of what would not come but what was already happening," Chris Paulk said. "The pressure of it all was over with and it's Christmas with everyone running around. You have those moments where Tammy was over on the side and she was just crying. There was Kenley staying with her dad so it was a celebration.

"It's a moment you can't take away. You watch all these movies like 'Remember the Titans,' and I think it was just one of those moments that just wrote itself. It wasn't a fake moment. It was just a real moment that encapsulated it all. You saw the testimony of what he stood for and you know that he knew where he was headed. He knew where we're going and he was fine with it. So, it wasn't the end of the chapter in the book."

"I said if it was anybody on this Earth that I would like to lose to," Coach Kirksey adds, "it would be him."

Chris was going through his own off-the-field issues. His 25-year marriage was coming to a close and it had been over the last 18 months. He had been spending a lot of time in prayer looking for guidance and his coaches were his rock as well in his life as his divorce was coming final.

"He's going through the biggest fight of his life, physically, for his life in a state championship game and I'm going through the biggest fight I've ever had in my life trying to save my marriage," he adds. "The two people that the Lord put against each other here in the state championship game...? I just felt like I thought that's very ironic to that situation. I felt very blessed to be there and, obviously, Buddy and his staff have done an excellent job over the years. I just had a whole lot of respect for how he carried himself and how it was handled."

"We were excited about just finally getting it done," Kasey said. "There wouldn't have been anything in the world that cancer couldn't have stopped him from getting up to get the trophy. He was determined that was something he deserved. To be able to get up there and experience that moment, I think, it was really special for him. It was still special for us as a family.

"I'm standing in the back of that group not looking like I'm ready to cry, but I was holding it in pretty well. Right then, it was emotional and it was good for the kids to be able to hear him come talk. It was good for the town that supported us and everybody that has been there for us throughout this year and throughout the rest of Dad's time.

"I think it was important for him to be able to get up there and address everybody. He's got a way of words with people and I thought that was about the most fitting and just speech for him that there ever will be. I wouldn't have expected him to lead with anything else. He got up there and he professed his faith and didn't care who heard it. Then, he tells everybody 'We're about to have a party at the Red Light.'

After Buddy was escorted off the stage on the field at Georgia State, every person of the assembled media wanted to get a soundbite. And everyone that was there to celebrate for and with Irwin County wanted a hug, a kiss, or a word. It took longer than normal for the football field to clear for the next game to have its proper warm-up time. But, there was still a lot of celebrating to go- red light or not.

"For me, personally, it was something I've been looking forward to experiencing pretty much my whole life," Kasey adds. "Whenever I was in elementary school, my dad was a Defensive Coordinator with Coach Pruitt down at Union County (Florida) and they won 52 games in a row and back-to-back-to-back state championships. So, my whole childhood was just watching them when I was a waterboy or a ballboy through all those years. Watching them win just made me hungry to get my own and I would talk constantly to my dad about winning a state championship.

"I'm sure I was annoying talking about it so much. But at Union, the first year we had a night we played, like, 40 freshman and sophomores and it didn't go well. The next year, we went to state and we lost that first trip to the state championship. That was rough, but we were young and didn't have many kids graduating. We figured that next year was our shot, but I learned going through the years that it's not so easy to make it there and to win it. The NEXT year, going into the semi-final game, losing by 2 points and turning the ball over, I think, seven times...in my high school career I've gotten so close...

"When I got to college, we made it to an ACC Championship game and fell just short. So, getting that feeling of knowing what it's like to celebrate on the field and in the locker room after, I think for me personally it was just years and years of striving to get to that. I thought this year was a perfect time for it to finally happen with everything that is going on that season.

"I wanted to win the state championship because we won it when I was a freshman in high school in 1975," Marty Roberts says. "I wanted to win the state championship for a lot of reasons- for the school, for the kids, for the community, but I also said I wanted a state championship for Buddy Nobles. If anybody deserves a state championship he does."

"When you know a man has been through what he's been through and does that, that's incredible," Casey Soliday says. "When we went into the locker room and he asked the kids, 'What music is this?' Then, you have the celebration in the locker room and it was not the same as the ones before."

"I did take a deep breath and enjoy it," Irwin assistant Clayton Sirmans says. "But in the last few state championship games we weren't so fortunate. To win was heartbreaking in a way, but to win convincingly and have a few minutes just to see those smiling faces on the big screen of fans and Coach Nobles was awesome. It was just a special moment for me to see Coach up there and give that speech that he gave- giving the glory to God. Seeing the emotion on his face, with what he was going through, I'm just glad he was able to be there and experience that.

"I wouldn't expect anything else coming from him and what he said. That's who he was. Everything the family did, they gave glory to God and I wouldn't expect anything else from Buddy in that moment. It was exactly what I was anticipating."

Everyone crowded around Buddy in the locker room, taking pictures with him and the trophy in his wheelchair. More often that not Buddy also had his index finger extended skyward as well. Irwin was, indeed, Number One. Everyone, and that word is accurate, "Everyone" got to celebrate a long season and a special season.

The song...??? "We Are The Champions" by Queen... and the players knew the chorus. Buddy had his right index finger in the air from his wheelchair seat in the middle of the group. It was a part of it, but the words spoken underneath the bleachers were ones that will stick for a while:

"Enjoy this day. It's the last time you walk out of here until we get to the banquet. You'll never be together again at one time. That's the hardest thing. I'm gonna tell you right now. I told y'all about love. I appreciate y'all loving me. I mean that with all my heart. You guys never understood what I'm going through. It's a battle. But you know what? You guys kept me getting up every day. You guys did a great job. Appreciate y'all. You're a team of destiny. We love y'all and I can't wait til they put some of those street signs up..."

The players cheered and broke off to their lockers before heading to the bus...

As state champs...

Everyone made it to the stoplight as Buddy said on the podium-even, as we are reminded, there's really two stop lights in town. The buses stopped and the talk was that close to a thousand people were back home to see the Irwin County Indians make their way back from the big city with a title in tow. The crowd started on the sidewalks to welcome the county "yellow hounds" back where they came from, but the standing was temporary. Anyone with a sign, a t-shirt, a banner, and anything they wore or carried on that Saturday showed that the collective had Buddy's back and could celebrate one of the most successful seasons anyone has seen in the smallest classifications in quite some time.

Fans of high school football are drawn to the Herschel Walker-Johnson County team from his time in school and his dominance as an athlete at the time. But those who saw Irwin

County work through the "Region of Doom" in Region 2-A with all of its collective firepower and come out the other side in as dominant a fashion as they did by mid-December will have a quality argument going forward.

Not to mention plenty of pictures of a heck of a celebration in two separate cities simultaneously that weekend…

Kasey would be there in Ocilla, but the day had taken a lot out of Buddy, Tammy, Kenley, and the rest of the family. They would stay behind in Atlanta.

"Some coaches ride on the buses with the team and I had equipment duties," he said. "Dad said he would not let me back out of any of that. I was loading and unloading trailers. He said, 'You better go do it.' But I hear he wanted me to ride home with the team just because that's a little different trip than what we're used to. Driving home from Atlanta used to be a sad and long ride home if we lost. But without that, it was a pretty dang fun ride every year.

"After the state championship, we would go to the Buckner's restaurant between Atlanta and Macon and eat. That's one thing I wanted to do. I wanted to go to Buckner's feeling like a winner. On this trip home, I enjoyed seeing those kids celebrate and be happy there while we're eating. That's a big difference in this season. To see a whole team of kids silent and devastated there in the past and, this time, I really wanted to go- and I know that might sound weird- and see the different tone."

After the restaurant, the buses were detoured once they got to the main intersection in Ocilla. The whole town was, basically, shut down as close to a thousand people decided to greet the Indians back home. Everyone had their chance to tell any player they could hug or shake hands with that the town could not have been more proud of everything they accomplished in the toughest of circumstances.

"It was kind of heartbreaking for my dad not to be there at the party at the red light because that's something he had started after beating Fitzgerald last year," Kasey continued. "He, kind of, coined the term and I'm not sure if it got approved by the city or anything like that the first time, but I don't think it mattered at that point. This is the second time we shut it down. Not being able to be a part of the thing that he started after finally achieving what he's been trying to achieve, it was certainly bittersweet."

There would, eventually, be a photo that would circulate with Buddy asleep cradling the championship trophy. It was a picture that was fitting to how the year was over on the football field, the day was over in a hotel room overlooking the city of Atlanta, and the mission for an entire community was shown in the hands of someone universally loved.

Everyone was drained emotionally and they were drained emotionally for one another...

"It is a perfect ending to a perfect season," Kasey said.

Kenley's memory of the locker room celebration is filled with little moments that make up one big moment: the speakers playing a song the players, initially, weren't all that familiar with, her Dad talking to her in her ear, taking pictures with one another, and then the unveiling of the championship ring.

"He also told the players they could keep their red jerseys from the game," she said. "A BIG roar went up and they went nuts about that."

"To get that monkey off his back and then, off of our back and get it, after everything that they had gone through- all the health scares and illnesses, nights at Emory and in Tifton- was the most fitting ending," Kaleb says.

It was the fairy tale ending and a cool moment across the board. Kaleb got to have some substantial FaceTime conversations with everyone for a good hour or so after the celebration. He had to multitask a bit preparing for his game at the same time he was wrapping his mind around the events at Georgia State. He had to take care of business as UWF took on Ferris State for a chance for the Argos to play for a National Championship. It was a tough thing to do, for sure...

"I kind of felt just like a massive relief once he got it done," Kaleb continues. "That was one of the coolest things combined with our staff at West Florida keeping up with how my dad seemed as well."

There would be consistent hugs all season in Pensacola from everyone in Argos colors, but before their game there were tears as well with what was happening in Atlanta. Kaleb just had to make sure the tears didn't freeze on his face as he got ready for his game up north.

Jared Luke got his hugs on the field as well...

"It was something I will never forget as long as I live," he says. "It was so enjoyable, so fun, you know. I'm so glad that we got to do it and Buddy was right here with us. To look around, I have tears in my eyes. My wife, who has been great with me, had tears in her eyes. We're kind of laughing, too, because Buddy's up there and he's got that big grin on his face.

"I can see it right now. It was so just so humbling to see this man that is put in so much work in this game of football to get to the pinnacle. There would be times where we would talk in his office- just me and him about life, but it always went back to God's plan and always went back that he's got a purpose for you in life."

"When he lost those previous title games, it felt like I lost," CJ Spiller says. "That was one of his first things that he always said after those games- I'm sorry I couldn't get it done for you. But he and Mama Tammy go give you a hug and kiss right after. You can just see the disappointment in Buddy's face when they fall short, but he would always tell people to win with class and lose with class.

"I let a few tears come down just because I know he wanted it so much. I, obviously, know the battle that he was going through. To be able to witness it and be there to see all the love that he got after the game on that stage, it just capped off a great career. To be a part of that journey...? I wouldn't trade it for the world...

"I wouldn't trade it for the world..."

CJ and Buddy wouldn't talk about his illness all that much. Buddy would always tell CJ, "CJ, we're gonna be okay. We're gonna be okay.' And he would always make a point to ask how CJ was doing as a priority. CJ could see the toll cancer was taking on his Buddy's body, but the focus was always selflessly on others.

"I think he knew this team was special," Matt Thomas said. "He was a humble guy, but he just had this way as he was talking about this team. Ironically, that's what happened when he was coaching me in high school. We got to the championship game the year we should have won it. We lost and it broke us apart. Then, we went back and steamrolled everybody the next year. It was almost identical to what this path was.

"I can say as a coach I was cautiously optimistic every inch of the way, because I wanted him to win so badly. Obviously, when the diagnosis hit, you knew this would be an amazing story. That experience for him and his family was perfect. I can't imagine a better story on someone's life and how many people he impacted. To get this horrible diagnosis and then finish on top, you couldn't have written a better story. I think anybody that knows Coach Nobles knows exactly what he was going to say in that moment and to put the focus on the kids, Jesus, and not himself but his family reminds us Buddy is a champion.

Thomas feels it was a great ending to an amazing season. But he also feels the moments that we all saw with Buddy in the 2019 season were already planned...

Planned by a power all its own... it was etched in stone and played out the way it was supposed to play out. Buddy walked the walk as he "talked the talk' all his life.

"I sent him a text about how he was holding that trophy later that night," Andrew Zow said. "If you put his thumb in his mouth, he would have looked like a baby for sure. He's holding that trophy like they teach you to hold it. I was teasing him about that. He texted me back and we talked about it. This game of football was given something more than we could ever fathom from having Buddy in it."

Mike Posey thought it was an honor to be at Georgia State Stadium to watch that final game of Irwin County in 2019. His memories come back to him every day. He'll text back and forth with Tammy when he can't sleep- and she can't either. She'll put the championship game every once in a while to remember the day.

"His speech on the platform," Mike adds, "that's what we were talking about. But I remember the story about the wheelchair just as much from that day. He's coming out of the locker room. It gets caught. He falls out of it. Tammy, at the time, tells me Buddy fell and we're all running around trying to find them like

chickens with our heads cut off. It all ended up being something we would all laugh about. We all know what he's going
through. No one knows the pain and suffering that he was going
for a second.

"But, Buddy did not want anyone to feel pity for him or feel sorry
for him. He has changed my life more and more every day. I
sit back at the house when I'm doing something, and I think
about what Buddy would do in this situation. I'll try to handle
it that way. Buddy has always been there for me and he is still
there for me.

"Buddy wouldn't change his love for you no matter what. Very
few people like Buddy come along in our lives."

"The thing about it is that his love for us all didn't start in
the last 6 or 7 months," Andy Paulk told GPB Sports on their
"Football Fridays in Georgia" podcast in January of 2020. "He has
been touching kids in a positive way as far back as we all can
remember with his time in Fitzgerald, Coffee, and Irwin. He left
a huge, positive footprint. In the last 6 months, people watched
him through his struggle. Buddy did his day-to-day with love.
That's his secret and it was love that brought it all together- the
kids and the sport of football.

"My transition into loving Buddy was pretty dynamic. At first, I
would be the guy questioning calls on the air, but I've come full
circle and have for a long time. Tell you right now... I'm a Buddy
Nobles guy. He won me over and I can't explain how much
he meant to me. What makes Buddy's success, too, is that he
doesn't forget anybody- the chain guys, the people who clean
out the little coolers, and the radio guys...

"The season has been surreal and the point where he's on the
stage holding the trophy is the pinnacle. And the picture of
him sleeping with it is my next moment of feeling happy. To
see him end up in storybook fashion, they weren't going to be

stopped. It was the power of God and Buddy. Everything pales in comparison..."

"Buddy had something I have yet to lay my hands on," Andy's partner, Kelly Wynn, admits. "How he motivated his kids at Irwin County wasn't just reloading. They were manufacturing kids and those kids never gave up. We watched a great leader in Buddy here.

"There was a shot of him in the fourth quarter on television that we saw on the big screen in Atlanta. There was a shot of joy in him and he was happy. He knew then he had control of the game. I look at that moment. You'll see Buddy Nobles at his best."

"After they beat Clinch, I knew they were going to win it," Fitzgerald's head coach Tucker Pruitt admits. "So, I wanted to be up there just to tell him congratulations. I knew he might not be coaching the whole lot longer. He lost a state championship in Florida with Kasey and CJ and then he'd come to Georgia and I think they had lost three or four. He had been there in that game so many times I knew he was going to get over the hump.

"I definitely wanted to be there just to tell him I love him and tell him congratulations. I know that day has been a long time coming and it couldn't happen to a better guy. It was just a joy to see his face and his family faces after the hard year with everything they've been through. To finish that way was, really, an awesome thing."

As a coach himself, Tucker also was reminded of all the hours spent away from your family to invest in working toward a title. When Buddy finally got his, the talk wasn't about politics or soundbites. Tucker saw a man speak from his heart- a good Christian man, a great role model, a great coach, and a great father figure to his kids.

"In years past," Bill Barrs says, "we really didn't get to enjoy the ride because we caught up so much at every play and every pass. Going back to Atlanta this time, we got to enjoy the ride a little more. There were times we were a really good team going in and it just wasn't our day. When he was the first guy on the platform, you can see the look of disappointment in his face. This year, just to see the look on his face versus the photos I have for the previous years is absolutely priceless.

"He was always about doing the right thing- either teaching your kids to do the right thing, mold them to be good husbands, to be good employers, to be good employees, and that's what he preached. Basically, the whole world got to see on that podium that Saturday."

"I was on the field after our call," Kelly Wynn said, "and I had tears in my eyes. But I was tickled to death for Buddy and his family." He wouldn't make it back for the party at the red light, but was able to share in the moments back in Ocilla through the technology of the day.

Live streams can be a wonderful thing...

"When Buddy was taken off the platform with a few minutes left in the game, he put his hand over his heart when he was looking at the Irwin County fans that made the trip," Marty Roberts recalls. "Everybody started chanting 'Buddy! Buddy! Buddy!' I started crying like a baby. I couldn't stand it. That's the way I am in the way I cry over everything. That was so well deserved for such a good man.

"After the first offensive play in the game for a touchdown, something came over me and I looked at my son and I said, 'We're winning it this year.' I just felt it in my heart. Then, we picked off the pass and went up 14 and we won the one we were destined to win."

Marty went home to Ocilla for the Party (capitalization intentional). He wasn't going to pass up the chance to put his arm around any player's neck and give them a big hug after everything the town had been through.

"We called ahead," he continued, "and told folks: 'We're just getting off the exit. We're turning into town.' It had already gotten dark by the time we got there, but it went on for almost an hour right there the red light. They were just rerouting traffic around us and there must have been over 500 people at that red light."

Marty's one wish from that night, like a lot of other folks, was that Buddy could have been there to be a part of a very special moment.

"I feel so heartbroken about it. He never made it back to his office at the Fieldhouse. He never got to go back in the weight room. He never got to go back to the school, go through and shake people's hands, and get the accolades he deserves. He never really got to celebrate like he should have been able to..."

"What he said getting the trophy didn't surprise me," Irwin assistant Troy Fletcher said. "That was the man that he always has been- putting God first in his life. He never wavered one bit and I, myself, will never question God through the whole thing."

Fletcher remembers the meeting where Buddy told the coaching staff he would be fighting cancer. After that day, there would be a time where the two of them would sit together and Buddy would lay the whole situation out for Troy. Those talks would be a part of his heart all year long- even as he would be a part of the buses that would head to the red light.

"I almost couldn't get the bus through the crowd. They were trying to keep the people back but they kept squeezing in on the buses when they got there to town. I was the first bus pulling in and I just shut the bus down right there. I let the kids off and, literally, when I got off the bus I think I made it almost to the back tires and you couldn't go anywhere. Everybody was coming up and hugging me and congratulating us for what we did."

For Irwin High School Principal Scott Haskins, it was a week of preparation that ended in a mass of celebration back home. There is all the ticket distribution, sales, getting the kids the clothing they need, and making sure they're in the frame of mind to go on one final business trip.

"It was a little bittersweet for me," he admits. "You're planning for any kind of celebration ahead of time. You're planning for a pep rally. But, it's all so special because it was in the air that this may be our year to win the title. It didn't surprise me that as many people came up to see the game in Atlanta that did. I think it speaks well about everybody who loves Irwin County, loves Ocilla, loves the school, loves the kids, and loves a family.

"The fans made every effort to be there in the cold weather. We're always so proud of being heavily supported by the community and by their families."

It is hard for Irwin Superintendent Thad Clayton to explain what it meant to see Buddy get the championship trophy. For one of your closest friends to be able to accomplish a lifelong dream after being a bridesmaid so many times before, it meant the world. He is fairly certain that Buddy's name was a popular one for vacancies around the state because of all of his success at Irwin. But, the two of them would talk as friends do. Buddy's sense of pride in his team and community showed in the moment when he turned to the crowd atop the platform in Atlanta and put his hand over his heart as time was running out.

He stayed with the family in Atlanta and got updates about the Party. He would come back the next day to a town that was the same, but at the same time, felt a little different about itself.

Luke Roberts was one of the bus drivers to bring everyone back from Atlanta and to see the police shut down traffic at the stop light was special. Chip Rankin rode in the equipment truck from Atlanta. He got his job done and doubled back to the red light.

"Just to see that many people there was unbelievable," he said. "You couldn't even walk around since there were so many people there. Where Buddy is concerned, I just think he was a great example of what a Christian man is supposed to be. He loved his family and he absolutely adored Tammy. He wanted his players to be good men most of all- even above being good players. He really tried to help them turn into good men."

"I could feel his happiness and I was sitting way up in the stands," Eddie Giddens adds. "it was just a great feeling when he got that trophy and he showed you what kind of man he was, and what kind of life he lived when he answered all those questions."

Troy Fletcher got to enjoy the fourth quarter as well. He saw a lot of the coaching fraternity in the state on the field walk over and congratulate Buddy on the platform. He remembered Robby and Tucker Pruitt on the field and he got to have his conversations with him as well. He stayed in Atlanta as well after the win but the images that were sent to him and the images he saw will always stay with him.

And you had a win that impacted coaches out-of-state as well... and not just in the idea of football and winning the last game of the year.

"I was as excited about that as anything that's happened in my coaching career," Jeremey Andrews said, "because I know what it meant to him and I know how special and important of a person he is to so many people. Everybody says we're all equal in God's eyes, but I don't think we are. I mean Buddy was a unique person and I feel like he just deserved more than anybody. I can't think of anybody that deserved it so much. I was more excited for him than I ever could have been for myself based on who he was as a guy when it comes to legacies- and I'm not just talking as a football coach, but as a husband, as a father, as a coach, and as a human being."

"We had some pretty good heart to heart talks where Buddy would tell me, 'I'm good. I'm good where I'm at," Kevin Erwin admits. "He said, 'I want to live and this is the hand I'm dealt.' He said he wasn't spiteful about it. He's not upset. He said that he wished he could have more time with his family and Tammy. He said 'this is what I've got to deal with and this is what we're going to do.'

Buddy also told Kevin over time not to cry with Buddy because if one of them started crying, the other would follow. Buddy knew what was coming and he was okay with it and he was okay with his God. It didn't matter who it was that was a part of the people that Buddy loved, you had to make sure you cried outside of Buddy's room. The conversations between the two of them would go to football, some new tires on a car, or something current.

The family had their share of close calls along the way- even one that presented the question of whether or not to resuscitate in the hospital on one occasion. There would be conversations with notepads and pens once Buddy regained consciousness. There would be the wonder of how Buddy even made it out of the woods on some hospital trips. But when Buddy would open his eyes after a time when he was almost lost to everyone, Kevin knew it was nothing but God that kept Buddy with those he loved.

Buddy would tell Kevin: "I ain't done yet."

"Buddy was not going to miss anything that season," he continued, "even if he had to be wheeled into the end zone in an ambulance. He was going to be sitting there as long as there was life in his body. Whatever it took to get that situation done is what we were going to do. Anything that was asked of me about it? I don't care. Everything else in this world was put on hold and I do it again in a second.

"Anytime my phone rang it was 'I got it. I got it. I got what you need. What do you need ?' My work was good enough to me to let me off on Friday nights so I can make it for our ride down there every Friday night to Ocilla. I think I missed two games in 2019. You just realize at some point this has some greater importance. It's not just a football game with numbers on a board."

"Those kids knew why they were there and they were playing for more than a ring.

For Kevin, getting to see the expression on Buddy's face in the fourth quarter knowing Irwin was going to win was an incredible feeling. If you ask him, there wasn't a game or a play that Buddy wasn't prepared for on a Friday night in his career. He always seemed to know what was coming.

"It was like when Steve Young finally won the Super Bowl and got the monkey off his back," he said. "There's not a whole lot of times where you can say somebody, absolutely, deserved something. Buddy ABSOLUTELY deserved the championship.

Kevin went back to the hotel with the rest of the family and saw that Buddy was completely wiped out. Inasmuch as there were smiles, tears, and laughter among the family at the hotel everyone was mentally, physically, and emotionally drained.

Understandably so...

December 16

Yes! He has put the trophy down. No! He hasn't stopped celebrating.

We were at the oncologist office from 8:30 until 4:30 today. We had a Doctors appointment followed by chemo. He had so many congrats from the doctors, the nurses and several other patients. It was amazing that so many watched the game and are following our Indians

We had surgery scheduled to put a feeding tube in this Tuesday. The Dr has postponed the surgery for the feeding tube because Coach's weight loss has leveled off a little. Dr wants to avoid the feeding tube for now if possible.

Coach's levels were good today so Dr proceeded with chemo. Coach got treatment #4 today which is one cycle. Dr wants a scan done on the 30th to see if the chemo is being effective. If it is, we keep on with more chemo, if not we regroup and discuss other options.

Thanks for all the congratulations and well wishes. Please pray that the chemo treatment does not cause him any bad side effects this time but puts a hurting on the cancer. Also pray that Coach is able to keep eating and put some weight back on. His body needs the nutrition to help the chemo attack that evil tumor.

Kaleb's focus on Ferris was warranted...

Big Rapids, Michigan was a tough place for folks to go in 2019 as the Bulldogs went into the national semi-final at 12-0. They had run the table in the Great Lakes Intercollegiate Athletic Conference and their undefeated regular season actually gave them two weeks off before their playoff wins over Central

Missouri and Northwest Missouri State. It would be their third semi finals appearance in the last four seasons and they would come in as the number two-ranked team in the country.

It would also be their first-ever semi at home...

It wasn't anything strange for the Argos to be on the road trying to take care of business and a tenacious defense was their answer all day long.

The game was tied going into halftime as Austin Reed and Tate Lehtio combined again in the first quarter to give UWF the lead, but FSU's Tyler Minor ran in from six yards out for the sevens on the scoreboard. The Bulldogs actually took the lead in the third as Dion Earls rushed in from 11-yards to give the home team the lead. Two Austin Williams field goals made it 14-13 early in the fourth. And that's when UWF took over...

On Ferris' first play from scrimmage after the Williams kick, Earls had the ball knocked out by Ty Cox. Reed and Lehtio hooked up again from 18 yards and the two scores in less than a minute gave the visitors a 21-14 lead after a successful two-point conversion. A bad snap on the next possession gave UWF another short field. Three plays later, Reed and Quentin Randolph combined for a 6-yard score of their own and the final margin appeared in, basically, a four minute span.

UWF won 28-14, causing six turnovers along the way, and would be making their second appearance in the national championship game. In 2017, they also won four consecutive road games over higher seeded teams. They would get Minnesota State on national television in McKinney, Texas after MSU blew out Slippery Rock, 58-15.

Eric J. Wallace of the Pensacola News Journal caught up with Head Coach Pete Shinnick once again after the game and asked what the lesson was:

"Never giving up, never losing heart ... it's just a great, great team victory. "We're now going to our second national championship in three years."

Austin Reed finished 18-for-44 on the day for 299, 3, and 1 as Lehtio caught seven for 118 and 2 of those TD's.

"We just kept believing," Reed told Wallace. "We had a bunch of guys coming up to us and kept saying to keep grinding. We know the kind of team and players that we have. We knew eventually it would all work and we would get into the end zone."

The Argos had beaten #16, #1, #6, and #2 to get to their last game of the year...

Kaleb had more work to do...

Marion County 14

Eagles

Irwin County 56

Indians

1	2	3	4	F
7	7	0	0	14
14	14	21	7	56

WEST FLORIDA 28 (12-2 , 7-1)
-VS- FERRIS STATE 14 (12-1 , 8-0)

1st	12:16	UWF–Tate Lehtio 34 yd pass from Austin Reed (Austin Williams kick) 8 plays, 75 yards, TOP 2:44	7	0
1st	00:50	FS–Tyler Minor 6 yd run (J. Dieterle kick), 11 plays, 61 yards, TOP 4:32	7	7
3rd	12:10	FS–Dion Earls 11 yd run (J. Dieterle kick), 7 plays, 65 yards, TOP 2:50	7	14
3rd	05:36	UWF–Austin Williams 21 yd field goal 8 plays, 44 yards, TOP 2:44	10	14
4th	10:56	UWF–Austin Williams 25 yd field goal 14 plays, 72 yards, TOP 4:36	13	14
4th	10:01	UWF–Tate Lehtio 18 yd pass from Austin Reed (Tate Lehtio pass) 2 plays, 16 yards, TOP 0:32	21	14
4th	06:59	UWF–Q. Randolph 6 yd pass from Austin Reed (Austin Williams kick) 3 plays, 33 yards, TOP 1:21	28	14

Chapter 18

DECEMBER 23- UWF WINS

It was another week of being a double-digit underdog after the win over Ferris State and one final road trip for the 2019 football season- regardless of the end result. The NCAA Division II Championship Game would be in McKinney, Texas. The northeast edge of the Dallas-Fort Worth Metroplex has, like most states that view high school football Friday nights, just as impactful a cathedral for the community as a Sunday sermon.

Legacy Stadium is just off the Sam Rayburn Tollway and cost just over $70-million to build for its 2018 unveiling between McKinney and McKinney North High Schools. It seats 12,000 folks and looks to be a home for the DII title game for a while. West Florida and offensive juggernaut Minnesota State would each get 2,000 electronically-produced tickets that they could do with as they saw fit.

The Nobles family wanted one person to be there if he could make it with one of those tickets...

"Honestly, my dad was trying to get figured out where he could fly out of to get there," Kasey said. "Everybody was against it because of his health, but I'm sure he would come to every game if he could. So, for him not to be able to fly out there was tough on him and he was unrealistically trying to figure out how to get out there all week. He was serious about it and it was another bittersweet thing because he couldn't be a part of it. But that whole entire trip was fun to take- from winning the state championship and then a week later having your brother go up for the D2 National Championship, it was special."

It's another week against an unbeaten opponent coming in as the Mavericks came in at 14-0. Their first two games were in Mankato- knocking off #9 CSU-Pueblo, 35-7, and #21 Texas A&M-Commerce, 42-21. They had to travel to #8 Slippery Rock but the Rock was dismantled 58-15. The game was even tied at 8 in the first quarter. Nate Gunn was the star rusher for the Mavs in the semi-final with three TD's and the Rock was hand-cuffed for an awful 4-for-19 on third down conversions.

It would be #4 versus #20 at 2PM the Saturday after the first title came to the Nobles family in 2019.

MSU averaged over 48 points a game in 2019 and gave up less than 13 on average. Gunn was also on the finalist list for the Harlon Hill Trophy- the DII version of the Heisman. UWF, on the other hand, played a schedule with an opponents' winning percentage of .675- the toughest in the Division. But Head Coach Pete Shinnick's team had only the 97th best defense against the run playing, in theory, into the Mavericks' hands. This is only the Argos fourth year of existence as a program in Division II, but it's their second appearance in the last game of the year. In 2017, they were a #6-seed. In this new format for the playoffs, there was no such number in parenthesis to the left of the boxscore.

Pundits and predictors didn't have them favored- again...

"I was walking around with a big smile all week," Kaleb said. "With the relief of Irwin's season being done, it was 'Now, hey, we've got to go take care of business, too.' Because it's the first time that I don't have another team to worry about all season long. It was a breath of relief because I was always worried about the Irwin game the night before our game all year long. It was pretty cool in some parts, even if it wasn't going to work out with Dad health-wise to be at the game. But it was pretty fun to do a game plan and not have to worry. He was trying his hardest to get to the game that week by plane and a lot of people were trying to make it happen but it just didn't feel safe with his current health status."

UWF left on Wednesday and were in and around McKinney on Wednesday, Thursday and Friday. There were all the events on your standard championship-week itineraries. So coaches were around the players 24-7. UWF players were sheltered but knew, somewhat, what happened with Kaleb and his family this football season and they, like Irwin County and Kasey, wanted to take care of their business one last time. There would be big hugs and pats on the back all week long.

The game turned out to be a whiplash of chunk plays, yardage, and scores that would take up most of the afternoon.

Quentin Randolph and Tate Lehtio combined for 23 catches on the day- Randolph had 3 TD's and 254 yards receiving. UWF would put 38 points on the board in the first half as QB Austin Reed completed passes for 399 yards in the first 30 minutes- shattering the DII record for yards in a title game in only half the time. He would wrap his day going 33-for-54 for 523 yards and 6 scores. The 38 net rushing yards would be the smallest total ever in a title game, but with Reed's handiwork, the running game set up the pass as a temporary distraction. MSU would mount a furious comeback by the fourth quarter and come within one score, but UWF would hold on in a game that the Mavericks actually outgained the Argos, 562 to 561. Two teams would go into McKinney looking for a title for the first time in their respective school's history...

"We just had to keep throwing it, they couldn't stop it," Reed said after the game to Eric J. Wallace of the Pensacola News Journal. "Our guys kept making big plays out there and we were doing what we needed to do to keep moving."

And West Florida would get their first after coming close two seasons back. Kaleb got his title to go with the one his Dad, Mom, Kasey and Kenley picked up only a week before.

"With a little over a minute left, we stopped them on 4th Down to seal the game and got into the Victory formation. I always wear a 2-Ear headset to block out the crowd during the game. So, for about 30 seconds on the sidelines, the coolest part was just taking the headset off and hearing the crowd go crazy. We had a lead, the ball, and Minnesota State didn't have any time-outs left," Kaleb said. "They couldn't stop the clock and we're going to win. Just hearing the crowd and realizing 'Oh my gosh, we are National Champs.' I just kind of listened and just closed my eyes and thought: 'Oh my goodness, what has happened this season with our family is the most crazy thing ever and now we both won it within a week of each other.'

"You can't write a better ending. This is the good Lord taking care of us. We were in the midst of the worst battle of our life and we're getting to do this with each other. I couldn't find Kasey, Kenley and Katy for a while after the game because our crowd rushed the field. When I finally spotted them, it was one of the most special hugs ever. We embraced for a really long time and cried of course. We immediately got Dad and Mom on Facetime to celebrate together on the field. He called me K-Man a lot while I was growing up. I'll never forget him saying 'You did it K-Man, you did it.' What an emotional moment that was on a FaceTime call.

"Dad stayed awake and alert the whole game. He's going crazy. He's crying and, probably, about an hour after the game ended and everything started to die down, Katy and I were in her rental car. Dad and I have always talked about, if we won a title, being able to listen to 'We Are The Champions' over the loud-speaker. I was on FaceTime with him to do it the week before while we were on the bus to play Ferris State. So, we got in the car, blasted 'We Are The Champions' and met on FaceTime together one more time.

"We're all crying of course and singing together, but that was one of the coolest moments ever of being his son, on FaceTime, and both of us being Champs. The whole family was just looking at each other going 'We did it! We did it!'"

And the fact they all did it in a week on the calendar was one of the coolest moments of all...

"I was FaceTiming mom running onto the sideline," Kenley said. "We found Kaleb, and all embraced in a big hug. It was a fun 10 days for the family. We had been through so much and, that whole week, was just a great distraction with everything that is going on."

When Wallace caught up with the Argos after the game, he found a bunch that was looking back at a magical time- knocking off a bunch of undefeated teams to set records along the way for their first-ever football championship.

"We felt in 2017 that it was an extremely special run and as unique as there was out there," Argos Head Coach Pete Shinnick said. "We were just kind of experiencing it while it was happening.

"This one, we had a little more purpose, drive and knew what we wanted to accomplish. And we knew how to. The experi-ence of 2017 allowed us to be in this place now."

"(2017) left a bitter taste in our mouth," UWF wide receiver Quentin Randolph said. "...You can Google UWF-Texas

A&M-Commerce and there are bad photos on there of us losing. Now when you Google 'UWF national championship,' you're gonna like what you saw."

So, suffice to say, there was a little more hardware in the Nobles household over the holidays than had been in years past. It had been a long road on the field and off, but Christmas was a true time to rejoice.

Christmas

Each and every day I have with my husband I view as a gift from God. Christmas Eve and Christmas Day in the hospital....still a gift from God!!! Thank you God!!

This is a great opportunity for me to put in perspective the true meaning of Christmas!! Our lives have been full of doctor visits, football games and many days just sitting with Buddy holding his hand because he felt horrible. I have not stepped into any stores shopping, I have not been able to get out my Christmas decorations or put up a tree. As fun as all of the decorating and shopping and wrapping presents (not really, I hate wrapping) are those things are not Christmas. Christmas is about the birth of Jesus. Christmas is about Mary and Joseph and no room in the Inn. Christmas is about baby Jesus in a manger. Christmas is about God sending His Son to be our Savior. I am celebrating Christmas Eve and Christmas day in a hospital room with Buddy, Kasey, Kaleb Kenley and Katy and Grandma. This might be one of the best Christmas' ever. I realize this day is truly a gift from God!!

Merry Christmas! The Nobles are truly blessed!

"We flew back later that night after the game as a team," Kaleb says, "and Katy flew back the next day into Fort Walton Beach. So I picked her up and we headed to Fitzgerald immediately. So we were finally all together on the 22nd late that night. It was awesome to be all home together and just sit there and watch both our championship games again. He was just as sharp as ever watching both games.

"We hadn't been together in months outside of the hospital so it was great to be at home and just sit and talk and cherish time together. It was kind of relaxing and then I think we went to the hospital around Christmas Eve or Christmas Day. But the Christmas holiday itself was different as Mom said in that Facebook post. The best thing we can do is all be together and just hang out at the house. We weren't five hours apart at the most for the first time in a long time. It was definitely a tough Christmas but it was a great Christmas too as well."

Especially as the family got to pick Buddy up from the hospital Christmas Day and bring him home for a little while. Buddy told everyone he wanted to take a drive through the school property on the way back. For the man who invested so much, and for the family that invested right alongside, it was a chance to see everything the community had unified to present to anyone who would come to Ocilla as "the 2019 Single-A Public Champ Irwin County Indians."

In the quiet of the holidays, it was a chance to smile, reflect, and be thankful...

Even if there were still a lot of football games to watch and just cheer for teams and give good-natured ribbing about instead of having a family member attached to the end result for good or bad...

"The last communication that Buddy and I had was the night of the Ohio State-Clemson playoff game," Jeremey Andrews said. "I graduated from Ohio State and I'm originally from Columbus, Ohio. So I'm a bit of a Buckeye fan and he would always tease me because, in the South, everybody hates whatever their school's rival is and it seems like it's always Ohio State.

Andrews starts laughing about the memory...

"The SEC has their own special little hatred for everybody else and then there's their own rivals. Traditionally, we would text on Saturdays and it would revolve around the previous night's game and whatever Ohio state was doing or whatever was happening in college football. In true Buddy fashion, the morning of that game, I sent him a text and it just said 'O-H.' I didn't get a response. After the game was over and Ohio State lost, his only response was: 'I-O.'

"My response to that was: I hate football.'"

But Jeremey loved the back and forth with a mentor and a role model any chance he could get...

WEST FLORIDA 48 (13-2)
-VS- MINNESOTA ST. 40 (14-1)

1st	09:22	UWF–Kevin Grant 5 yd pass from Austin Reed (Austin Williams kick) 13 plays, 72 yards, TOP 5:38	7	0
1st	06:09	MSU–Arnold, Justin 38 yd pass from Schlichte, Ryan (Williams, Luke kick) 7 plays, 68 yards, TOP 3:05	7	7
1st	03:38	UWF–Ka'Ron Ashley 12 yd pass from Austin Reed (Austin Williams kick) 5 plays, 69 yards, TOP 2:24	14	7
1st	00:53	MSU–Gunn, Nate 2 yd run (Williams, Luke kick), 7 plays, 60 yards, TOP 2:38	14	14

2nd	13:18	UWF–Q. Randolph 2 yd pass from Austin Reed (Austin Williams kick) 7 plays, 59 yards, TOP 2:26	21	14
2nd	10:58	UWF–Austin Williams 31 yd field goal 5 plays, 21 yards, TOP 1:20	24	14
2nd	06:21	MSU–Gunn, Nate 6 yd run (Williams, Luke kick), 9 plays, 75 yards, TOP 4:37	24	21
2nd	05:31	UWF–Q. Randolph 34 yd pass from Austin Reed (Austin Williams kick) 3 plays, 72 yards, TOP 0:44	31	21
2nd	00:18	UWF–Q. Randolph 48 yd pass from Austin Reed (Austin Williams kick) 4 plays, 99 yards, TOP 0:38	38	21
3rd	08:12	UWF–Tate Lehtio 8 yd pass from Austin Reed (Austin Williams kick) 7 plays, 40 yards, TOP 2:27	45	21
3rd	03:48	MSU–Sleezer, Kaleb 15 yd punt return (Sample, Jalen pass)	45	29
4th	14:39	UWF–Austin Williams 30 yd field goal 6 plays, 33 yards, TOP 1:24	48	29
4th	09:52	MSU–Williams, Luke 24 yd field goal 10 plays, 45 yards, TOP 2:36	48	32
4th	04:03	MSU–Zylstra, Shane 7 yd pass from Schlichte, Ryan (Arnold, Justin pass) 13 plays, 90 yards, TOP 3:48	48	40

Chapter 19

ONE FINAL LAP

One major holiday passed in 2019 and there were two more coming in short order to finish the calendar year...

Christmas and New Year's...

One celebrates a birth while the other is about renewal, rebirth, and the hope of the future. The entire Irwin County/Fitzgerald/high school football community was looking at 2020 with possibilities and that Buddy and the Nobles family could fight cancer and come out the other side in this fight that started back in the summer.

Was it hope against everything else...? In some circles, perhaps... But hope is always a part of the discussion that miracles could happen. For a miracle to happen in any circle, the bottom line is that you have to keep fighting. The Nobles family did just that in an as big an uphill battle as you could find anywhere.

"Dad went back into the hospital the day after Christmas," Kasey admits. "He had gotten so weak and couldn't really do much on his own at that point. We had a doctor's appointment when we got there and they couldn't do what they needed to do- which was a common story throughout. He just wasn't strong enough to get the proper amount of chemo so we were going to start immunotherapy, but it was the same old story.

"Things were bad and we were getting ready to go home and I think he almost passed out. That's when things, kind of, really went downhill. Through those next few weeks, he was in the hospital in Tifton."

Buddy would end up at Tift Regional Medical Center.

"Mom stayed at the hospital with him the entire time," Kaleb said. "She never left his side a single day. We hadn't done chemo in a while and his body was kind of trying to make that final push to fight against things. There were some tough decisions to be made and tough things that were said. We're in the middle of it and we're right in the eye of the storm having to make these decisions, talk about certain things, and things that as a kid you don't ever think of as Dad was having a really tough time."

Buddy had players come and visit from his time in Florida- all the way back from the eighties and nineties.

"People started coming to visit because you kind of had a feeling and, I think a lot of people did, that the end was near," Kasey continued. "People wanted to see him and, eventually, we were able to get him out of the hospital. He kept talking about how he just wanted to be home. We got the home care finalized and had him set up in the living room where we all had space to stay around him from the time. We all started sleeping in the living room on the couch just to be near him."

"I think they were trying to do everything they could," Kenley admits. "I was back at school in Statesboro when Mom called me that night. She told me 'We're taking him home.' I didn't know how much time we had left with Dad, so I knew I had to get home.

"We spent the night in the hospital and finally took him home. He was asleep the whole drive. Our uncle was there for almost everything from then on as Mom and Dad had moved downstairs from their room upstairs. I had to write emails to my professors and got two classes moved online. We just spent the next couple days just sitting by his side and talking."

It could have been about football. It could have been about the Daytona 500. But, most importantly, it was just sitting and talking. The sign on the door about keeping your visit time became just a sign on a door. Everyone that dropped by, whether they went to high school with Buddy and Tammy, or went to high school to be coached or taught by Buddy and Tammy, people would just show up.

To sit and talk... throughout this whole time...

"I remember the night before he passed," Kasey said. "He had deteriorated a little mentally. But he was still really sharp. Even at that moment, he knew players that he coached back in the eighties and nineties. He could think of a specific call he made in a game. But you could just tell he was starting to slip a little. I remember that night for about probably a good hour to an hour and a half, he just was talking and basically coaching.

"We just sat there and talked," he continues. "It was a little funny at the time because he would be calling out kids, but he called out a kid that I played with when I was in high school. He was also going through the phases of calling a game that night. In his head, he was coaching as hard as he could. He was telling the kids to turn their hips and not get beat and he just went through coaching a game right there as he went to sleep.

Then, Buddy was gone...

He didn't tell anyone. Buddy had coached his last game. He won his last game on a football field and while he was lost to all of us, he won a larger game in getting to be with his Lord and Savior, Jesus Christ. He let his family get some rest as he had put them through a lot since his diagnosis and, after a night's sleep, Kasey and Kaleb were the first to know their father was no longer with them..

"It was pretty early in the morning," Kasey says. "I heard Kaleb moving and I looked over. I asked him if everything was all right. I could just see the tears in his eyes again and we went to wake my mom and Kenley up and tell them."

"I was there the whole time we got back from our national championship game until after his funeral," Kaleb remembers. "With the direction things were going, I was always in communication with our head coach at UWF and he was always telling me, 'Do what you need to do. Take as much time as you need. You don't have any obligation to be here in Pensacola.' I got to stay with everyone and then didn't leave until early February after everything kind of calmed down a little bit.

"There were a lot of tough moments to go through during that time period. A lot of things you can't even imagine going through as a kid growing up. The medical teams we were with were very good at telling us what to expect in the weeks after New Years Day and they were pretty spot on with the ending stages. Following him home , with him in the ambulance, was probably the toughest thing to do because you knew this was the final step. We all slept downstairs by his bed but nobody really wanted to sleep because we wanted to spend as much time with him as we could. So there were a lot of sleepless days and nights but for the right reasons.

"It was very humbling and was very eye-opening to see everybody come together and see the things that were done for us this whole time. Even before we were home on hospice care, people would make sure we were okay at the hospital. I remember that we knew that food was coming to the house- a lot of it. We didn't want to waste food and we knew that we didn't have time to make food or go get food. We had to get a second refrigerator.

"People did for us stuff like you see in a movie. There were donations and other things that people didn't have to do. And it was a testament to the people that are in both counties, but also a testament to what Dad meant to those people. People all over the southeast would come to visit before Dad passed. We had people driving from Virginia- people from their high school youth group with my mom and dad together- that they hadn't seen since those years come by. It was pretty, pretty, pretty humbling.

"But it's kind of cool for me to see the impact that he had had on a lot of people. You start thinking about how many people's lives he touched over the years and how lucky we were to have him every single second of every single day of our lives and how lucky we were to have been impacted by him on a daily basis, to be able to talk to him, and have him in my whole life. To have someone that special and we were blessed to call him ours. To call him my Dad, I don't know that there's anything I can ever be more proud of...

"We were home from the hospital for 8 days before he passed and a lot of people visited during that time. Those visits were very tough because you loved people coming by to see him but you knew that they were stopping by for a specific reason. To hear the words people said to him and the love that was poured out to him are very special to me and things I will remember forever."

"Being a loving Christian father to so many young men across the state of Florida and the state of Georgia, he was a father to many, many more than his immediate family," Troy Fletcher adds. "Players look up to him as a very devoted, passionate father. I was telling my own kids at dinner last night that one of our players texted me a video because we're in this Covid-19 time. Athletes can't work out. They can't do things and it is killing me as the strength coach. The video was of him running and he gave me a 'thank you' for teaching him the proper techniques. He sent another text and said 'Thank you for seeing the potential in me that I didn't see.'

"When you get players to send you a text or something like that out of the blue, it really touches your heart. We're not in this for the money. It's developing relationships and showing them that you care about them. You've got to be tough on them, too, sometimes in this day and age. But Coach Nobles really exemplifies that and he taught me that as I came up with him for the years that we coached together."

"When I would go see him whether it was in Atlanta over at St Joseph's, or if it was down in Tifton, or even when I went to go see him in Ocilla, I always made a point to tell him that I loved him before I left," Robby Pruitt says. "For me, since I couldn't be there every day and I could only be there over the phone or something like that, it was just as important to tell him that kind of stuff every single day- knowing that the family was fighting as much as they were.

"You couldn't ask for a better head coach for your kids. Not only as a role model, but also as someone who had to tell football players what they needed to hear. He would always tell me he loved me and thanked me for everything."

Robby was on his way to go quail hunting when he got the phone call that Buddy had finally passed. He immediately turned around and came back to find out what he could do for the family as quickly as he could.

"Other than being the all-time winningest coach in Irwin County history, and winning more region titles than anybody ever has, I really don't know how to say it other than no one will ever forget Buddy Nobles," Marty Roberts says. "I will always love Buddy Nobles and his family. If you didn't like Buddy Nobles, maybe you need to look in the mirror, because there's a problem with you if you don't like Buddy Nobles. He was a Christian man. He was friends with everybody he ever made acquaintance with and had the biggest heart of anybody. He always wanted to do for others. He never wanted accolades for himself and he always wanted the best for his team and his coaches."

The afternoon turned gray on the day Buddy would have turned 54.

2500 people joined the Nobles family, friends, coaches, and the 2019 Irwin County Indians at the football stadium in Ocilla to say good-bye. People were dressed, mainly, in red, silver, and black- the Indians' colors. But you did have your share of the previous coaching stops for Buddy and his family. You had purple from his time at Fitzgerald and Union County and Blue and Gold from his time at University Christian. You had your share of the maroon of Coffee High as well who made the 20-mile trip from Douglas. Kaleb even had support from his fellow coaches at West Florida as some made the trip from Pensacola.

The Rev. Percy Cunningham, the Rev. Dr. Lloyd Stembridge, the Rev. Bill Horne, and the Rev. Billy Stephens officiated.

As Kaleb made his way from the front row to the platform that his dad coached from all season long, the wind picked up and the field became colder.

Thank you to everyone that has come out today. These are obviously not the circumstances that we want to be gathering for but we all would not be here if it weren't for my Father, Buddy Nobles, having an impact on everyone here at some point during his life. My Father had an ability to talk and relate to anyone

he came across and we have joked with him for years that he could talk to a brick wall and if he talked long enough he could probably even get the wall to talk back to him. Dad never met a stranger and never met someone who he didn't care for just as if they weren't his son or daughter, as shown by the number of people who have shown up here today,

As you all know, our family's world revolves around the football calendar and we all look forward to the days counting up to the beginning of football season. This year was no different, with Dad, Mom, Kasey & Kenley here prepping in Ocilla & me in Pensacola preparing our team for this season. As many of you know, we received news on August 7th that changed the course of our lives forever. Mom gathered Kasey, Kenley & I on the phone to deliver the news: Stage 4 Cancer, non-operable, terminal with no length of time given to us only with the warning that this battle did not have a good ending.

He would break down as he looked down at his dad's casket on the elevated brace below

If you know our family, you know that we are very quick to jump to help others, especially in our family. Our Mother & Father taught us as young children to be quick to put others before yourself & Dad gave us a great example of this every day. There were no lengths that Dad would not go to to ensure that Mom, Kasey, Kenley & I were taken care of. And now, as we received this heartbreaking news about our Dad, we could only feel one of the worst feelings in the world: Helpless. I cannot express in words how hard it was to see Dad, the person we love more than anything in the world, be diagnosed with such an ugly disease and not be able to help him in his most time of need.

Then what has happened over the past 5 or so months has amazed me and shown us the type of person that my Dad was, not only to us but to everyone he crossed paths with. Only my Dad could turn his personal battle with cancer into a way to

spread the message about his Lord & Savior, Jesus Christ. Dad told us over the years that the game of football can teach us lessons that will stick with us for the rest of our lives. What he also taught us is that football provides you a great platform to spread the message of your personal faith & to lead others in the correct direction & towards the Lord. My Dad had a very good grip on how large his platform was, and knew he had the ability to impact hundreds of young kids on a daily basis in whatever school he was in.

As many of you already know, Dad's body started working against him early in the season and he wasn't able to stand for an entire game, which is where this platform that I am standing on came about. This platform gave him the ability to continue to do what he loves while also showing what Jesus meant to him. This platform gave him the ability to lead others to Christ and be a light for others, even when he was the one in the midst of a battle for his life. After all the years of telling us about the platform we are provided with through football, I find it nothing short of amazing that Dad chose to turn the biggest battle of his life into a way to spread the word of Jesus to others. So thank you to everyone who had a part in this platform and allowing Dad to be part of such an amazing season for our family.

As many of you know, Dad coached at Fitzgerald & Coffee County before making his way to Ocilla almost six years ago. Fitzgerald is where I played under him and a lot of other coaches that are here today. Leading up to our last season at Fitzgerald, we unfortunately had a teammate pass away by the name of DJ Searcy. DJ was much like my Dad in that he had contagious positive energy and an ability to talk and spend time with anyone. As you can imagine, his passing was heartbreaking to everyone involved and was something that we struggled with understanding. I can remember the morning after DJ passed that my Dad walked into my room and woke me up to ask how I was doing. I being the 17-year-old kid did not understand why things like this happened. One of the questions I asked my Dad was

"Why do bad things happen to such good people, especially out of nowhere?" His response is something that has helped clear up tough moments for me ever since. Dad said "Kaleb, there are going to be tough times in life and many things that you may not understand why they are happening. But what you have to understand is that God does not wake up every morning & make decisions like we do. God has already planned out our lives long before we were born and long after we have left this earth. God does not make mistakes & how we handle these tough times in a positive manner for Him is what matters the most". As mad as I wanted to be about losing someone close to us, Dad's words had a way of giving me a calming peace about tough situations & I feel even prepared me for his battle over the last 5 months.

Over the last few weeks, we have seen the impact that Dad has had on countless lives across the entire world. We have had hundreds of people reach out and stop by to see us with amazing stories of how Dad impacted their lives. But one story has stuck out to me about Dad that I think sums him up the best. One of Dad's close friends stopped by the house last week and told us about a conversation he had with Dad back in August.

He told Dad "Buddy, I know you don't want to hear this but I am mad. I'm mad that you are having to deal with this because you're too good of a person."

Dad responded with "I'm fine. I have come to grips with this & I'm okay with it. I know the battle I have ahead & I'm not afraid."

His friend came back with "Of course you're saying that Buddy cause you're always able to find the positives in tough situations. But this isn't right. There are people out there that do a lot worse things than you that are probably more deserving of this than you are".

Dad's response are words that don't surprise me but still amaze me. Dad said "You're probably right, but I'm not worried about

that. I'm not worried about it because I know where I'm going after this battle. I know that I'm going to Heaven. What a much worse tragedy it would be if God gave this battle to someone who didn't know where they were going. I would much rather those people who don't know have more time on Earth to find the Lord & have an opportunity to go where I am going to go."

And that was who my Dad was. Selfless & more worried about leading others to Christ, even in his battle that would end up taking his life. I can't stand here today and say that I am doing great because I am not. This is a very tough situation to deal with & is something that will take plenty of time to adjust to. What gives us peace is: knowing that we prayed for healing for Dad, whether here or in Heaven, and it is reassuring to know that Dad is walking the streets of Gold right now, smiling down on us as we gather to celebrate his life.

But the one presence that couldn't be ignored as he spoke started from far away at first, but as Kaleb kept talking, the noise grew and grew. A cardinal would circle the people assembled on the football field and would pass over Buddy's youngest son as he talked about making sure he represented his name as best he could every day.

Over the years, my Dad taught us many lessons. He taught us about being tough, how to love our Mom and also our future wives & husband. He taught us about perseverance & dealing with tough times. He taught us to lead by example & to get our job done. But the one thing he stressed to us the most was to Represent Our Last Name. I heard my Dad say this hundreds & even thousands of times. Growing up, I didn't fully grasp onto this message but I have come to understand as I have gotten older. The reason I have understood this more is because Dad gave me the blueprint of this on a daily basis. You showed me what it meant to be a good teammate & coach. You showed me what it meant to be a good man, husband, & father. But more importantly, you showed me what it meant to be a good

Christian, a servant for the Lord who should never be ashamed of my relationship with Christ.

Dad, I cannot thank you enough for the life lessons you taught me over the years and I thank you for teaching me to represent my last name. Because I could not be prouder to be a Nobles because that means I had the most amazing person in the world as my Dad.

When the ceremony was over, the six pallbearers that included Kasey, Kaleb, CJ, Robby Pruitt, Casey Soliday and Drew Tankersley and those that were chosen for that honor escorted Buddy off the stand and moved him to the hearse that waited on the track. The hearse would make its lap and those seated on the field made their way to the far side of the field to form a cordon to say one last farewell. Each Irwin County player raised their hand as high as they could to salute their coach, friend, mentor, and leader who had been taken from them all too soon.

The crowd would head to their respective homes while the family would lay Buddy to rest in Irwin County's Frank Cemetery.

The season had ended with a title and Buddy would even get to wear his championship ring before he was called home.

"I remember he didn't want to have the memorial service at the stadium," Kasey says. "We'd suggest it because he was one that was going to plan everything and he planned out every detail of his funeral- from the songs played, to everybody speaking, how much time they had, and he was a stickler for details. It was either in late August or September, whenever his first trip to the hospital was and when things weren't looking good, that he was sitting around and Kaleb was on his way up there and we sat and planned his funeral.

"I mean, he wrote down everything- pallbearers, what the coaches would wear, what the kids would wear, the most minute details... He had it figured out, but said 'no' to having it at the stadium. He wanted to have it at church and we were never able to convince him that there's not a church around here that's going to be able to hold everybody. I completely respect that that's what he wanted but, realistically, we had to have it out there at the stadium.

"It was the perfect venue for it. It was fitting. Doctor Clayton and everybody did such a great job getting everything set up and preparing it out there on the field. I remember walking up and walking out to go where the casket was going to be and, I remember, I looked up once and looked in the crowd. There were a bunch of people that some of my family hadn't talked to since high school. it was just bringing a lot of memories from over the years.

"I remember walking up and carrying the casket. That was tough. But, probably, my favorite memory of that day is seeing all the kids walk up as we were leaving. We're walking around the track and seeing the kids all with their hands in the air. To see all the kids who loved and respected him- and he was a father to a lot of those kids- they didn't have much at home. He knew that and he did everything he could to be that figure.

"Thanksgiving meals were never normal. When I was a little kid, all the way to coaching with him here, they were not just family. We always planned on practicing Thanksgiving morning and those morning practices were the best feelings in the world. Families talk about the best feeling you can have is waking up Thanksgiving morning to know you're still alive still practicing. But our Thanksgiving meals were, like, 10 players over on Thanksgiving eating with us. He was able to get through to so many kids and I think that showed with the procession. As it was going by, you see all the kids there with tears in their eyes. Their hands in the air just kind of showed how much he meant to those kids.

"Dad was a great family man- which came first. Family came before football- even though we were diehard football. And I think he wasn't afraid to let people know how important both those aspects were in his life. Everybody knew football was important, but I think his legacy is of a phenomenal football coach- one of the best I've ever seen or learned from. Everything I know is from him. But it's also as a great family man, a father, and as a great Christian."

"I don't think I realized how big the crowd was until I turned around and looked in the stands when I was walking up to the platform," Kaleb admits. "I wasn't surprised at all because of all the people that loved him and he loved back."

"I don't feel like I'll be able to talk about Dad in a past tense. I know that's probably a little different but I don't know that I'll ever be able to make myself say 'My dad was or my dad did this' because I still feel him every single day in every single thing I do. It will be very hard for me to talk about him in a past tense form. It'll probably take a long time for that...

"Mom and dad have a textbook example of what a Christian love should be. They were dating and married, combined, for 37 and 1/2 years and married for 34 and a half. I don't know that you can put into words the love they have for each other. I think that everybody realized that during the whole process because my mom wouldn't leave his side. We offered to her that we- Kasey, Kenley and I- would sleep with him and she would sleep in the house when Dad was in the hospital, but she wouldn't do it.

"In the end, I think we all knew she wasn't going to do it. But she could be up there for him and it was an example of what they were their whole lives. They were always comforted by the other at their side. Not that we never saw them bickering or we never saw them fighting. It's not that everything was smooth sailing all the time, But they never argued in front of us. They never got into a fight in front of us and there was never a moment where Dad left the house or Mom left at the house to get away. They were always together and always insisted on making sure their love for each other was the same the day before that it was the day after, and the next day, and the next day, and then the next.

"I'm 26. I saw what true love is supposed to be. Dad gets a lot of publicity because he is a head coach. He has a major platform to share his life with Christ and Mom's the same way. She's just as firm in her Christian beliefs as he is. They both understood what it meant to love each other. I also think they understood that they had a duty to make sure that we understood what it meant to love somebody and to treat your husband or wife with love every day."

That has, definitely, rubbed off on Kaleb and Katy. Kaleb is following in his dad's council with the goal of marrying her one day. And Kaleb has secured that goal as the two have since gotten engaged with plans of marrying in 2021. Kaleb had been able to see his parents every day and it's a combination of game film analysis, on-the-job training and getting two of the best life coaches you could find anywhere. He got to see what love is supposed to be. He knows how to treat someone he loves in that way- even as life's ups-and-downs greet you in the only way they know how to greet you every sunrise.

Katy has been there all this time as well. She has slept uncomfortably in hospital waiting rooms. She has driven long hours and been a car passenger much the same. They have walked side-by-side juggling school, work, and travel to appointments and games on weekends. Seeing his parents as they were makes Kaleb feel that he wants to have that same kind of marriage when that day comes.

"The memorial service was the only thing that didn't go as he planned," Kenley says. "Dad had it like a game plan for him. He wanted the players to be wearing their red jerseys because you wear red when you're playing at home, or you wear dark when you're home, and when he was planning everything, he said he was 'going home'. When you look at the people that were filling the football stadium, it was insane to think that many people showed up for my dad."

"Dad was so passionate about everything that he did. I don't even know if you can even put him into the words to describe him. He was the most amazing dad and I got almost nineteen years spent with him. I got to work with him on the sideline for about eight years. He was always so amazing to me as a daughter and when I worked for him. He always told us to represent our last name and now, when people hear it, I just want them to think of him.

"He always told Mom 'If you leave me, I'm going with you. You're not leaving me alone with the kids.' That's how they were. They were always together. Theirs was the type of marriage where they always supported each other no matter what.

"Mom went through everything in that 5 and 1/2 months. It's just something that no woman should ever have to do, no person to ever have to do. They just loved each other that much that there was nothing that was going to stop them. They're the best role models to have."

CJ Spiller would alway look at Tammy and Buddy as a second set of parents- not as a substitute, mind you, but an addition to a family. He would add a sister and some more brothers as well. The Nobles family would always be there as a significant part of his life. He also got a great recipe for banana pudding out of the deal. The Nobles family wanted to share God with CJ and opened their doors for him and anyone else along the way.

"Mama Tammy, literally, is a second mom to me," he said. "She's, probably, one of the strongest persons I ever seen- especially when they had to go through what they went through as a family. To see her hold everything together the way that she did, it was like something I have never seen. She made sure everybody was okay even as people would come by and check up on her.

"I knew it was taking a toll on her because I don't even think she got to cry. We had a couple of conversations about Coach's condition early on. I could just see it was starting to upset her. I think that's when it hit me this is serious. As strong as she was, she had to be strong for Kasey, Kaleb, and Kenley, too. Mama Tammy has always had a giving spirit and a giving heart. She is very generous and always made sure that you were okay first. She was always giving you a hug and to see her and Coach was like a match made in heaven."

"Because I've known Buddy for so long, it's awesome that people that only get to know him for a year, six months, or one football season love him as much as I do," Kevin Erwin says. "His legacy is: what you see is what you get. He's helping young boys become men and become better men then they probably would have been without him in their lives. It was nothing for Buddy to walk over to a player on an opposing team on a night Irwin beats them and talk to him. He would say, 'I loved his game and I want to find him and talk to him.' That's just everything that should be done by a coach and Buddy did it.

"I don't know that there will ever be another Buddy. If you can find somebody who doesn't like Buddy Nobles, it's probably somebody you don't want to be around because I have known him forever. I know a lot of people and I can't find somebody to say a bad word about Buddy."

Kevin's influence from Buddy didn't stop. Right above the head rest in his truck, a "Nobles Strong" band keeps its place. For

Kevin, he has had his share of loss in his life. He lost his parents close to one another in the calendar, so he understands what it means when it happens to someone else.

Selfishly, though, he still is upset. He just wants to see Buddy... and you can't blame him in that opinion. He, certainly, isn't alone...

Kevin is also one of the first people to give Kaleb all the credit in the world for what he said at the memorial service.

"I just absolutely couldn't have done that, but his strong Christian faith just got him through it. He just spoke from his heart and it was just beautiful."

If you ask someone like Luke Roberts, he'll mention Buddy's legacy is built around Buddy being steadfast in his beliefs and defended that every day. Buddy was a true brother in every sense of the word. For someone like Andy Paulk, it was all those things that people didn't witness that made Buddy who he was as he made a difference to everyone he came in contact with on a daily basis.

"It really was tough," Fitzgerald Head Coach Tucker Pruitt admits. "I had to watch it all unfold right before my eyes and that was tough. Even though you knew that day was coming, I don't think it was made any easier knowing the finality of it and knowing that he's really gone. Then just remembering how much impact he had and all the good that he did while he was here, it was a sad day at the memorial service. You know what, though...? At the same time, you know he's not suffering anymore and he's in a better place. He did what he did and made."

When Tucker looked up toward the stands in Ocilla, it gave him a bit of a start, but it reminded him just how many people Buddy impacted. Whether it was at University Christian, Lake

Butler, Fitzgerald, Douglas, or Ocilla, you're talking about five different communities that came to show their respects. It was a testament to what he meant to all those places, families, and communities.

The coaching staff from UWF made the trip as well to be there for Kaleb... a true show of class...

One other moment crystallized what Buddy meant to his family...

Kevin's daughter graduated from college and would, eventually, end up getting a job in Ocilla as a teacher. She would live with Tammy and the rest of the family to add to the warmth that house gives every single day when the new school year would come on line.

As she crossed the stage after she received her diploma, she shouted to her family...

"Ocilla, we did it..."

Of that, there is no doubt...

Chapter 20

THE NEXT STEPS

Tammy and the family are taking it one day at a time going forward- like every family that has experienced a catastrophic loss...

There were Christmas days, a New Year turned, Valentine's Day, and everyone under the Nobles roof faced them together- including Kasey getting to spend his birthday in the hospital for the removal of his gallbladder. Casey Soliday was named head coach- as was widely thought. While there were moments of melancholy and a "To Do" list that Buddy left behind, CJ got married to the love of his life, Daysha Jackson in South Carolina.

Kasey

Made it the whole trip without getting too emotional, until I started looking at pictures and thinking how much my dad would have enjoyed this weekend. I know he used to pray for you to find a great woman, just like he did for the rest of his kids. He'd be so proud of you and would have been the first one to get up there proclaiming that you're that woman he prayed for Daysha. I think he enjoyed the visits up there to see you just as much as he enjoyed seeing CJ. Hope you guys have a great

marriage, and thanks for this great weekend spent with family and friends

Tammy

God chose to take my best friend to the mansion He had prepared for him in heaven. My heart has had an empty spot since then but as promised God has and still is providing me the perfect amount of comfort combined with the perfect amount of grace. My heart will always have that empty spot but God has adjusted my focus. I try not dwell on these painful months since Buddy died, but to put my focus on the 34 1/2 years we were married, the amazing children that Buddy and I called our "gifts from God", and the precious times we had since we first met back in 1982. When I focus on all the time that God allowed us to have together I am just thankful. Thankful for the devotion Buddy had to his Lord and Savior first then his devotion to me, to our children and to his job. The precious memories we created together are what helps me to survive without him.

Many people that I speak to have a "remember when Buddy _____" story to share with me. Those stories have been precious to me and my children. So today as I grieve not having him beside me I cling to my memories and the many memories that you have shared with me and I thank God for providing His grace, comfort and love.

"The last time I talked to Buddy was actually in the hospital" Clemson head coach Dabo Swinney says. "He had just stopped treatments. He was still hopeful and he had come out of there and was right back at it. When you think about the championship that he won, it's an amazing, amazing story. To see that community and all those kids rally around him and walk in that valley, that's something that will be with me for the rest of my life. And then, a week later, for Kaleb to win the national championship...? Thinking you could script something and write it as well... the story is powerful on every level.

"Buddy was peaceful at the time. He was focused and he was still fighting. I think we can learn that we can be strengthened with our faith. I think he had a peace that only God can give you and I just really believe that in every fiber of my body. I learned to study something is one thing, but actually see it in practice makes it even more of an affirmation or confirmation of what I believe with my faith. How Buddy accepted the challenge...? he did not lay down. We all have a circle of influence and I think he used his challenge to hopefully create positive change in other people's lives. No matter what you're dealing with, there's a way that you can still make a difference in a positive way to other people in your community. He did that and I think that's something that we can all take away.

"It wasn't just how he lived his life as a person. He's a great football coach, but there's a lot of great football coaches. It's the relationship with his players, and how he lived his life as a father and as a husband. All those things we should learn from somebody. And how Buddy honored God and put his faith first and wasn't ashamed of being all of those are things...? That's a great inspiration to me. He never sacrificed his family. He involved them in everything. His fate is being a great father and being a great husband goes with the things that drove him. He was what he truly loved and loved what he did. I think there's a lot of people who have jobs and they don't like their job, but he loved what he did."

In mid-June, almost as an early Father's Day, the school system gave a gift to a family, friends, and an entire community. The stadium that has so many memories for Irwin County will now and forever have a Nobles in-house.

The Nobles family considers it quite an honor that the ICHS football stadium will be named after Coach Nobles. Thank you so much to everyone who made this happen. Coach Nobles considered coaching at Irwin an honor. He loved his job, his players, his coaches and Indian Nation. In his humble manner he would try to deflect the attention off of him and onto his players. I consider it quite the honor and very fitting because he poured so much of himself into that stadium. Thank You Indian Nation!

"I thought it was clear to myself and the board members about some sort of naming of a facility," Irwin County Superintendent Thad Clayton said. "As Coach Nobles' health was deteriorating during the season, we were having a lot of conversations about how remarkable his career was then and what was potentially a great end to last season. Out of that conversation, the school started evaluating 'What is our policy in naming facilities?' It gives us the ability to understand, whenever we decide the name of a facility, that it really reflects what we believe. We didn't actually craft the new policy until February after the football season and the passing of Coach Nobles. Over two to three months, there was a really good conversation between board members, community members, and others about wanting to do something.

"So that Monday night was really cool once we officially had a policy. It was my first budget item and it became a real popular moment in Irwin County. We just had an awful lot of Facebook responses where a group of people were excited to be able to do the stadium in Buddy's name. The post from Tammy and the family was precious. That was a cool moment that I don't think I'll forget for a long time."

Mr. Clayton will always be struck by the notion of wondering how you take care of your loved one, and how did you make young men and women better adults by the time they leave school. He received those answers from watching Buddy Nobles. The other thing that sticks with him is seeing someone communicate all of the really important things in life- Faith, family, friends, and all the other issues of today.

David Pierce, who wrote the history book on Irwin County football, "Our Boys: A team, a town, a history, a way of life," adds his thoughts to the history of the accomplishment...

Characters who played on the fine teams of Irwin past take a bow.

Boys of Ocilla High first played football in 1922 with veterinarian T.B. Gissendanner as coach. The Terrapins rose of prominence under E.V. Whelchel before the little program died out in 1933 and stayed dead until after World War II. In 1949, the Ocilla team was re-named the Indians and in 1952, after a school merger, the squad became the Irwin County Indians. Since that time, fans of football in this farming community 170 miles south of Atlanta have whooped and hollered for some outstanding teams. The 1953 Indians of coach Herb Strickland went to state. The next great team played in 1964 under Ralph Cook but they did not make it all the way. The 1968 the team under Kermit Elliott lost in the final. Irwin still did not have a state champ until seven years later when Mike Battles led a scrappy, hard-nosed gang of under-sized farm boys to a perfect season.

Which raises some questions.

Could the Indians of yore hold up against Buddy's 2019 squad?

Oh, sure, quips Tommy Tucker, an outstanding guard on the team 55 years ago – "for about a quarter."

"No," Oscar Roberts, quarterback on the '68 team, says with a chuckle.

Even the '75 team might not give the most recent champs a run for their money.

The boys of 2019 leave a legacy as the most dominant team in the history of Irwin County football.

Lewis Hall was a half back in 1975.

"We had our time, and this is their time. Let them enjoy it," Hall *says, when asked to compare. "It's a different time and a different world.*

"These boys need to be in the limelight."

"We were talked about for years. Now it's their turn."

Certainly, no other team has played under such distraction than Buddy's boys did in 2019, but they used it for motivation.

Larger in number, bigger, too, stronger and arguably more talented than boys of yesterday, the 2019 club, if it needed any more incentive, was fueled by the fact that Nobles, a mentor and father figure to a large number of the boys, did not have very long to live, cut down by stomach cancer, and there was no way they were going to lose it for him. The boys in the silver helmets and red jerseys wanted to send him out with a championship.

Nobles went out as the winningest coach with a record of 67-13-2, taking the Indians to the state title game five times in six years of "Buddy ball" in Ocilla.

There is nothing in Ocilla quite like winning football.

As a growing boy, all Buddy wanted to think about was football. Now he leaves a legacy richer than football, and if you knew him you were better for it. Buddy showed young men how to live for Jesus and how to take it courageously when life deals you a bad hand.

Father's Day

Kaleb

Every day of the year, I always feel blessed to have the Dad that I have but I am always reminded yearly of that even more on Father's Day. As imagined, this Father's Day is a little tougher than years past because it is the first we are not able to celebrate the day with our Dad. I am reminded today of how precious every single moment is with family because this time last year, we had no clue of what the next 365 days would be like and certainly no idea that would be our last Father's Day all together. Over the last year there were a lot of sleepless nights, middle of the night car rides (mostly driving way too fast Thea Katy Kuhlmeier), and certainly a lot of tears shed. I cherish every one of those long days and nights because of the conversations and moments we had together that showed me more than ever the type of Father my Dad is.

There have been plenty of rough days since January but also countless reminders of his legacy left on this Earth. What I will miss the most today is his prayer at lunch and him telling the Lord how thankful he is for the Wife Tammy Nobles that he has and the three children Kasey Nobles Kenley Nobles he was blessed with. My Dad always says how blessed he is to have us, but even more today I realize how blessed I am to have him as a Father.

35th ANNIVERSARY- June 22

From the day we met on August 23, 1982 and became high school sweethearts to the day we married 35 years ago today to today I never once doubted how much Buddy Nobles loved me! I am so thankful for the time God allowed us but wanted

more!! We planned to grow old together! We had things left to do! God has a perfect plan though and for reasons I will probably never understand He decided that 34 1/2 years was enough and took Buddy to his heavenly home. Today I am trying to focus on the good times we had. During the 37 years, 9 months and 30 days since we met we had a love and devotion for each other that will last a lifetime.

Mark 10;7 "For this cause shall a man leave his father and mother, and cleave to his wife;"

Matthew 19:6: "So they are no longer two, but one flesh. Therefore what God has joined together, let no one separate."

Thank you God for allowing me the time I had with Buddy. We laughed, we cried, we followed where God led us and we had fun. I cherish every moment. I could not have asked for a more devoted husband who was an amazing provider, father, gentleman, protector, soul-mate and much more. Thank you Bud my man! Thank you God for the time we had! GOD IS BIGGER!! NOBLESSTRONG!!

Kaleb also popped the question to Katy in mid-August 2020... Tammy let everybody know after Kaleb proposed on the Gulf of Mexico...

I am so excited! Buddy and I prayed from the day our children were born that God would prepare and send Godly mates for our children. God always answers prayers and he sure did this time also. I can tell you what Buddy Nobles would say to the news of Kaleb & Katy's engagement, "Kaleb, you outkicked your coverage"!

I watched as Katy stood with our family through Buddy's battle. She was there with us and she was there for Kaleb through the toughest of situations. Her love for God is evident and after that her love for Kaleb is just as evident. I have watched as she

calmed Kaleb down at times, comforted Kaleb during those tough times, stood in the stands supporting him as he coached and loved him unconditionally. When Kaleb could not be at Buddy's state championship game because he was in Texas preparing for his national championship game Katy came to Atlanta and FaceTimed the entire pregame, game and post game celebration with Kaleb. She made sure Kaleb could be with his Dad on that special day. My heart is overflowing, I am so glad Katy said "yes" because Katy is that Godly mate that Buddy and I have prayed for for Kaleb. Thank you God for you blessings. Katy you have been a part of our family from the time you met Kaleb but it is official now! Welcome! We love you, appreciate you and will continue praying that God will bless and lead both of you through this engagement into a long Godly marriage! Kaleb, you have had the perfect example from your Dad how to treat your wife. Follow Dad's example and you will be an amazing husband! Dad would say you did good Kaleb, outkicked your coverage, but you did good! Love you guys!

He did, in fact, outkick his coverage...

It has been a difficult year for the Nobles family (local, extended, or otherwise) and it gave a lot of people time to think, time to remember, and time to continue Buddy's impact on an entire community that can't be measured by geography.

"I spent some time thinking about the legacy question," Kenley concludes. "We have a notebook that Dad has kept over the years. In one of his entries, he has written, "I am in Clemson working CJ's camp, and a dad of a camper said 'football is so temporal.' I have thought about it all night. How things of this world do not matter other than the love I have for my family and the love that I have for the kids I coach! All of these things (material) on the Earth will disappear, but I hope and pray I have made an impact on the people I have been around. That is what really counts when it is all said and done!'

"I think that this represents him a lot. His time spent coaching was more than just teaching kids how to play football. Wins and losses are important in coaching, but being able to connect with the players on a personal level and be there for them was far more important to him. That's the type of man he was, and that's how I hope he's remembered."

Chapter 21

WHEN YOU THINK OF BUDDY

As we all move forward, folks were asked one final question...

When the name "Buddy Nobles" is mentioned, what comes to mind...

Here is a portion of their answers...

Tucker Pruitt

"He's just a special man, you know, a real special man. I know the next Irwin game will be a little different without him. That'll be kind of tough to get through, but thinking about it, I'm just glad that I got to know him and have all the experiences that we got to share together.

"When it comes to being a gentleman, being a husband, being a father... that kind of stuff, when you look at Buddy and Tammy, I just don't think you'll find any better. When I think of them, obviously, they're great people. I mean, that's first and foremost. They'd give the shirt off their back for you. They would take you in and feed you, but at the same time, they're going to tell you what's wrong. You know if you're doing something that isn't right, they're going to tell you. They stand for what's right. They're very strong people, very kind people...

"I think they have what it takes to be successful- no matter what. If you would have taken Buddy Nobles- he would have been a football coach, he would have been a painter, or a carpenter, or a doctor. I mean, he would have found a way to be special and build relationships. He would have made other people better in their walks of life, too. I just think they're great parents. I think they're great people and I think they obviously have a special love for each other and a great relationship. They just let the love that they have for each other bleed right down to the kids and right down to his players."

Robby Pruitt

"I think he'll be remembered as a guy who loved Christ and lived that life. In his life, it was God first, Tammy and the three kids second, and football third. I don't know of anybody that's exemplified that. He's one of a kind. We had a great adventure, man. Everybody that was around him... and I think it will continue... all those guys together that he coached and all the schools and all the coaches that he ever coached against will never forget his legacy. I really struggle with him not being here- especially early on."

Bill Barrs

"I told people, with Buddy, when he came to Irwin County that there are football programs throughout the state they can associate somebody with it- like Valdosta, you associate coaches like Bazemore and Hyder... Lincoln County...? You associate a coach like Larry Campbell. I told him we don't really have that person to associate with at the time he came, but we do now. So, it is Buddy now. A while back, I told my wife when I was sitting in the parking lot by the red light, and I sent her a message and told her that I really miss my Buddy. You know, you're sitting there seeing the red light in Ocilla and it all replays in your mind."

Marty Roberts

"I remember when he broke the record for wins by a head coach. I set it up with Kenley to get me the game ball from her and I had a Sharpie in my hand. I was going to write it real neat on the ball and present it to Buddy after the game. I had a silver Sharpie for some reason and my silver Sharpie quit. I had to find a black Sharpie quickly. Buddy's talking to the team and I'm over behind him writing on the football the record and score of the game. I told him, 'I got something for you.' He looked and he saw the football in my hand and to see the reaction from him...? He's just a humble man- no buts about it. I went to his house the next week and the ball is up on his mantel at his house. He just would have rather done it in private instead of in front of everybody.

"I just also remembered to tell him 'I love you my friend. I love you.' And to do that every time I saw him. The Monday before he died I was over at the house. I stayed about an hour with him. I didn't really realize he knew I was there because they'd gotten his championship ring and Tammy called me. She wanted me to come over and see the championship ring. I went over, but he was awake enough to greet me. I put the ring on him and I took the picture everyone saw. We got ready to leave and I walked around the other side of the bed. I leaned over. I said, 'Coach I love you.' He was close-by, but he said 'I love you.' That's the way we ended every conversation. He and I always did. It's going to be really hard this year. It's really going to be hard."

Pete Snyder

"Back in 2014, we went to our first state championship game vs Hawkinsville and you know that we lost that game. Like all the other state championship losses, it was tough for everyone, but for Buddy and Tammy it just got worse after that loss. Within just a few weeks after that game, Buddy lost both his father and his step father. It was a difficult time for the Nobles family. But through those tough times, I saw such a resilience and positive outlook in Buddy. He never complained or was negative in any way. He trusted God through those circumstances and believed in the vision that God had given him for Irwin County and it poured out on those around him.

"I'm also reminded of times when it wasn't all peaches and cream during the season. In his third year we started the season 1-3. We had just played in consecutive state championship games (2014 and 2015) and won consecutive region titles. However, we were really young overall in 2016. Not to mention that in those first four games we played Fitzgerald (AA state runner up), Macon County (A state champion), and Clinch County (A semifinalist). But in the eyes of the public, we lost and losing is not a good place to be, especially when we had been so accustomed to winning. Those were tough weeks for Buddy. People were coming at him from all directions. In the midst of that time Buddy constantly held his ground and did not waver in his commitment and vision for our players and Irwin County in general. As a coach, when angry parents verbally attack or stir up trouble in the community, there may be a temptation to hold that against the player connected to that person(s) and treat him negatively as a result. Buddy never did that in any way. He consistently and completely loved all of his players through the good and bad times. Ironically, that season had a great ending even though we lost in the quarterfinals. For me the season ended with such a great sense of accomplishment when we were so young as a team and had little depth on top of it. Buddy was the backbone of all of that."

Casey Soliday

"Everybody just, somehow, became friends with him. How he was able to do that and be able to introduce the kids to God was one of those things that he did with you- by being a strong and religious man for these kids."

Drew Tankersley

"When you have an impact like he had, not only on players but coaches... people in the school... people that you go to church with... people that you interact with daily... when you treat people how you want to be treated, you know people you can gravitate toward. He's someone who put Christ first and persevered. He ended up getting the Ultimate Prize of being in heaven. But, then secondary to that because of his perseverance, he ended up getting the state championship trophy- something that he always longed to do as a head coach.

"Winning that game, it was just like it made up for all of the other ones that we didn't win. Those other losses were really hard and winning gave so much excitement. That's the only way to describe it- just a celebration.

"The day of his memorial service in Ocilla was such a sad day. But it was such a celebration of Buddy's life and just the person that he was. The year before he came to be head coach, we had, kind of, established a winning attitude. Honestly, it was hard on Buddy when he came in because there were those who were really upset that the previous coach left. He has to come into this type of an atmosphere and he didn't blink. He just did his thing and decided we're going to do it and we did it. Buddy was also wise in that he didn't try to reinvent the wheel, though he has his way in 'this is how we're going to do it' at the same time.

"He didn't bash anybody. He didn't say, 'We're going to do it this way.' There were some things that now, over time, that changed but he didn't try to reinvent the wheel when he came. I think that was one of the wisest decisions he ever made. But, at the same time, he was leaving his mark and it was completely in terms of the legacy that he will leave. The legacy of love, family, hard work, discipline, and teaching our kids not just how to win, but how to prepare for life.

"When he first got here, he was still (kind of) in that mindset of 'I've got to do everything. We're going to do things exactly this way. We're going to do this on defense because this is what I've always done.' But, as the years passed, he realized that I have to let my coaches coach. He just, basically, said to the assistants 'You got it.' Buddy would put trust in his guys to the point where he would say, 'I don't even even know what y'all are doing.' In the middle of games, sometimes, it would get heated. He would get on the headsets on the defensive side and he would want to know what's going on with press coverage. He would do the same with the offense.

"Some of the funniest memories I have in this are about those times. Please don't misunderstand me here... it would be hilarious when he and Kasey would kind of argue over the headsets. Buddy would be saying 'I want you to do this,' and apparently Kasey had a devil of a time getting his microphone to cut off during the season also. There would be times where he thought that he would do enough to lift the microphone up enough to where it would cut off and it wouldn't do it. But Buddy would hear him yelling at the officials and that was one thing that he had he did not want anyone to do. No one could speak to the officials but him."

Scott Haskins

"Coaches just respected, loved him, and liked him because he was such a real humble person. Buddy was one of those rare breeds who was really good at his job. I think his legacy is one where you try to do things the best you can the right way. He was big about representing your last name and doing things the right way to those kids- about doing what you were supposed to do in the classroom and in those hallways at school- represent the school well and the represent their their their name well- and just adding to the legacy of trying to help kids develop into good future fathers, citizens, employees, military, and first-responders. Whatever he wanted them to do: do it, do it the right way, and do it the very best.

"He portrayed what he expected from his kids and that's always the mark of a great leader. Do you like to walk the walk if you talk the talk to me...? Well, he tried his best at everything he did. But he did it the right way and nobody could ever question his commitment or his effort. That showed tremendously to the kids and then that transcended into their their ability to perform year-in year-out.

"I, unfortunately, didn't spend a whole lot of time with Buddy compared to a lot of people, but if he loved you, you knew. Because he told me and that was so comforting as the new guy coming in. Buddy thought more about promoting you than himself and if he loves you- you knew it. Because he told you and he wasn't afraid to share his feelings."

Jared Luke

"I mean, he's going to go down as one of these is the winningest coach in Irwin County history. That's going to be a hard feat for somebody to beat his legacy. He would be the kind of guy who would just stop by my house in town and throw the ball with my kids in the yard. I would never know he was there. I'd be inside watching TV and he would do that because he loves me and he loves my kids. He loved our lunchroom staff. He loved our cleaning staff. He loved everyone. The family did things for everyone here. We got biscuits every Thursday morning after practice and he took those biscuits around to the cleaning ladies.

"He was a guy that didn't see you as 'I'm the head football coach' kind of a bigwig. He saw you as the same person that he was and he loves you for that. He was one hell of a football coach and a man of faith that never wavered."

Chip Rankin

"With any college coach that would come around looking at our guys, I'm just a middle school coach, but Buddy always made it a point to make sure he introduced me to the college guys and tried to talk me up. Buddy was handling things in his office and he always took time out to talk. He would always try to make other people feel important, but he always took time out and did stuff like that for me and Pete and Tim. It was just nice for him to do stuff like that."

Chris Paulk

"I just was awestruck at the amount of people- I mean there must have been 2,500 people at his memorial service- and I've just never been a part of the ceremony like that before. It was quite the accomplishment of testimony and respect and just how people felt this man was in their lives. He was just that loved by people and they just wanted to pay their last respects.

"Buddy saw the best in people and he loved people. And how he was with people is what endeared him as far as he was more than 'this person is Athletic Director/Football Coach.' It was more than winning. Winning was secondary and for him winning being secondary was doing it the right way, doing it his way, and his way was going to work. We didn't win every game. We didn't win every state championship game we played. But we won so much more. It was more than a game. It was about staying the course and his body of work will show that."

Lloyd Stembridge

"I love that man. I walk every morning and every time I walk by their house, I think about it. We had a plaque where we've recognized him at churches as an elder, but we just couldn't because of his physical condition. We just never got to that... Most people loved him and he was just a super guy. You know, you can't say that about everybody. I knew he was a super guy helping the church as he did and you don't have a lot of guys with the love their players that he did.

"Buddy was a Christian man and, I guess, if I have a question... he, probably, had 10 to 15 more years of coaching. Why God didn't allow him to see those seniors make an impact I don't know... What I do know is He had a better plan for Buddy and he made the impact that he made in his steps. But there were so many folks he could have been impacted that I just have that as of one of my questions.

"One thing about Tammy, too. She never left his side- being in hospitals or at his hand- she was absolutely a rock behind him. She never once complained and I never saw her leave him in the hospital or anywhere else. She was right there with him the whole time."

Eddie Giddens

"You can tell they came from a good family. All the hard work they did and their children are 'off the chain' courteous and well-mannered. It is 'Yes' or 'No, sir. Thank you.' And Buddy and Tammy are the same way. But he never failed. Everything that he asked me to do...? Every time that I asked him what could I do...? We would do things to help out the team like cooking hamburgers and we would try to raise funds for the team once, sometimes twice, a year.

"I had a guy over at the pecan company here in town. I went in asking for some money. He gave me like $150 or so. A couple of weeks later, he says, 'Listen, if you need some money for this, you can ask me again and I'll help.' That gentleman said he got the best thank you note card from Buddy. He couldn't believe that. No one had ever done that for him. Just thinking about what he said, it's things like that I can talk all day. And I could talk about what a good man Buddy is, but he was a great coach. And Tammy...? She's worked her butt off to make things happen here."

Matt Thomas

"As a mentor... as a friend... as family... as someone who taught me about fate... he should be remembered as one of the greatest coaches in Georgia and Florida high school football. You know his story on how he fought through to become a head coach. It is also a story of not complaining and just keep fighting the fight. He was also a great friend and someone that I miss dearly.

"I could go on for hours about what we used to talk about in the car, but you have these experiences that you remember. I won't forget he was always so humble, but he also could get so excited in the locker room. I've never seen somebody be so humble and then go into the locker room and just let let loose. I got that experience as a player and coach. You would see this humble, fun-loving guy. But, man, when you messed up he disciplined you.

"I was out there too many nights 'til 10 doing up-downs and rolling down the field because I talked back to a coach. So, when I became a coach, I get it when a player talks back to me. I did the same, exact thing even if it's a different dynamic nowadays. I was a player back in the 80's and 90's, but it's still the same foundation. Buddy had an amazing way to discipline his players and they respected him at the end of the day. That's why he had the ability to have people play for him. They trusted each other and believed in each other."

Andrew Zow

"I think he completed what he was supposed to do from living a Christ-like life and it wasn't just a put-on. He did an outstanding job of loving people so his legacy goes way beyond football. It goes way beyond anything-not just athletics-because of the impact they had on my life.

"When you look back and think about the small things people say... I would be just heading out of the house, and I'll say 'I love you' and those types of things. We're in a manly world and we live in a time of, where as a grown-up, you never really said those kinds of things until recently. I repeat this every day- 'I love you.' And I say 'I love you' again and again to everyone around me. His legacy is very impactful in why God brought him here- not just as a winner but how he reacts to losing. I've seen this since I was 15 years old, and you're now talking 20 to 30 years of seeing his legacy.

"He left it on my family, my boys, all my teammates, and everyone that I come in contact with... that he came in contact with... Everyone talks about it. I know we all feel like we have a very close relationship with our coaches and that we were the only one in the room whenever they talked to you. When Buddy was on the phone with you, he made you feel like you feel if you were a member of his family. Everyone that came in contact with him left with a piece of him as well. Now, those folks can go out and impact someone else's life. Buddy did that as a coach and you would get better as a man, as a father, and as a husband.

"He had an unbelievable spirit of God with him."

Gerard Warren

"Going up to get that championship trophy, it gave him the chance to say, 'Hey! I ain't too bad, either!' It is one of the reasons, but not the total reason why you coach- to reach the point of being the champion. But Buddy had the same amount of joy winning a championship than seeing someone going to graduate and go to college. That was the ultimate goal- to get those young men out and go to school.

"I know... I KNOW... my great friend, my coach... we identify him as a husband, father, coach, and brother. We give recognition and knowledge that he was a born-again Christian and a True Believer in our Lord and Savior Jesus Christ first and foremost. Buddy and Robby Pruitt brought something of a different element for me personally. In a simplified way, what's greater of a man...? There's much greater things than just being a football coach. It's things away from the field that helped shape me as a human being.

"I would get a ride home from Coach in high school. He lived, like, three minutes from school. He would put as many of us in his car as he could and drive us all home. If we needed a 7-mile drive, a 14-mile drive, or a 20-mile drive, he would do that for us. And the love that he and Miss Tammy showed you...? There are things like that still in my mind to this day as I've grown up. Even something like her banana pudding and my mama's pancakes.

"Parents willingly turn their kids over to coaches and, with coaches like Coach Nobles and Coach Pruitt, they knew their children were in the hands of a good man. If Buddy wanted to include me in a trip to Jacksonville with the family on a weekend, I could go. You can't put a title on what he did as he went above and beyond his coaching duties. It was personal and I will always love them.

"Buddy wasn't just a good man. He was a great man... a great, great man..."

Eddie Giddens missed the party at the red light- the first one he missed. The city officials didn't like it the first time it was called, but it became an important event in the fabric of Irwin County.

"His legacy, in my mind, is that Buddy is one of the best football coaches we've ever had or will ever have. But he will also be remembered as being the best man to have that position I have ever seen. Buddy never raised his voice at anybody other than the football players- and only when you needed to... he's a winner. No matter if you lost the game or not, he is still a winner and he'll never be forgotten in the halls of Irwin County."

Dwayne Vickers

"In seventh grade, these kids won a championship in football and recreation basketball as 13 and 14 year olds. They were undefeated the whole time. I knew they were going to be a special group. Buddy's legacy will come from his faith in

God, speaking God's word over to the kids, and letting them know- no matter what the situation is- that you can come out a victorious person on the field and with your God in heaven."

Clayton Sirmans

"There's a lot of lessons to tell... One of the most important lessons is he didn't complain. He didn't do it. I know he didn't ask 'Why?' He just thought through it and continued to be the man we all knew. He was a Christian man who loves his players, loved his family, and loved Jesus Christ. His willingness to continue to be that person and be an example for everybody else is just incredible. Seeing him go through that terrible disease, but never waver on this, showed he was the same person throughout this whole process. From the seven or eight years that I have known him, he's the same guy from from beginning to end."

Tim Talton

"It's all about being a person, first and foremost, of Jesus Christ. It's also about the kids you're around and that you coach, and how much you care for everyone. Buddy will always be known as a very caring person to me."

Jeremey Andrews

"I first met Buddy when he got the job at Union County in Florida. He just put out an ad for an assistant coach. I had been coaching for three years at Columbus South High School in Columbus, Ohio and I just was looking to move somewhere warm. So I sent out some resumes and Buddy's position was one of the ones I applied for. I spoke with him for several nights and he was trying to figure me out as I was trying to figure him out. He, finally, just kind of said, 'I think I would like to offer you a job.' I drove down there and we talked some more. My degree was in political science and I've never taken an education course. I was in the process of getting ready to go back to school, and he said he wanted to hire me.

"He took me into the principal's office and she said that the only spot she had was in English. Buddy said, 'Well, that's fine just give it to him,' and she said okay. He takes me across the street. We talked to the superintendent and I was hired. Our paths had never crossed. We had no background. It was just God's intervention putting us together. So, it was an interesting experience to say the least.

"I moved down there. I was only 23 years old and my 19 year old girlfriend was moving down there with me.I was down there for about 2 weeks before she came and he knew that she was coming. Coach and his family helped move me and they, sort of, adopted me in the two weeks I was down there. Buddy was riding around and he saw a car with an Ohio license plate going down our road- which never happens. He decided to follow her just knowing it was her. He'd never met her, but he decided to follow her. He was blowing on his horn, messing with her, and they pulled into the driveway. She has no idea what in the world's going on and that's how my wife first got to meet Buddy. He made quite an impression on both of us."

When he got to witness Buddy and Tammy as husband and wife, it was another example of how to be there for each other and for those around you...

"I don't think I've ever seen a husband and wife love each other as much as those two did. He was crazy about her and he loved those kids. He was a great example for me. My girlfriend actually ended up pregnant soon after we moved to Florida. She's now my wife and we've been married 18 years with two kids. But he was a great example for what it was to be a good husband and a good dad. My wife and I both come from great families, but they were both up here in Ohio. We're down there in Florida, we were newlyweds with the baby, and I'm trying to figure it all out.

"They were just such great examples of how to be spouses and how to be parents. One thing that always stuck with me is whenever a conversation ended between buddy and one of his kids or Tammy it would always end with 'I love you.' It doesn't matter if it was on the phone or they were walking out of the coaches office. I do that with my family now and that was a direct result of being with Buddy. My son is now 17 years old and every time he leaves to go somewhere... every time we're on the phone... our call ends with 'I love you' and I got that directly from Buddy and how he dealt with his family.

"I think his legacy is, primarily, a leader and as a leader of people. It's by his words, by his actions, and by his example- whether it's pushing somebody to be better or dragging their behind along to be better. I think, ultimately, it is just as a leader of men- whether it's in personal life, whether it's athletics, or whatever... Whether we're sharing texts and always being there going back and forth, he tells me he loves me. We would end our conversations telling each other we loved each other and I think that, ultimately, you could tell that he just had this love for people. That was more important to him than anything- for anyone to be just be the best that they could be and Buddy would make sure that everybody knew that they mattered to him."

Zach Smith was planning on spending his senior season at a private school, but decided as he sat with his teammates at the memorial service that he was coming back to Irwin County for that final year. He found out quickly that Ocilla meant too much to him.

He was coming home...

"Nobody can say anything negative about Coach Nobles, so it's all going to be good things.

"I only want to say that I wish he could have gotten on me one more time as a player for my senior year. They're going to, definitely, talk about his coaching because he went to a state title game 5 out of 6 times. He's a great coach. He's a great person. He's a Godly man. So, you know his legacy is going to be remembered and I'm definitely not going to let it die. I still have all of our 'Nobles Strong' stuff and our 'We got your back, Bud' bracelets and I'm not going to take it off.

"I knew that with all Coach has done for me, I wanted to finish with my friends. There are a lot of Juniors in 2019 that are going to be seniors this year. I can promise you that I want to try my best to see if I can win again as a senior.

Zach will also remember what Fanta orange and purple Power-Ade meant to Buddy. So, don't be surprised if he has them in his hands going forward as a drink of choice.

Garland Benyard

Words can't describe how heartbreaking this is to me. You've lived a good life and touched so many people's lives throughout your days. I was really looking forward to you coaching me all four years, but that didn't happen. You've set a great example for me and I'm sure for others too. No one knew the pain you were going through but you were still here for us.

Throughout these three years i have learned a lot from all your coaching skills, the man you were, and how you always fought in everything you did no matter what the situation you were in.

Nobles was a man of his word and always told us how he felt about his team. Also he would do anything to make you succeed and make you a better person.

A memory from last year's season I would like to share is the night we were leaving Ga Southern with a couple of teammates . As we were on the road, half of us were sleep. All of sudden Javon wakes me up laughing, saying " aye coach nobles eyes keep closing. As we woke everyone up they found it funny and started laughing. As Coach nobles rapidly open his eyes looking back asking "guys what's so funny?"

Shaneka Paschal (the mom of the Benyard twins)

Coach Nobles has also told me, "Shaneka I want you and Tony to know that you have some special boy's. They are Awesome and I want you to take care of those boys. They are a Special gift from God because they are some great kids and they have a great future ahead of them". I will always hear Coach Nobles tell me how unselfish they are in everything they do and how great they are in the class room. Coach Nobles was God sent to Irwin County. #ACOACHOFDESTINY

Tanique Howard (she's one of the biggest fans for the Indians... you can hear your yelling and cheering from the other side of the field)

So many memories! One of my favorite was watching Coach Nobles plan the tomahawk. Notable mentions the entire Indian nation singing the war chant, watching Coah Nobles finally get his ring, and "wont back down" locker room fun!!!

Tissy Smith

Thinking back on the life of Coach Buddy Nobles, so many great memories flood my mind. Our family became acquainted with Coach Noble through the Irwin Co Football program. My youngest son, Harmon Smith #58, has always loved playing football. In the 6th grade, Harmon started playing on the Irwin Co Middle School team in 2014. We would see Coach Noble at some of the home games catching a glimpse of the future players. He would always take the time to compliment players for playing well. Like most coaches, he corrected any mistakes they made to help improve the team. He always encouraged them even at that age to stay the course and finish the drill. In due time they would be playing under the Friday night lights. I admired Coach Nobles' dedication to the program.

Harmon's 7th-grade year was when we got to know Coach better. Harmon had Mrs. Tammy Nobles for 7th-grade math. At the time, we didn't know Mrs. Nobles had been going home telling Buddy stories about Harmon. Harmon has always been very smart and has a personality that everyone loves. After a middle school game one afternoon we noticed Coach Nobles had pulled Harmon to the side and talked to him before heading inside. Many laughs were exchanged and a big ole pat on the back. Kevin and I are standing at the end of the field waiting for Harmon to exit the fieldhouse. Coach Nobles approaches us and has the biggest smile on his face. After introductions were made, he starts telling us what a special young man we were raising. He told us some stories that his wife had shared and said she talked about Harmon every single day. So, he had to meet this kid that she spoke so highly of, and Harmon did not disappoint his expectations. He told us how proud of the improvements Harmon was making on the field and couldn't wait to have him as a 9th grader.

Since that time, we have had numerous conversations with Coach Nobles. Harmon's 9th-grade year, we joined the Indian Touchdown Club. Sitting in the first few meetings, it was evident that Coach Nobles was serious about football. But even more serious about being a good role model for those young men. In the three years of being involved with the football team, I never heard Coach Nobles say one curse word. Now I saw him chew out several for not making the right block or run the correct route. But never any foul language! After a long hard practice, he sat his guys down and told them what he expected out of them. He never dismissed without telling him he loved them and prayed with them. As a parent, you take notice of that! Especially in the times we live in today. That is one reason I loved Coach Nobles because he loved the lord. I didn't worry about Harmon because he heard Jesus at home, church, and the football field.

Another reason I loved Coach Nobles was that he always encouraged Harmon with football and, more importantly, his school work. Harmon is an intelligent young man. He has been one of the top students in his class each year. One day Coach Nobles approached Kevin and me to let us know that he was pushing Harmon hard to stay on top of his studies. He explained that in all his years of coaching, he never had a player be the Valedictorian, and Harmon had the potential to get it. So, Coach was continually asking him about his studies and how things were looking. I have always appreciated him taking the time to encourage Harmon to do his best at school. Even today, I use Coach as an incentive to push Harmon to do his very BEST. Harmon has one more year to get the job done. But even if he doesn't end up #1 on the list, he still knows Coach was cheering him on the entire time.

One of my favorite memories was the day the Touchdown Club gave him his bright red Indian golf cart. See Coach wasn't feeling well in July of 2019 and had expressed to the club that he needed a dependable golf cart to get around at practice. After a few phone calls were made for donations we surprised Coach with a golf cart the very next week after our Touchdown meeting. We had snuck the cart outside his office door while he was inside for the meeting. Tammy had come for the surprise also. After the meeting was over, we asked Coach to step outside to look at the field. I went out first to video the moment. I'll never forget the expression on his face when he walked through the doorway. He was taken back... thankful!!! After a minute he finally notices Tammy standing to the side. He beelined it to Tammy's arms, and they held each other tightly. That day I witnessed the love he had for his wife and vice versa. Trust me there was not a dry eye on the premises. No one was aware of the diagnosis that would come the next week. I'll never forget that memory! #wegotyourbackbuddy!

Even after being diagnosed with cancer, he didn't complain or give up. He let everyone know that he was saved and had faith in God that everything would be OK. Coach Nobles wasn't able to attend the remainder of the Touchdown Club meetings. I stayed in touch through text message about football business since I was the Treasurer of the Club. Even in the hospital he checked in to make sure we had everything covered. That was just who Buddy Nobles was. So thankful that Coach Nobles was on board with the idea of having the 2019 season videoed. I was somewhat nervous to ask him because if you knew Buddy you knew he wanted the same routine when it came to game day. I wasn't sure if he'd allow a new person to come in and video on/off the field. When we discussed the idea, we both agreed that 'this was Irwin's year,' and having that documented would be awesome. Through those videos, the world got to see what an awesome man of God Buddy Nobles was. The 2019 Irwin Co Indians were a Team of Destiny led by a phenomenal leader, coach, and, more importantly, a man of GOD!

I am so thankful that my family got to know such an inspiring man. Buddy Nobles will always hold a special place in our hearts.

Sherry Wilmot
President, ICHS Band Boosters

I am a band mom, so my Coach Nobles story is a little different. My husband, Kurt Wilmot, asked Buddy if he would mind speaking to the marching band during their summer band camp. We thought it would be an encouragement to our students. After all, they are a big part of the Friday night lights atmosphere!

Of course Coach Nobles agreed. He came the last 3 years and talked at length to the band, supporting them, thanking them, and encouraging them to do their best. Our favorite quote that he gave us was this, "Kids, I want you to play loud. Play until you get a warning from the referees. After the warning, put your horns down and scream as loud as you can!" He truly appreciated them as part of the football atmosphere.

Denise Hamby

On the night of Meet the Indians last year, Coach announced to us all that he had Cancer. Of course, as was everyone, I was upset. I started to leave and something made me go back inside. I walk up to Coach and asked if I could give him a hug. He said, "Yes Ma'am, I'll always take a good hug."

Steve Carter

My love for Irwin County Indian football goes back to 1981 when I played for the junior varsity team and was on the varsity roster. My highlight was two tackles in a win against Berrien.

If my memory is true I would not miss a single Irwin game from 1981 until 1992. I got my love of high school football from my pop. I lost him in 1989, but the only fall Fridays we missed were because there was no Irwin game or a game in our area.

Fast forward to the 2019 state title game and the only thing those guys needed from me was being loud and proud as I watched them win something I've been waiting 38 years for, a state championship. After that game and before I went back to Ocilla I kept thinking how excited my pop had to be in Heaven. He graduated from Sylvester High, but due to me and the friends we had made from our support of the Indians he was through and through an Irwin County man.

I should've mentioned this earlier but, at his insistence, there is no telling how many family members of players we would take to games. He did it to show his love and support for those players. Back to state championship night, after hugs and well wishes I sat in my truck and cried tears of joy for all of those athletes I had covered and how much they meant to my pop and me.

I know Coach Nobles had a positive effect on the 2019 Indians. He showed those boys to never quit, because he never did. And if he just got through to one member of Irwin's opponents, there is no telling how far his legacy will go. He got through to his guys, so his legacy in Irwin County will be forever. If he got through to the opposition, his legacy will be state-wide.

Tommy Palmer

"I think his legacy will be a great coach and being the right person for the right school in the state at the right time. I am amazed at how high schools and communities all just rally around certain situations- and this one with Irwin County is absolutely no different. Buddy Nobles will always be a loved man by two cities next to each other and two counties that he was a part of in his life."

EPILOGUE

COVID-19 put a hold on everything in 2020...

The high school football season in Georgia was pushed back from its original start dates and coaches, administrators, and... well, everyone, associated with their favorite programs had to be very adaptable to schedules, being at games in person, how they could attend if they were allowed, and how games actually happened.

You had to make it to 3:15 (or earlier in some instances) on game days and hope you could get on a bus to play. You had to hope you could get to your fieldhouse on game days for home games and hope the opponent made it and didn't give you one of "those" phone calls you dread.

The first two games for the Indians were on the road. But the dedication, so the town of Ocilla could now see games at Buddy Nobles Stadium, happened in Game 3 when Wilkinson County visited. It was a dominant 44-0 win over WilCo, but the fabric that holds the Irwin County indian community changed with the new name on the marquee.

Every time I walk into the stadium I am filled with a mixture of emotions. I cry because of what is no more, I smile because of what was and I cheer for what is! Now each time I enter the stadium I can add pride to my emotions. I am so proud of Buddy Nobles. I am proud to be his wife (I despise the term widow! I will

always be his wife)! I am proud to be the mother of his wonderful children! I am proud to have been beside him throughout his coaching career and I am proud of the legacy he left! What is so ironic is that Buddy had no idea the legacy he was creating. He was just doing his best to serve his Lord and Savior Jesus Christ, he was taking care of his family and he was coaching football.

Each step along the way he was touching lives.

WE ARE STILL NOBLES STRONG & GOD IS STILL BIGGER!!

A week later, Kevin's daughter, Emma, coached the Irwin County Middle School softball team to a conference championship. The trophy made a trip to check in with Buddy on a sunny afternoon.

Kaleb and Katy are planning a wedding after he popped the question on a beach and the family is taking it a day at a time. And another birthday for Tammy gave itself to the thoughts of the past year:

This is my first birthday since I was 16 years old that I was not able to spend with my Buddy. He always made it a special day for me. As I read some of the cards he gave me over the years I was reminded of how blessed I was. I miss everything about him, even his handwriting.

I still do not understand all of this but I do accept and trust God's perfect will. I am surviving by the grace of God and with the prayers and love of many friends and wonderful family. I love you all and am so thankful for you.

Everyone who has been a part of the story feels the same in return...

Guaranteed the feelings are mutual...

CREDITS/BIBLIOGRAPHY

Thanks to this list of folks from outside Irwin and Ben Hill Counties for all their hard work in telling the story in real time…

The staff at GoArgos.com and the Sports Information Department at the University of West Florida

The Tifton Gazette newspaper

WALB-TV in Albany, Georgia

Georgia Public Broadcasting and GPB.org

The Valdosta Daily Times newspaper

The Pensacola News Journal newspaper

Jorjanne Zorn Paulk's Southern Mercantile blog

CPSIA information can be obtained
at www.ICGtesting.com
Printed in the USA
LVHW070309040621
689238LV00023B/819